3-Color
WATER
COLOR

Published in 2024 by Search Press Ltd
Wellwood, North Farm Road, Tunbridge Wells, Kent TN2 3DR

Bookmarked Hub
For further ideas and inspiration, and to join our free online
community, visit www.bookmarkedhub.com

This book was conceived, designed, and produced by
The Bright Press, an imprint of The Quarto Group
1 Triptych Place, London SE1 9SH
United Kingdom
www.quarto.com

ISBN: 9781800922648
ebook ISBN: 9781800932630

The Bright Press
Publisher: James Evans
Editorial Director: Isheeta Mustafi, Anna Southgate
Managing Editor: Jacqui Sayers
Publishing Operations Director: Kathy Turtle
Publishing Assistant: Jemima Solley
Production Manager: Nathan Miller
Art Director: James Lawrence
Commissioning Editor: Sorrel Wood
Senior Editor: Izzie Hewitt
Text Contributor: Helen Birch
Designer: Joelle Wheelwright

Cover design: Emily Nazer
Cover illustrations: Katie Putt

Printed and bound in China

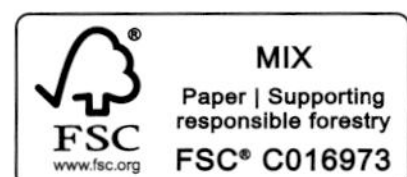

3-Color WATER COLOR

30 COLOR-MIXING MASTERPIECES

KATIE PUTT

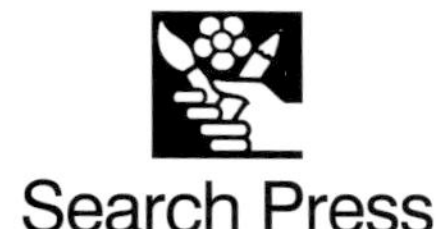

Search Press

Contents

The Palettes

Jewel Brights

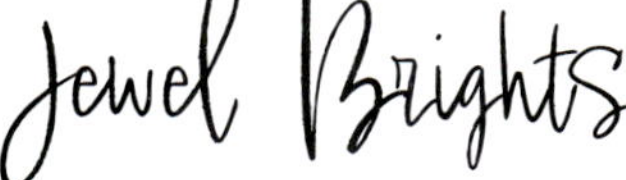

| 24 |

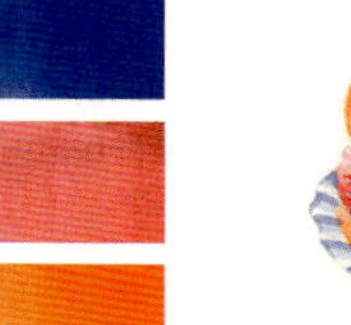

1. PATISSERIE

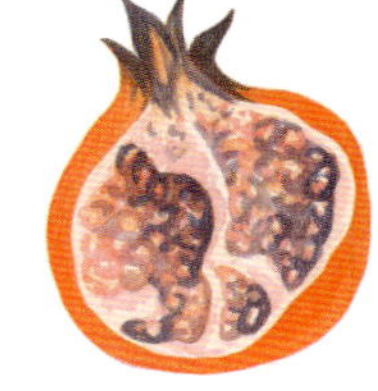

2. POMEGRANATE

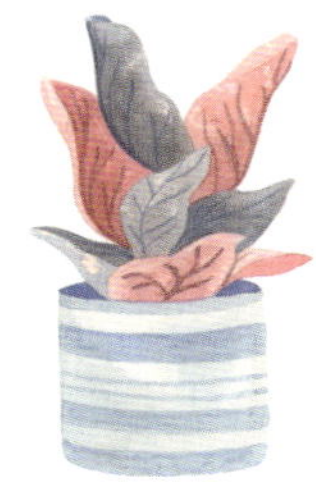

3. POTTED PLANT

Beach Spirit

| 34 |

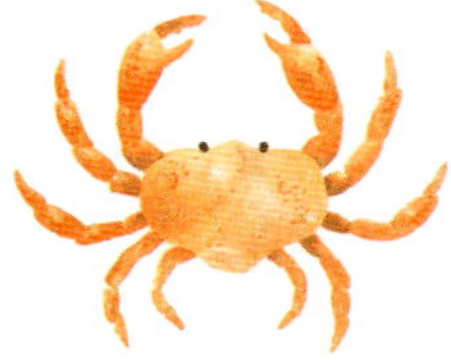

1. ROCKPOOL CRAB

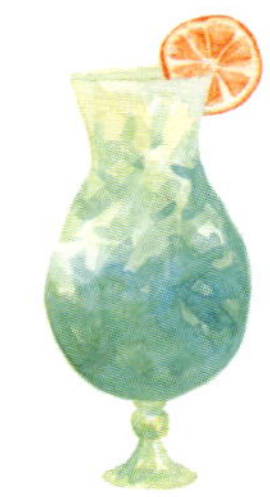

2. COCKTAIL HOUR

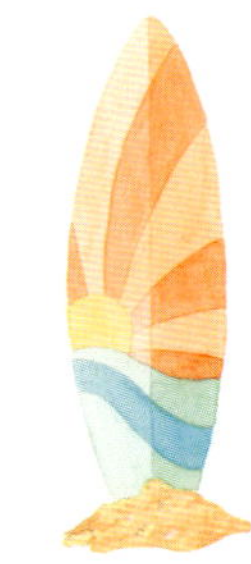

3. SURF'S UP

Scandi Calm

| 44 |

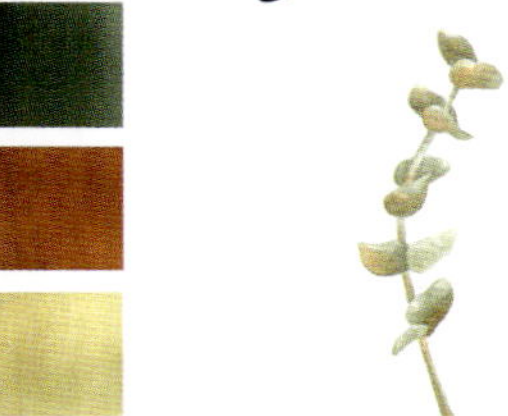

1. EUCALYPTUS

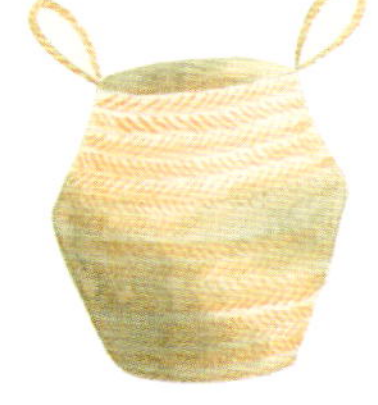

2. WICKER BASKET

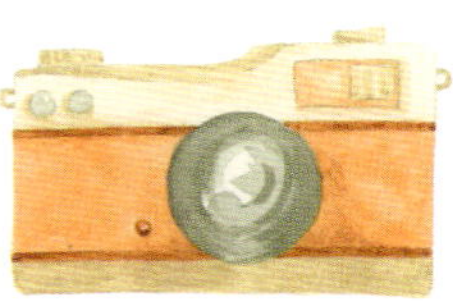

3. PHOTO TIME

54 True Romance

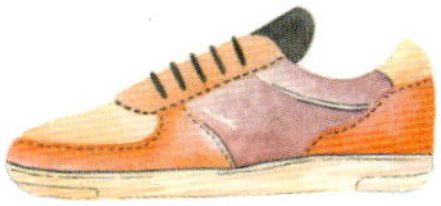

1. SNEAKER

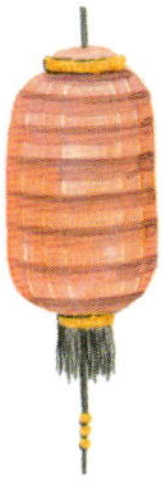

2. LANTERN

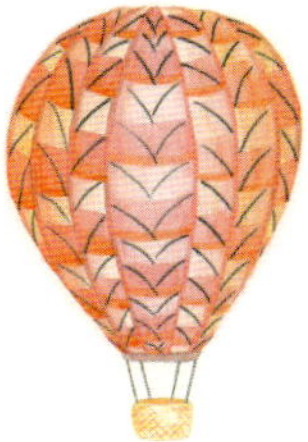

3. HOT-AIR BALLOON

64 Tropical Sun

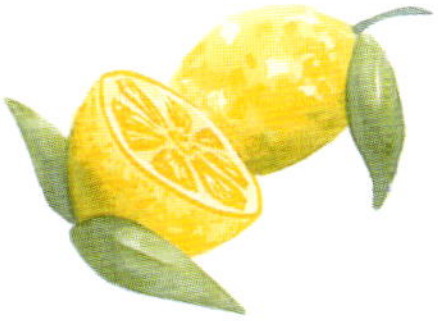

1. LEMONS

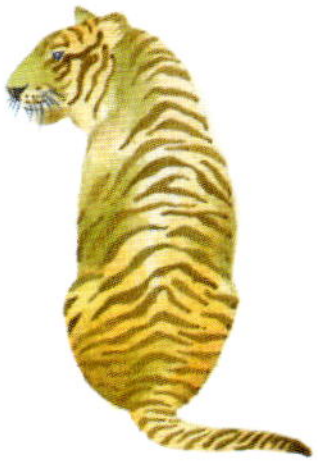

2. TIGER

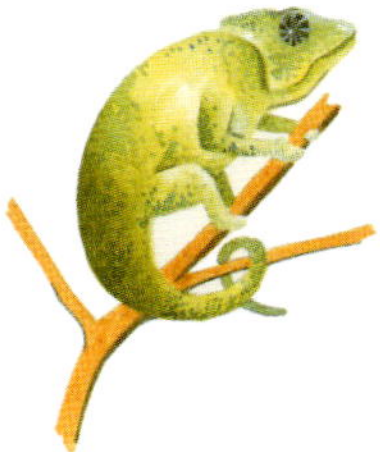

3. CHAMELEON

74 Magic Touch

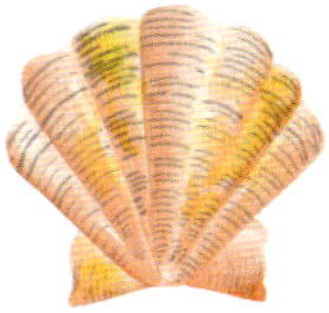

1. SHELL

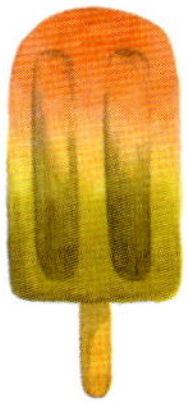

2. POPSICLE

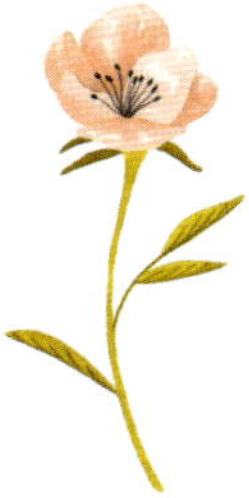

3. FLORA

84 Spring Fresh

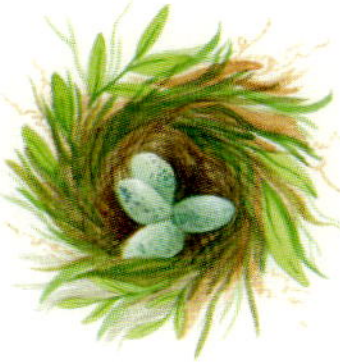

1. BIRD'S NEST

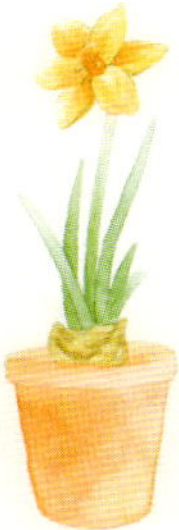

2. FLOWER POWER

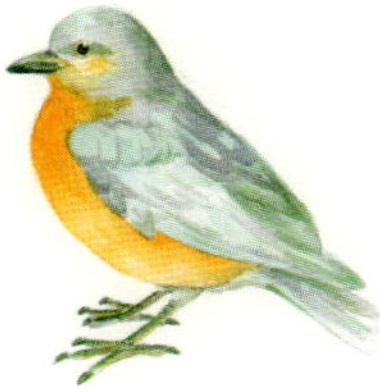

3. SPRINGTIME BIRD

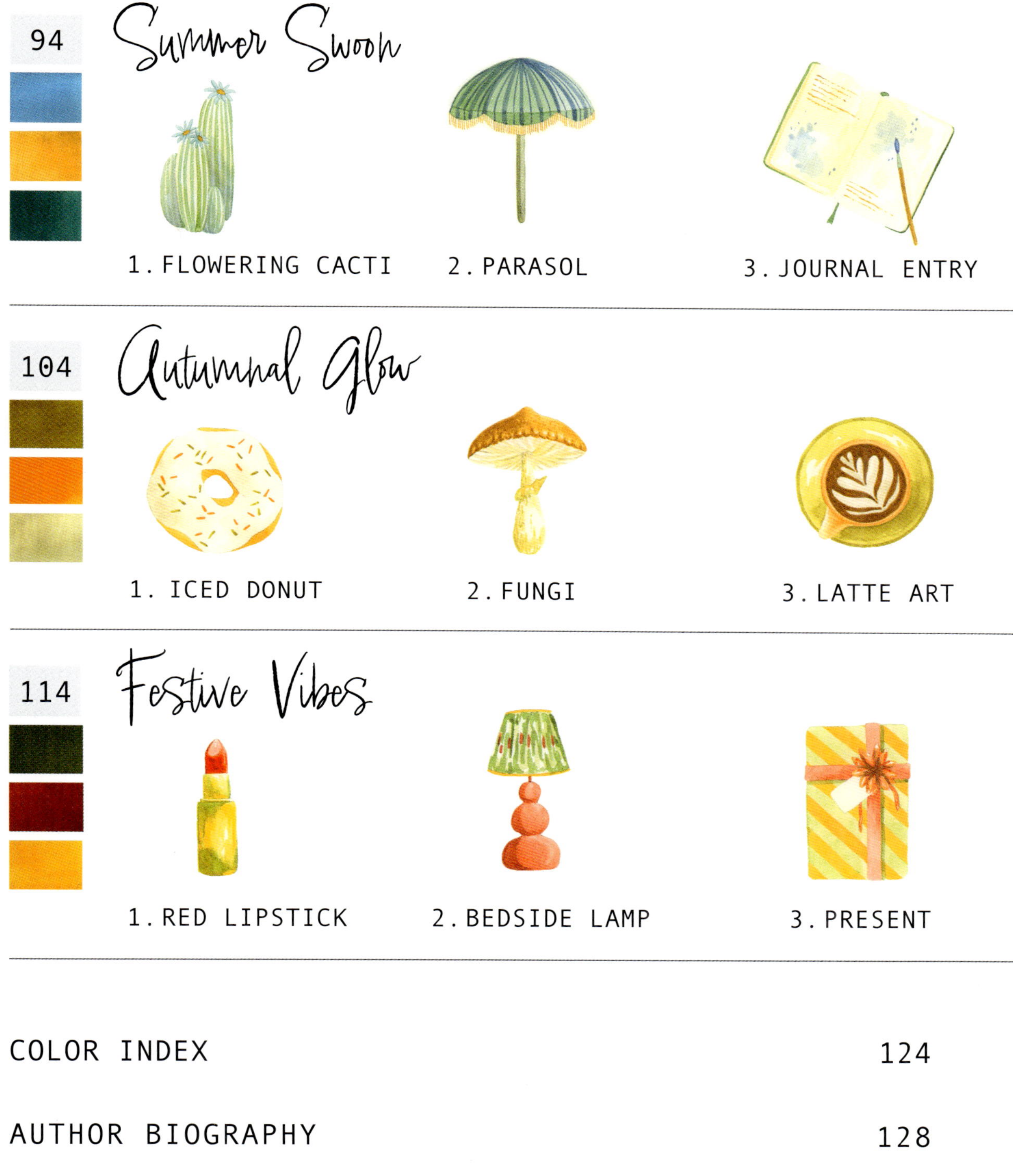

Introduction

Watercolor painting is all about color. The clue is in the name! Watercolors are built by layering washes of paint. Each layer is translucent. which is what gives the colors such a beautiful sense of vibrancy and depth. That's why a strong understanding of color is so essential for successful watercolor painting.

Each of the 10 chapters in this book is based around a different three-color palette. You'll need just three "pure" paint colors to make a start. From these, you will learn how to mix a surprising range of different colors—every hue you'll need to complete the three simple watercolor projects in each chapter. Whether you're looking for something bright, calming, or festive, there's a palette for every mood.

By working with three-color palettes, you'll get to know each different color of paint intimately. You'll gain an understanding of how different colors interact when mixed or layered, and you'll become a pro when it comes to the different characteristics of dark and light washes. By the time you've completed the projects in this book, you'll have a sixth sense for color.

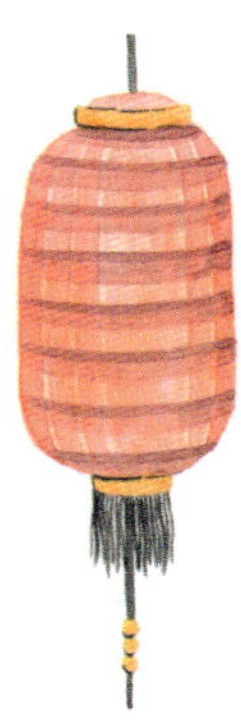 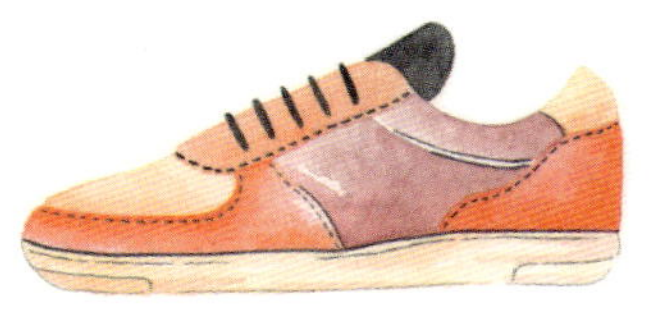 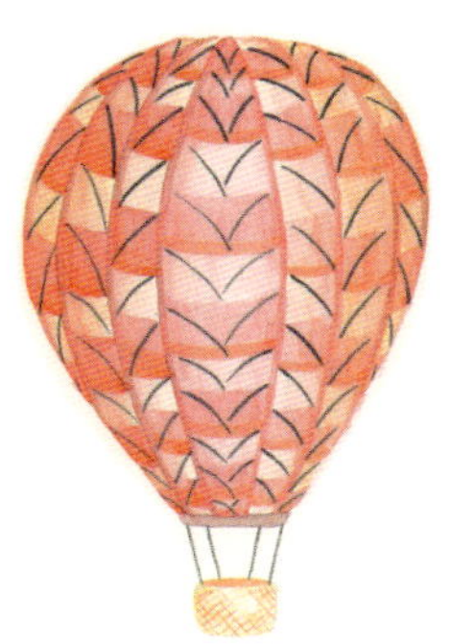

The first spread of each chapter shows a different palette, which you will use to create three watercolor projects. Once you have these colors, you're ready to get started.

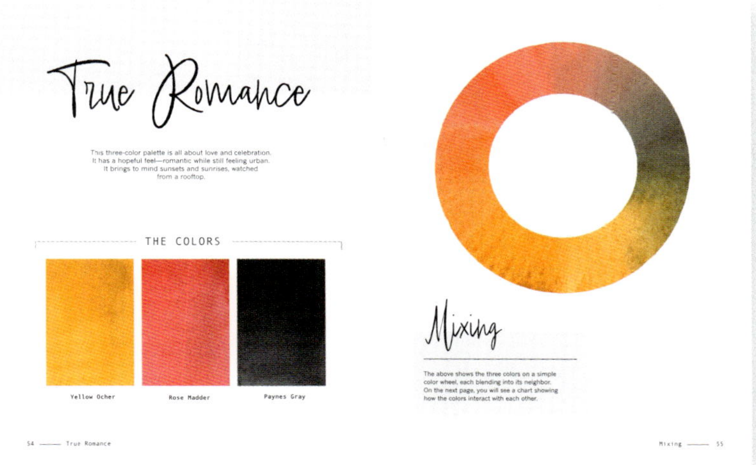

On the facing page is a color wheel, demonstrating how the colors will blend when mixed.

The second spread of each chapter shows a color chart. The color chart demonstrates the range of colors that can be mixed when combining different colors in the chapter, in dark and light washes. Turn to pp. 17–19 for more on color charts and mixing.

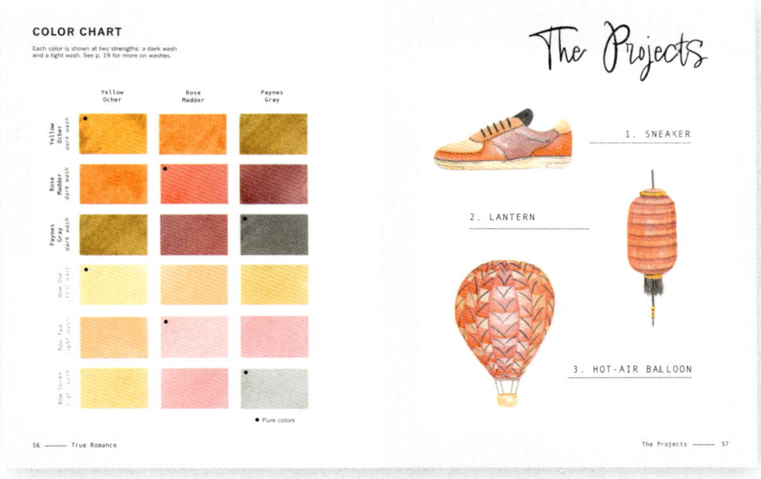

The facing page shows the three watercolor projects that you will create using this three-color palette.

Following the introductory pages in each chapter, you will find step-by-steps for each of the three projects. Enjoy!

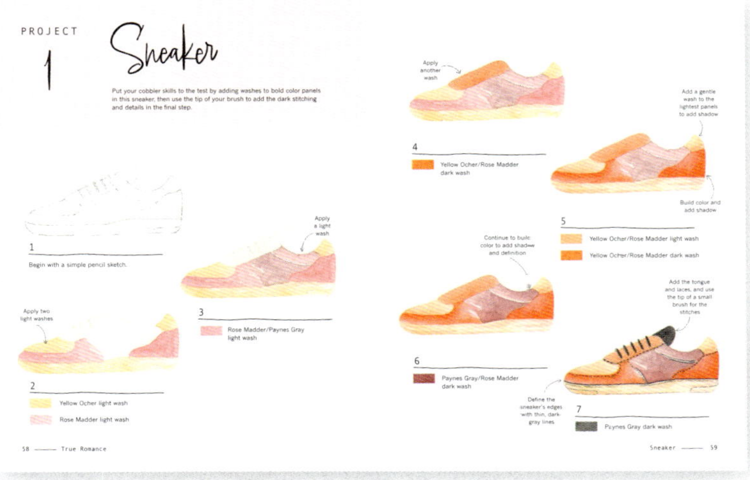

The Basics

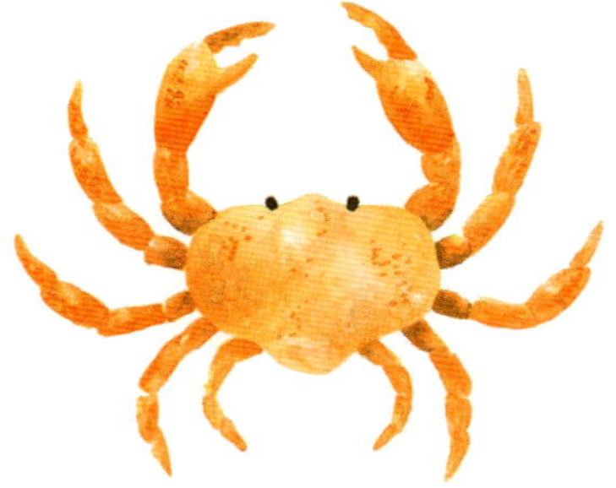

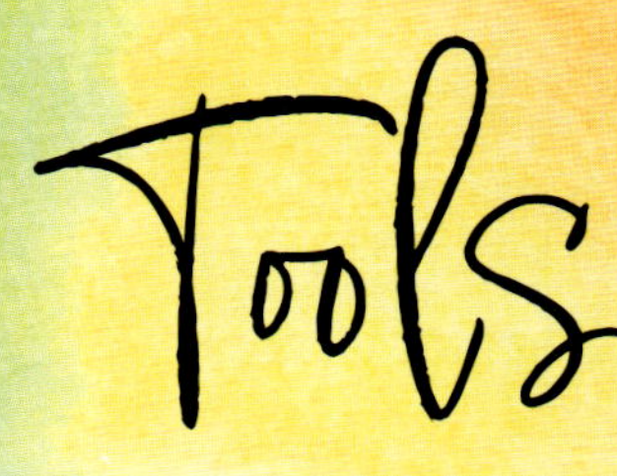

You can start watercolor painting with just a few simple materials: paints, paper, water, and brushes. Once you get stuck in and start to experiment, you'll build confidence: at that stage, you might find that you'd like to try out different tools and techniques. Here's a summary of everything you need to get started.

BRUSHES

The most widely used brush for watercolor painting is a round brush. It forms a point when it's wet, so if the tip is used very lightly, it is excellent for finer details, and you can also cover more surface area if you press the brush down.

For the projects in this book, you'll need just three round-head watercolor brushes:
1) A small brush for details (size 1)
2) A medium brush for general use and to build up layers (size 4)
3) A large brush to create washes that cover a large area (size 7).

Brushes come with natural or synthetic hair. The latter are less soft than the natural brushes, but they are more hard wearing and cheaper. You don't need to spend a fortune: great-quality student brands are available.

PENCIL

It can help to sketch a light outline of your project before you begin painting. Use HB or 2H pencils so the lines aren't too dark, and draw lightly, as watercolor will not cover your pencil marks.

PALETTE

You'll need a surface to mix your paints on (make sure it's white, otherwise you won't be able to tell what the colors you're mixing really look like). Watercolor sets with pans of paints usually have space for mixing on the inside of the lid. Special palettes with "wells" are great for saving colors you've mixed. You don't need these, though: a small white plate is fine!

PAPER

Use watercolor paper. It's specially crafted to allow paintings to dry evenly, to stop pigment soaking into the paper fibers, and to keep your colors strong and vibrant. Any paper over 270gsm (weight) will be best.

You have a choice of surface textures. If you like smooth paper, choose "hot pressed" watercolor paper. If you prefer a textured surface, choose "cold pressed" or "grained" paper. Both are good, it's a matter of personal preference.

ERASER

A regular eraser can be useful for cleaning your paper and for lifting pencil lines.

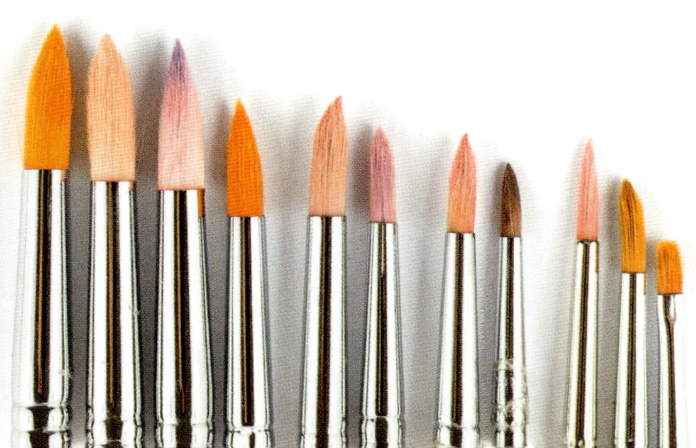

PAINTS

Most of the paints used in this book are from the brand Winsor & Newton. They are widely available, so if you want the closest match to the colors in this book, that's usually the best brand to use.

You may want to use watercolors from different makers. Confusingly, manufacturers often name similar colors differently! One way to find a color match is by looking at the packaging. On quality watercolors, a pigment number will be listed there. You can ask at an art store if they carry watercolor paint with that pigment number, or use it to search online. The name might be different, but if the pigment number matches, so will the color. You can find the pigment numbers for the colors used in this book in the color index on p. 124.

Look for paints labeled "student grade"—these are more affordable than the more expensive "artist-quality" paints, and are still good quality. Whichever paints you go for, you'll need to decide between tubes and pans.

Tubes v Pans

TUBES

Tubes of watercolor paint are more expensive than pans but they last for a very long time. A tiny dot of fresh paint squeezed directly from a tube instantly provides a concentrated amount of color. The paint is already moist, so it makes mixing speedy—just be careful, though, as this means there will be more pigment. You need much less paint on the brush than with a pan. When you squeeze tube watercolor onto your palette, it will harden if you don't use it. When that happens you can add water to reactivate the paint, like using a pan watercolor.

PANS

Pan watercolors come in the form of little cakes, which sit in their own recess in a tin. They are dry to the touch but adding water activates them. This makes them easy to store and transport. Pans are much cheaper than tubes, which makes them a great option for beginners and for trying out new colors. You could use these for the projects in this book, and if you find you're enjoying working with the colors, it might be worth investing in tubes for the longer term. You can then refill the pans with a tube when they run out.

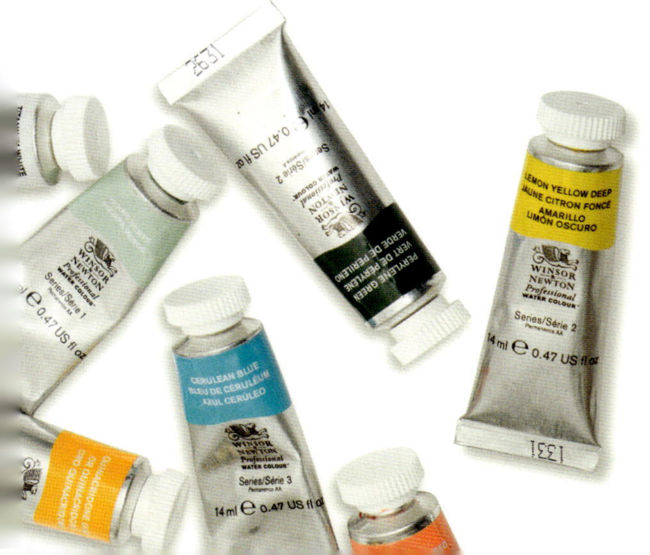

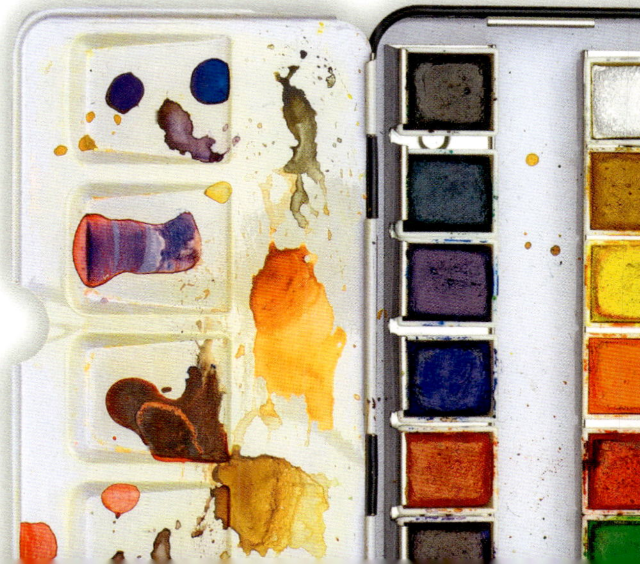

Color Essentials

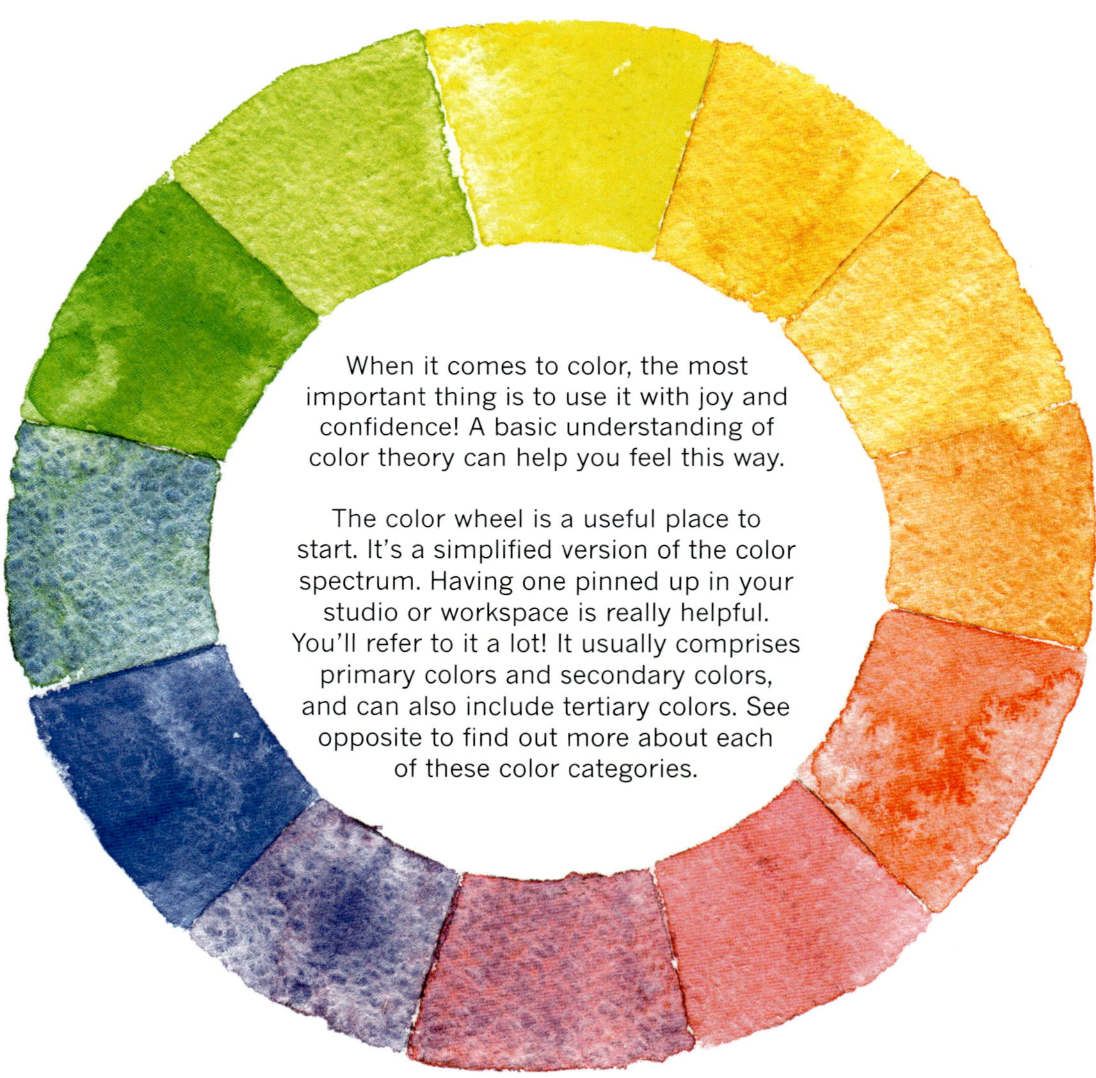

When it comes to color, the most important thing is to use it with joy and confidence! A basic understanding of color theory can help you feel this way.

The color wheel is a useful place to start. It's a simplified version of the color spectrum. Having one pinned up in your studio or workspace is really helpful. You'll refer to it a lot! It usually comprises primary colors and secondary colors, and can also include tertiary colors. See opposite to find out more about each of these color categories.

PRIMARY COLORS:

 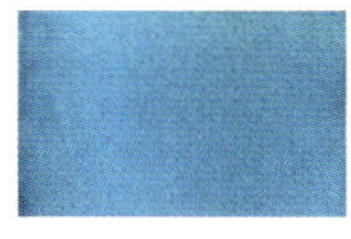 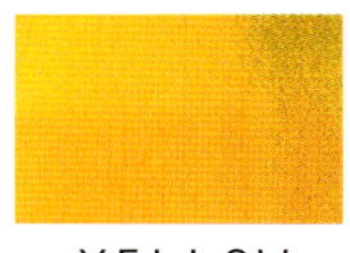

RED   BLUE   YELLOW

These are colors that can't be made by mixing other colors. Red, blue, and yellow watercolors come with different names. Alzarin Crimson, Delft Blue or Phthalo Turquoise, Cadmium Yellow . . . the list is endless. With use you'll quickly become familiar with these variations and their differing characteristics.

SECONDARY COLORS:

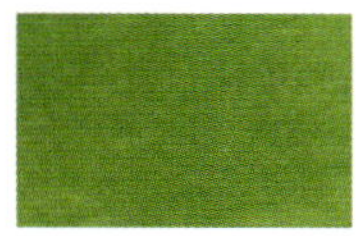  

GREEN   PURPLE   ORANGE

Secondary colors are produced by mixing two primary colors. The following combinations create each of the secondary colors:
Yellow + Blue = Green
Blue + Red = Purple
Red + Yellow = Orange

TERTIARY COLORS: ENDLESS POSSIBILITIES!

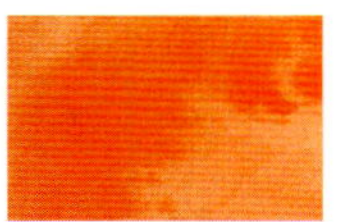 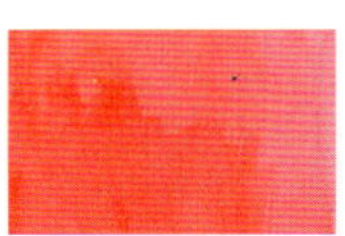 

VERMILLION   MAGENTA   VIOLET

Tertiary colors can be made by mixing one primary color with one secondary color, or by combining the three primary colors. And when you start mixing tertiary colors, it offers infinite possibilities.

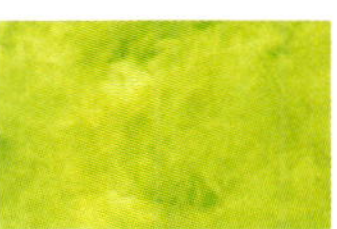 

TEAL   CHARTREUSE   AMBER

Top tip

You can buy secondary or tertiary colors ready-made, but you can achieve a greater variety of colors through mixing—and it's more fun that way!

COMPLEMENTARY COLORS

These colors sit opposite each other on the color wheel. Using them in combination will make your paintings pop: each brings out the opposite quality in the other. You'll often find complementary colors in nature—an orange sunset in a blue sky, or green foliage with red flowers. Complementary colors include blue/orange, red/green, and yellow/purple.

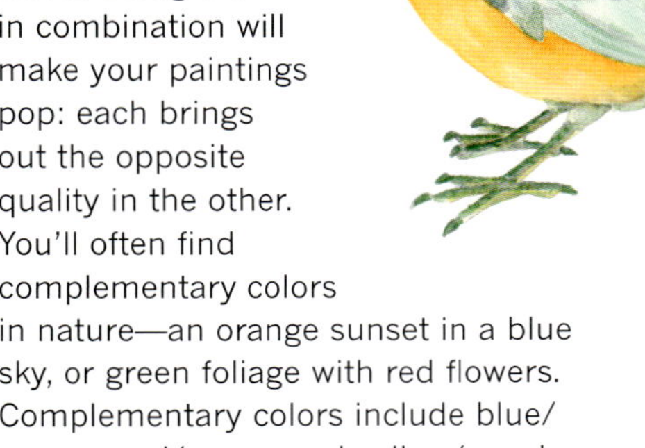

HARMONIOUS COLORS

Colors located beside one another on the color wheel are called harmonious (or analogous) colors. Their close relationship means that they always work well together. They're one of the simplest ways to achieve a pleasing outcome: they tend to produce calm, harmonious results.

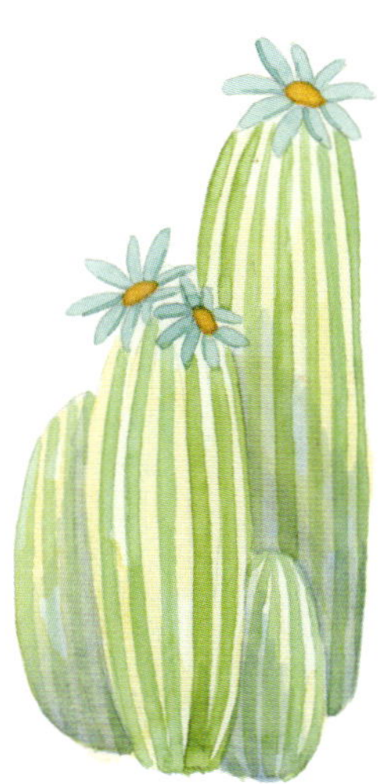

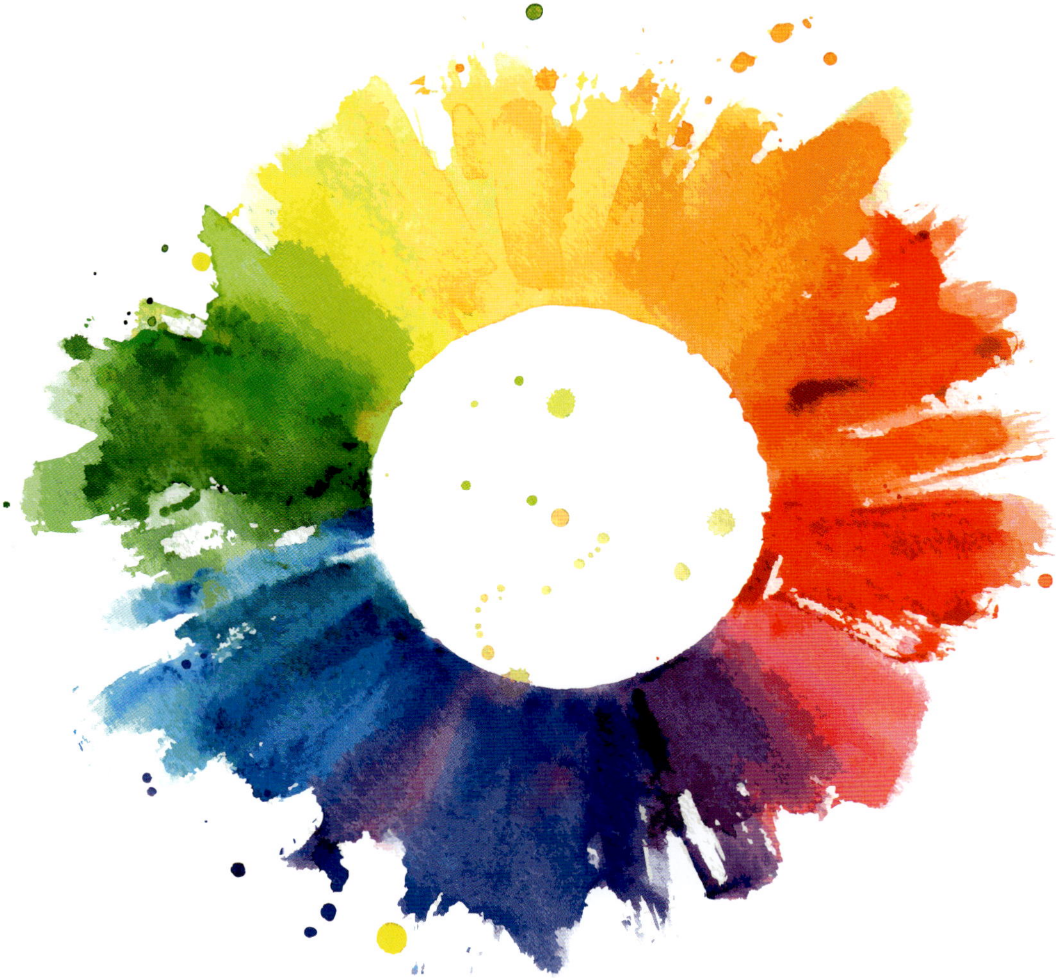

COLOR BIAS

Understanding something called "color bias" will help you understand the characteristics of different paint colors. This will enable you to anticipate the results when you mix colors.

Simply put, the color wheel can help us place our colors into warm or cool families.

Each "family" tends to sit on either side of the circle.
Warm color family = red, orange, yellow
Cool color family = green, blue, purple

Generally speaking, warm colors contain more red, and cool colors contain more blue. When artists talk about the "temperature" of their paints, they're referring to the color bias.

For example, you can get warm yellows, such as Cadmium Yellow, or cool yellows, such as Lemon Yellow. (Warm yellows are closer to orange on the color wheel, and cool yellows are closer to green.) When mixed with other paint colors, they will give a different outcome, even though they're both yellow.

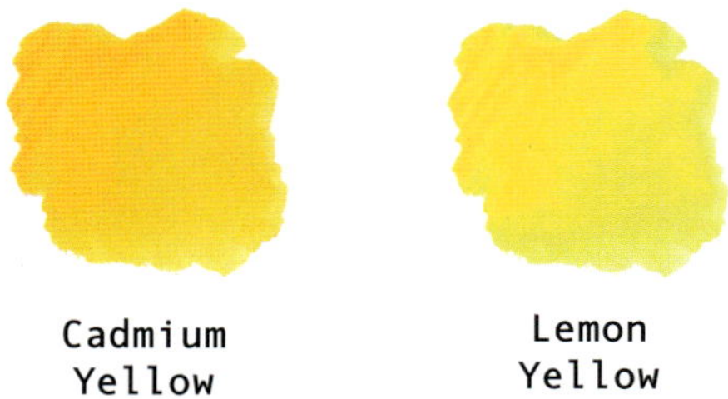

TRY IT WITH PURPLE

You can get a good sense of how warm and cool colors work by mixing purple. Mixing primary red and blue creates the richest, purest purple.

You'll get a different result if you use a cool red (which sits nearer the purples on the color wheel), such as Alizarin Crimson. Mixing a cool red with blue will create a cool purple.

Your results will be different if you use a warm red (which sits nearer the yellows on the color wheel), such as Pyrrol Scarlet. When you mix a warm red with blue, the yellow warmth it contains will turn your purple into a burgundy.

If you use a warm blue (which sits nearer to the purples on the color wheel), such as Ultramarine Blue, it will create a muddier purple.

Similarly, a cool blue (which sits nearer the greens on the color wheel), such as Winsor Blue, will create a purple that is closer to mauve.

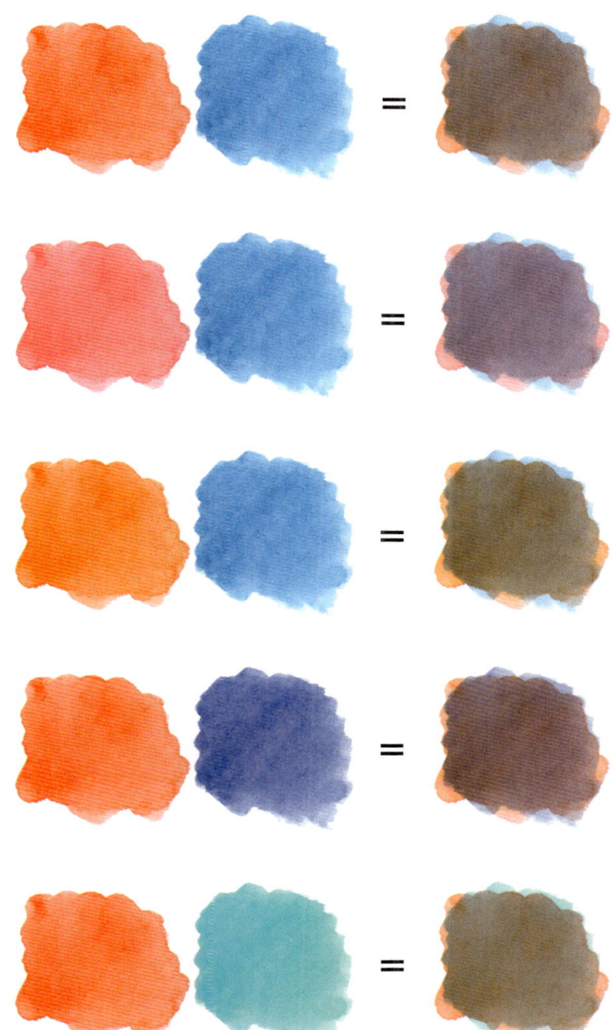

THE RULES OF COLOR BIAS (AND WHY TO BREAK THEM)

For vibrant colors, always look for the color bias that is closest to your target color on the color wheel. For bright purple, mix a cool red and a warm blue. For bright orange, mix a warm yellow and a warm red. For bright green, mix a cool blue and a cool yellow.

Once you understand the warm or cool bias of your paints, you can start to break the "rules." Try different mixes to get a sense of what happens when you play with different biases, and have fun exploring the rich color options that are suddenly available! For instance, try mixing a cool blue and a warm yellow: you'll find that you've made a lovely olive green.

TIPS FOR MIXING COLOR

There's no better way of understanding color than to mix it yourself. It'll help you understand color theory as a practical doing, trying-it-out thing, rather than as a theoretical, stuck-in-your-head thing.

When mixing, start with the lightest color and gradually add the darker one until you reach the desired color.

The basis for working with watercolor is not to add white paint to lighten colors, but to add water. By adding more water, the paint becomes more transparent, which makes it look lighter and paler. (White paint would make it cloudy and opaque.)

Three Colors

Limiting the colors on your palette will increase your color vocabulary and take your watercolor skills to the next level. Working with a three-color palette allows you to get to know each of your paint colors—and become really good at mixing them. You can focus on the impact of every color that you've used in a project, and learn the huge range of shades that each one can achieve. As an added bonus, you'll find that your paintings look more cohesive and harmonious!

The most obvious three-color palette is red, yellow, and blue. This is called the primary triad. When you introduce a secondary color as part of a three-color palette, things get even more interesting: your color world, and how you understand it, expands.

Explore the projects in the book to gain a sense of the variety each color has to offer, and the astounding range you can achieve by mixing colors together. Permanent Red Orange takes on a completely different character when used in the Jewel Brights chapter (see p. 24) compared to the Beach Spirit chapter (see p. 34)—all because of the colors it's combined with.

Some palettes will be zingy, and others will have a softer, pastel aesthetic. "Purer" primary colors will give you bright, super-colorful paintings, as in the Spring Fresh chapter (see p. 84), whereas more subtle outcomes can be achieved when your three starting colors contain complementary colors and a less saturated third color, as in the Scandi Calm chapter (see p. 44).

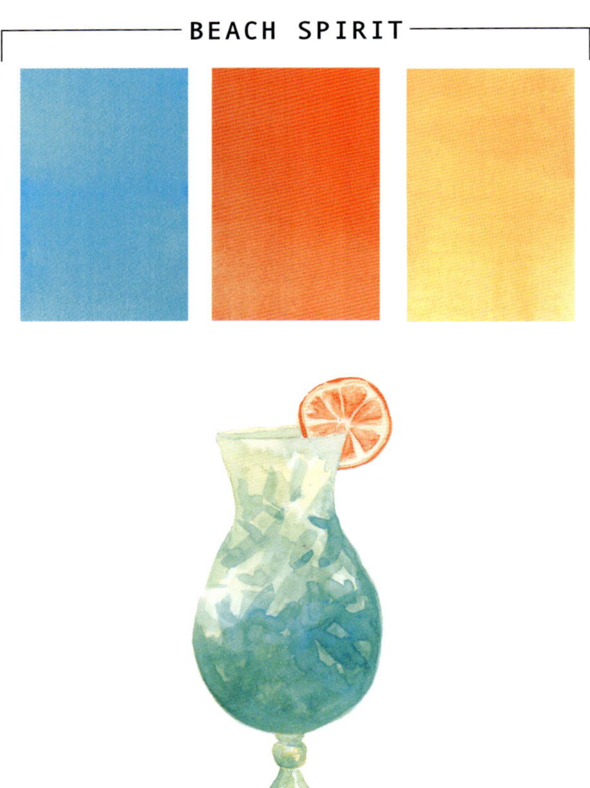

Color Charts

Each of the chapters in this book uses a different three-color palette. The palette is presented at the start of each chapter, together with a color wheel and a color chart to show how the colors can blend together and demonstrate the range of colors you can achieve from a three-color palette.

Each color chart shows 18 colors. Swatches marked with a black dot are the "pure" colors: the colors from your three-color palette. The other colors are achieved by mixing two of your three colors together.

The labels along the top and left-hand edge of the chart show which colors you need to mix to achieve a certain color swatch.

LIGHT WASH AND DARK WASH

Dark Wash

The first three rows of swatches on each color chart are richer in pigment. To mix these colors, you need more paint, and less water, on the brush. This makes the colors brighter and more saturated.

Light Wash

The lower three rows of swatches on each color chart are the same as the "dark wash" rows, but with a higher ratio of water to paint, so there is less pigment on the brush. This makes the colors paler.

Play around with adding different amounts of pigment to a wash to learn how to control the intensity of the colors in your painting.

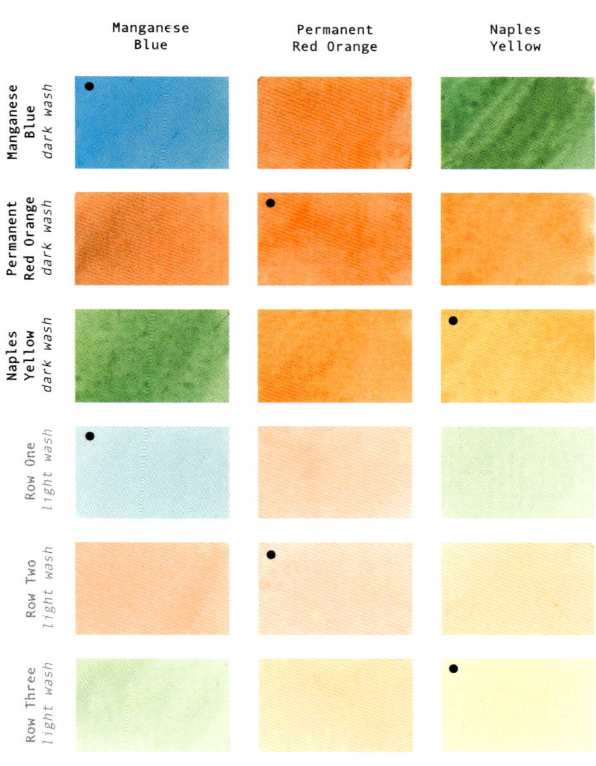

Layering

The basis of watercolor painting is building up layers of paint. Each layer of paint is called a wash, and the term for layering lots of washes is "glazing."

As watercolor is transparent, each layer shows through to the one below, combining the colors and brush marks of each. The trick is to build layers subtly and patiently: with each new layer the tonal value is increased, and you create a new, darker color. That's because you're building up layers of pigment, one on top of the other. This is what gives watercolor painting such a beautiful depth of color.

Glazes can be applied in two main ways: "wet-on-wet" and "wet-on-dry."

THE WET-ON-DRY METHOD

This technique of glazing is to paint a shape and let it dry completely before painting a new shade over the top. This is the most commonly followed approach, and is great for achieving bold color and details, and for crisp outlines and edges.

Start with your lightest shades, and when each is completely dry, add another layer. It can be a little frustrating waiting for paint to dry between glazes—using a hairdryer can speed up the process, but make sure your paper is taped down, and don't hold it too close!

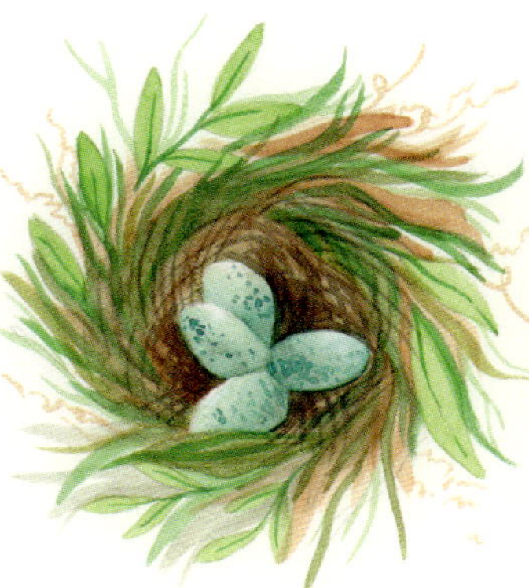

THE WET-ON-WET METHOD

This technique of glazing is to use wet paint against wet paint or paper. Areas of color blend and spread, creating beautiful bleeds or "blooms."

You can achieve this technique by painting an area of wet color, then mixing a different color on your brush. Touch your brush to the wet paint—because the first layer is still wet, your new color will spread into it.

Another option is to add to areas of wet paint on dry paper, and allow them to touch. The paint from one area will bleed into the other, allowing the colors to mix.

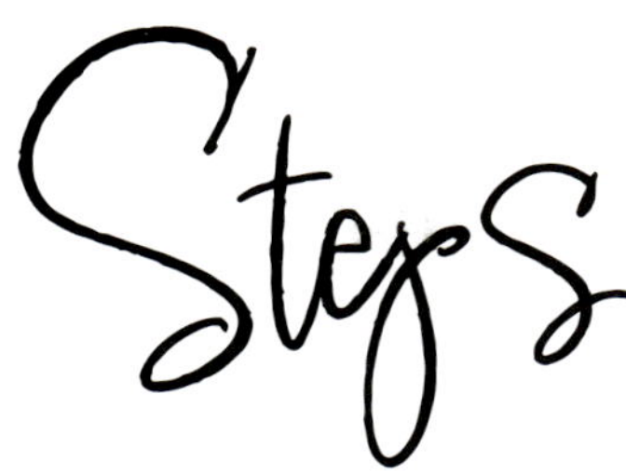

Steps

NEGATIVE SPACE

One of the first things you need to think about when you start a watercolor project is negative space. Negative space in a watercolor painting is where an area of the painting has no paint on it (or, sometimes, only a very light wash).

Negative space is used for the areas that are white, or the very lightest parts, of the subject you're painting. There is no "white" watercolor paint. Instead, the white of your paper acts as the white.

That means you need to plan for your highlights at the beginning of your project, even though you might naturally think of them as a finishing touch. Make sure not to add paint to the areas you would like to be highlights.

If you're worried about filling in your negative space, you can use masking tape or masking fluid to protect these areas if you like.

INITIAL WASHES

Initial washes are usually "light washes," or pale in color, which means they are made with a higher proportion of water to pigment than dark washes. These create a foundation, or background layer of color.

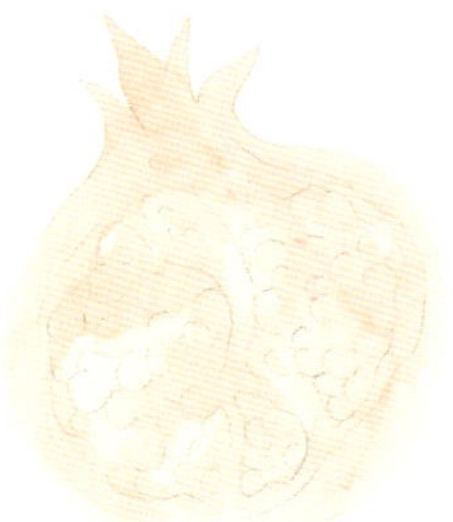

BUILDING COLOR

After the initial wash, build layers of progressively darker colors, with an increasing proportion of pigment to water.

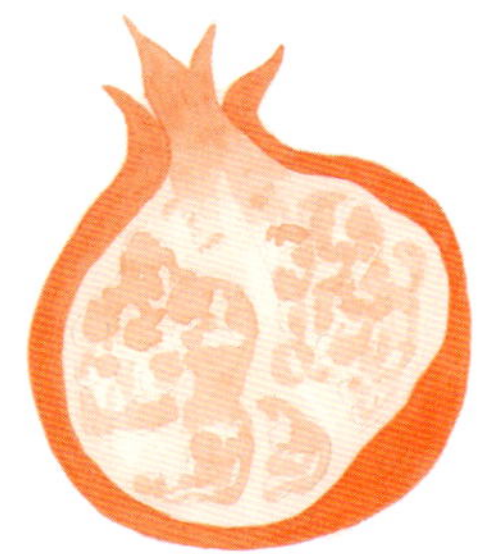

DARKER COLORS AND DETAILS

The darkest colors in the painting are added toward the end, and the final touches will be your details: elements such as the speckles of an egg or the pupil in an eye, which are usually added carefully with the tip of your brush.

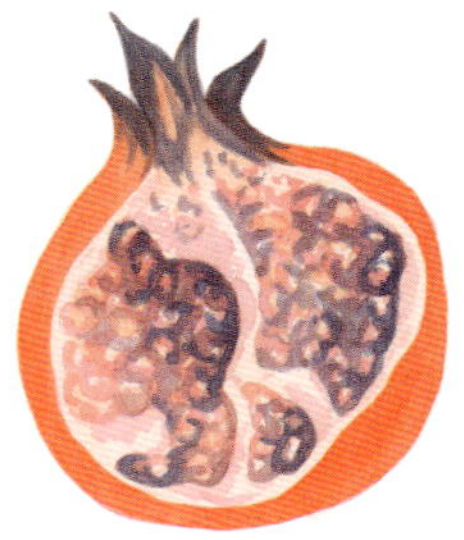

The Palettes

Jewel Brights

This three-color palette is inspired by the director Wes Anderson, whose movies are immediately recognizable for their richly contrasting colors and nostalgic pastel shades. It is a simple, fun mix that lends itself well to juicy fruit, brightly colored plants, and pretty pastries.

THE COLORS

| Permanent Red Orange | Rose Madder | Delft Blue |

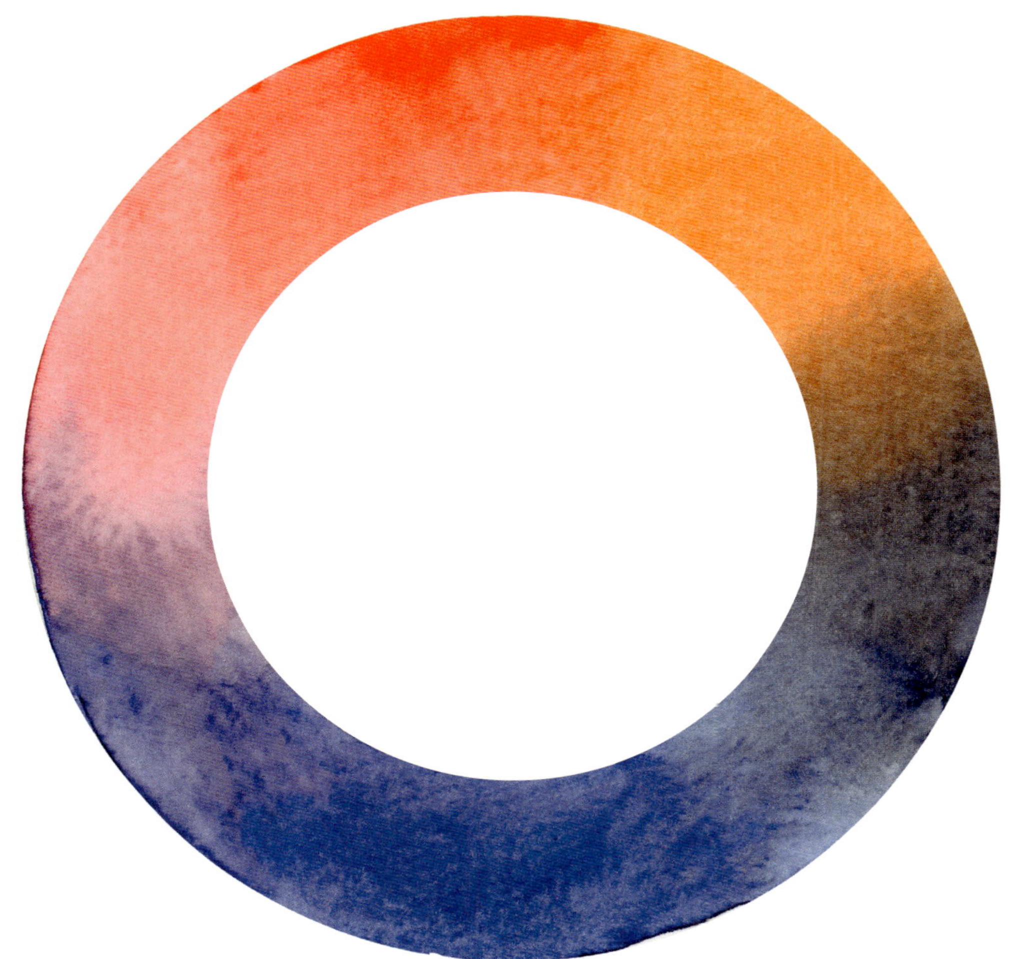

Mixing

The above shows the three colors on a simple
color wheel, each blending into its neighbor.
On the next page, you will see a chart showing
how the colors interact with each other.

COLOR CHART

Each color is shown at two strengths: a dark wash
and a light wash. See p. 19 for more on washes.

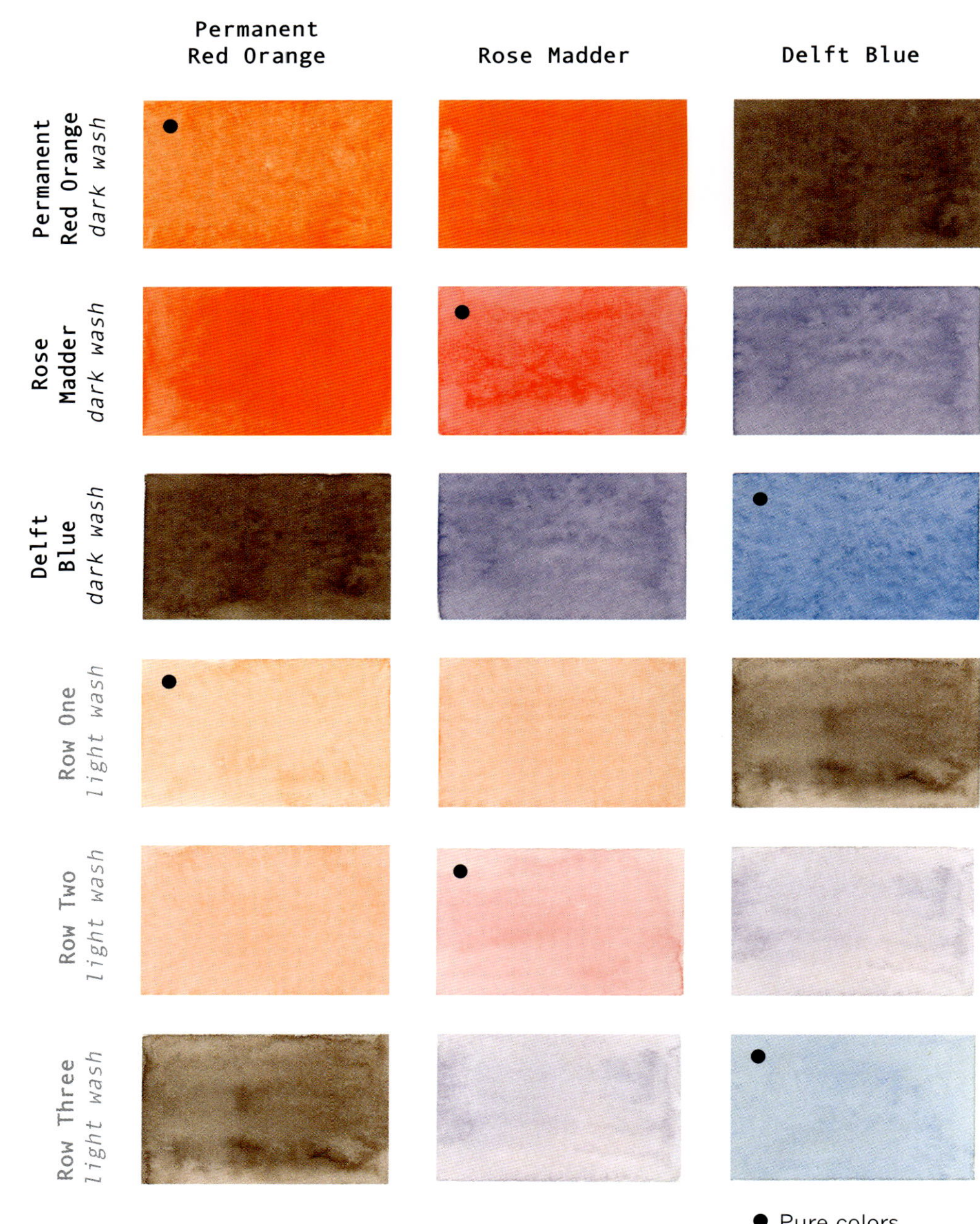

The Projects

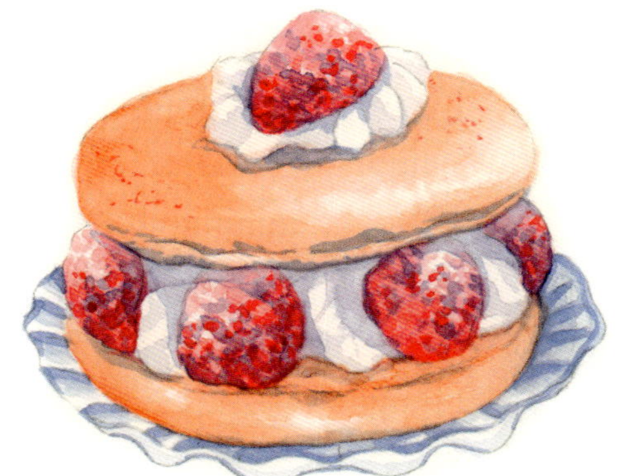

1. PATISSERIE

2. POMEGRANATE

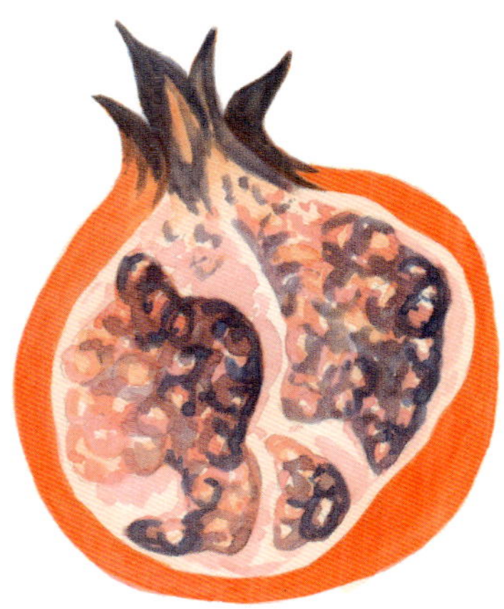

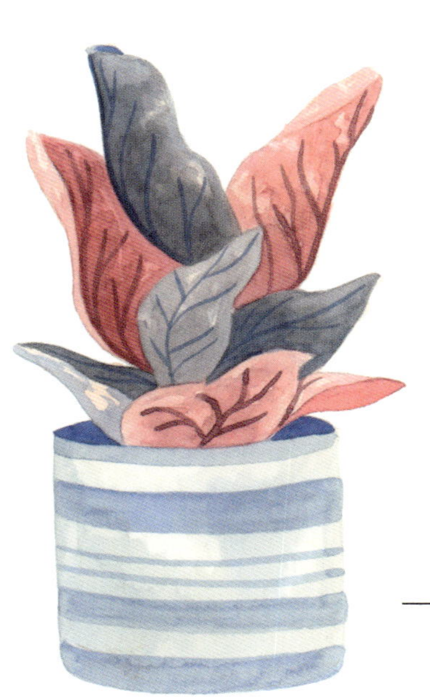

3. POTTED PLANT

Patisserie

Create a confection fit for Wes Anderson's *The Grand Budapest Hotel* with charming pastel tones, fruity raspberries, and plenty of panache.

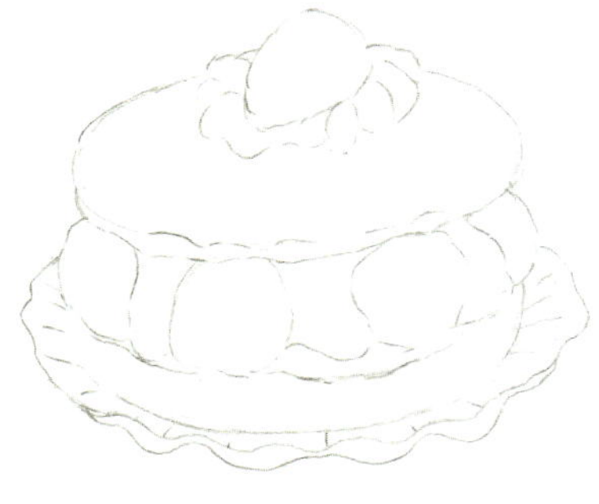

1

Begin with a simple pencil sketch.

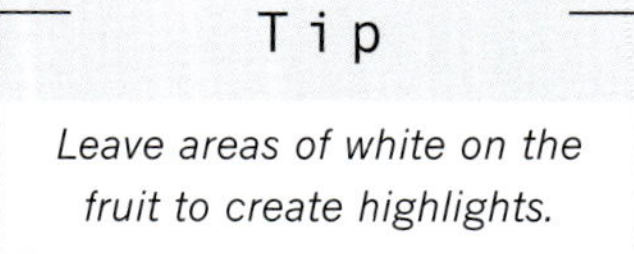

Tip

Leave areas of white on the fruit to create highlights.

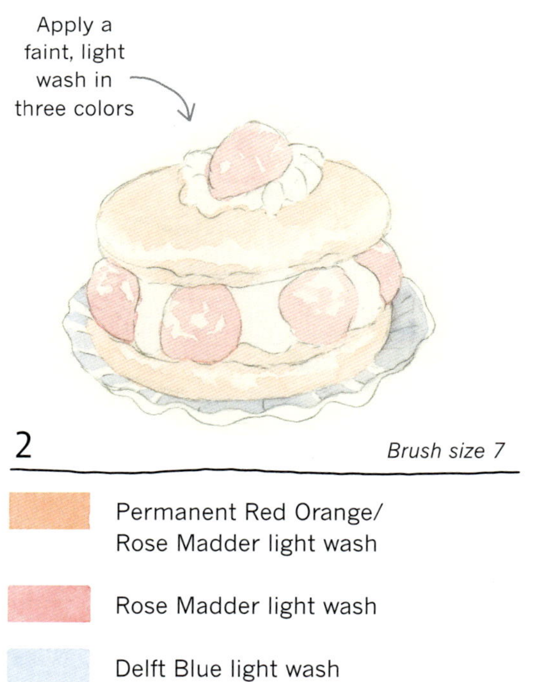

2

Brush size 7

Permanent Red Orange/
Rose Madder light wash

Rose Madder light wash

Delft Blue light wash

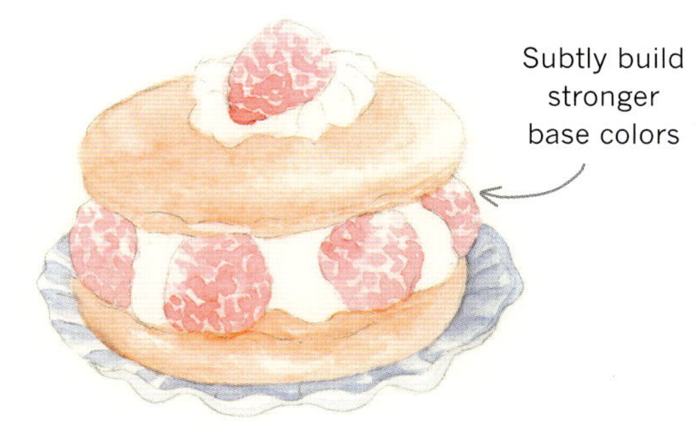

Subtly build
stronger
base colors

3

Brush size 4

Permanent Red Orange
light wash

Rose Madder light wash

Delft Blue light wash

Add shadows
and depth to
the fruit and
the cream

4

Brush size 1

Rose Madder/Delft Blue dark wash

Rose Madder/Delft Blue light wash

Add depth to the
shadows and pink-up the
raspberries

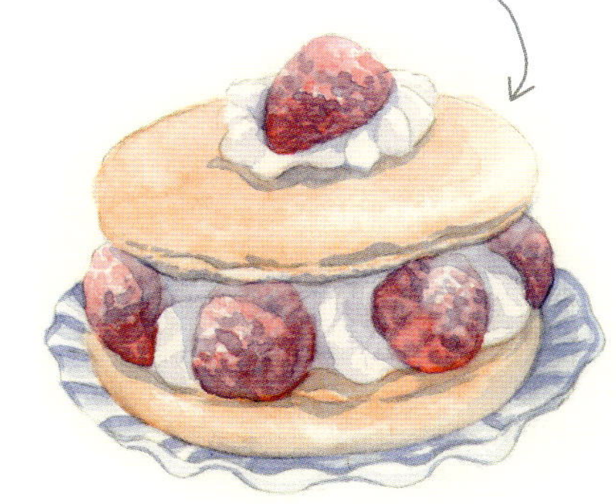

5

Brush size 1

Rose Madder
light wash

Delft Blue
dark wash

Apply a darker wash for
more depth, giving a
greater sense of three-
dimensionality

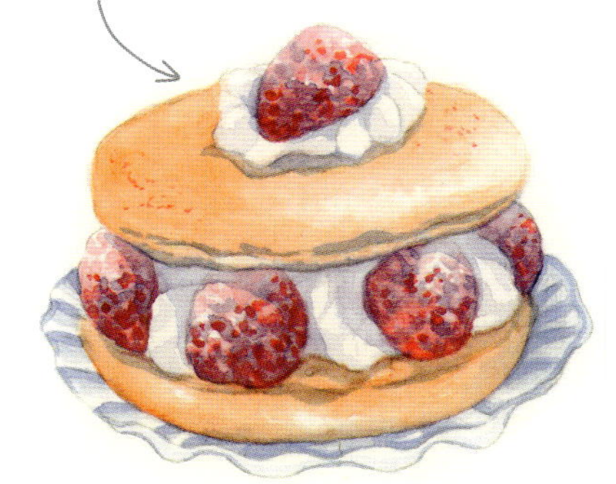

6

Brush size 4

Rose Madder dark wash

Permanent Red Orange dark wash

Pomegranate

The jewel-like pomegranate is the king of the fruit bowl. Use your three-color palette to serve up an enticing fruit with subtle flesh and rich, juicy seeds.

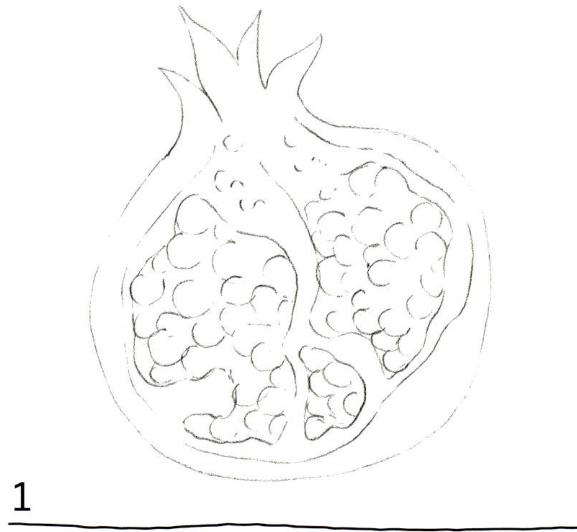

1

Begin with a simple pencil sketch.

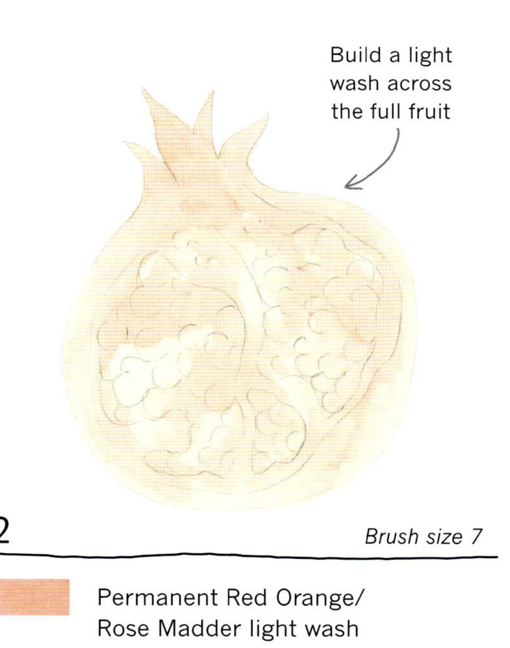

2   *Brush size 7*

Permanent Red Orange/
Rose Madder light wash

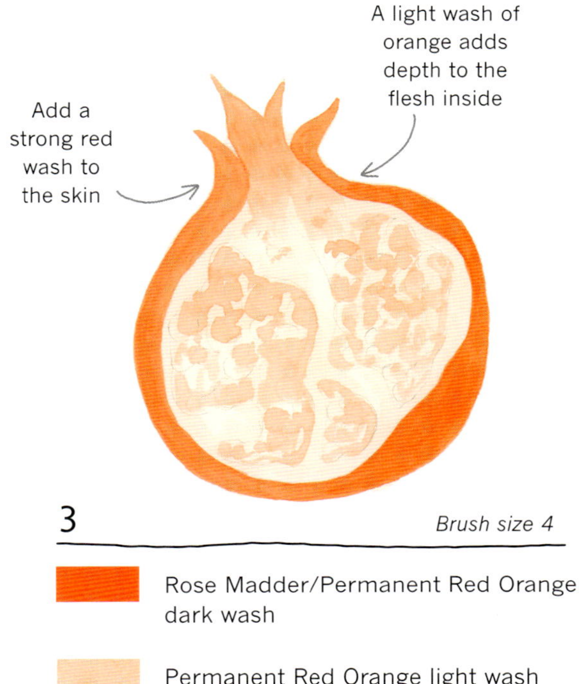

Add a strong red wash to the skin
A light wash of orange adds depth to the flesh inside
3
Brush size 4
Rose Madder/Permanent Red Orange dark wash
Permanent Red Orange light wash

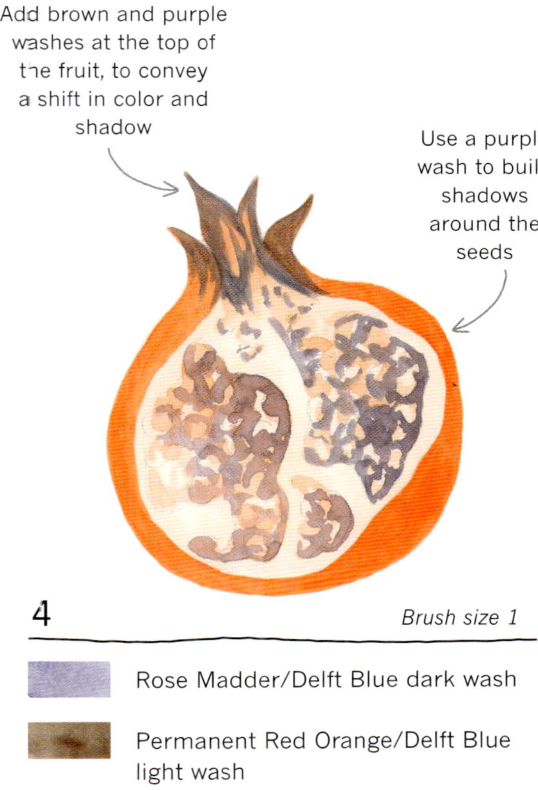

Add brown and purple washes at the top of the fruit, to convey a shift in color and shadow
Use a purple wash to build shadows around the seeds
4
Brush size 1
Rose Madder/Delft Blue dark wash
Permanent Red Orange/Delft Blue light wash

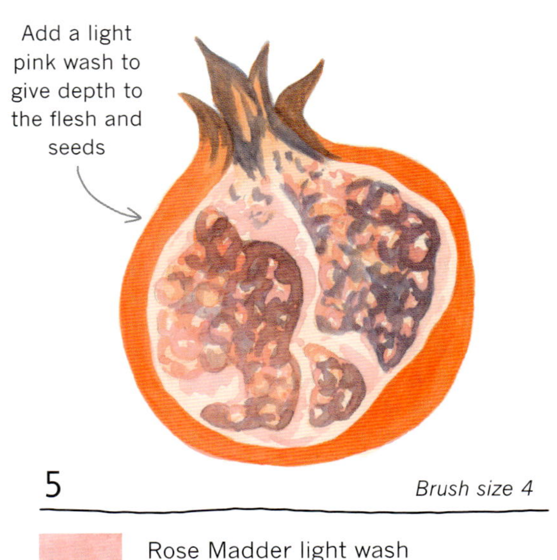

Add a light pink wash to give depth to the flesh and seeds
5
Brush size 4
Rose Madder light wash

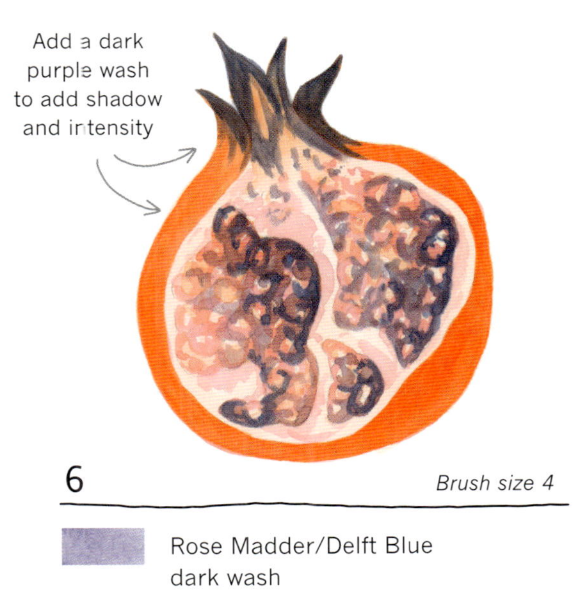

Add a dark purple wash to add shadow and intensity
6
Brush size 4
Rose Madder/Delft Blue dark wash

Potted Plant

Do you have a thriving jungle at home, or perhaps you have a flagging houseplant on your conscience? Either way, here's one plant you'll be sure to nurture. Dreamy, calming tones are the name of the game.

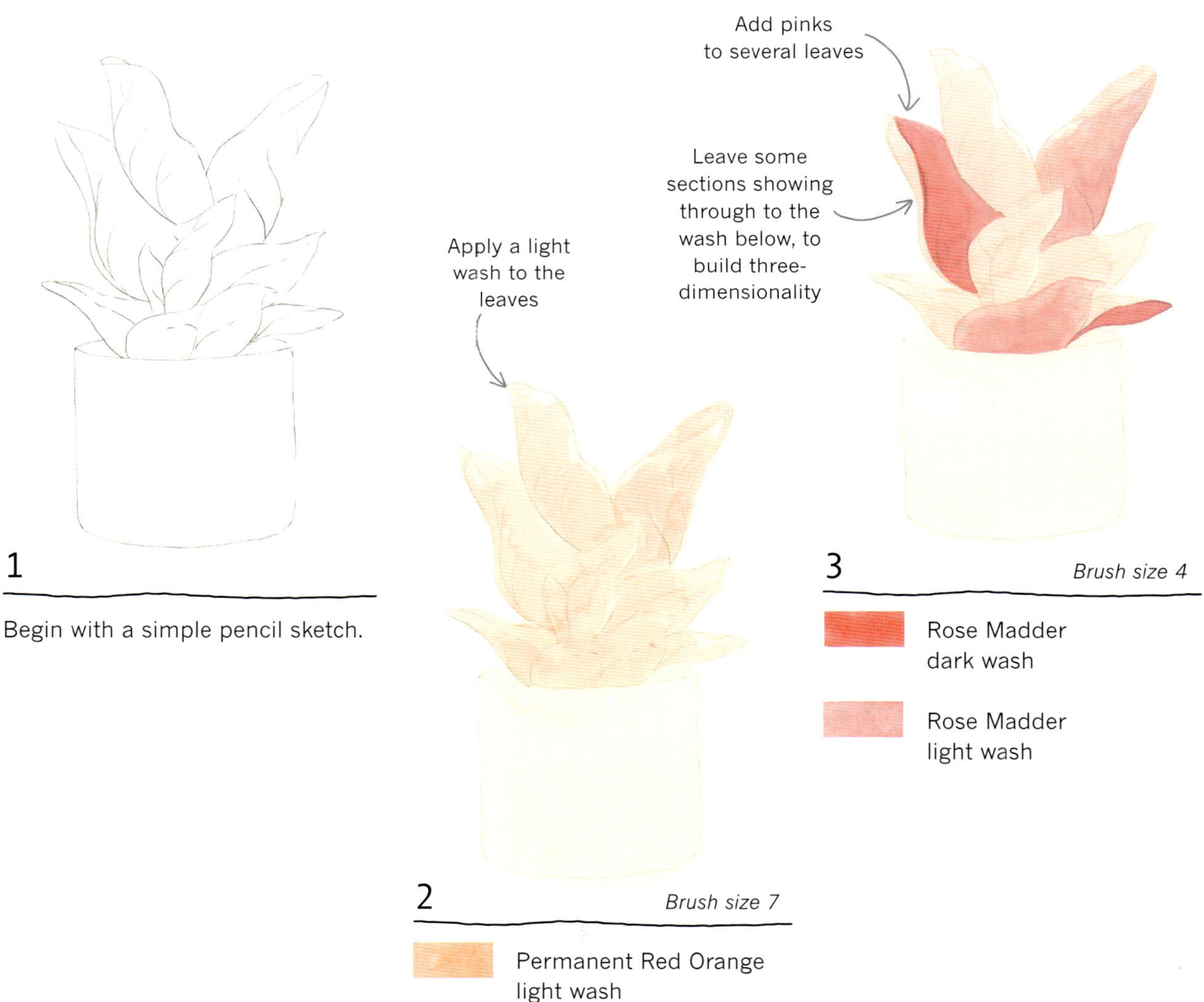

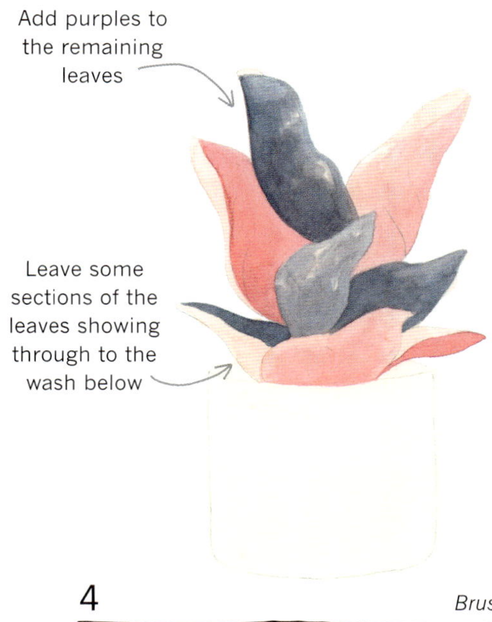

4 *Brush size 4*

Rose Madder/Delft Blue dark wash

Rose Madder/Delft Blue light wash

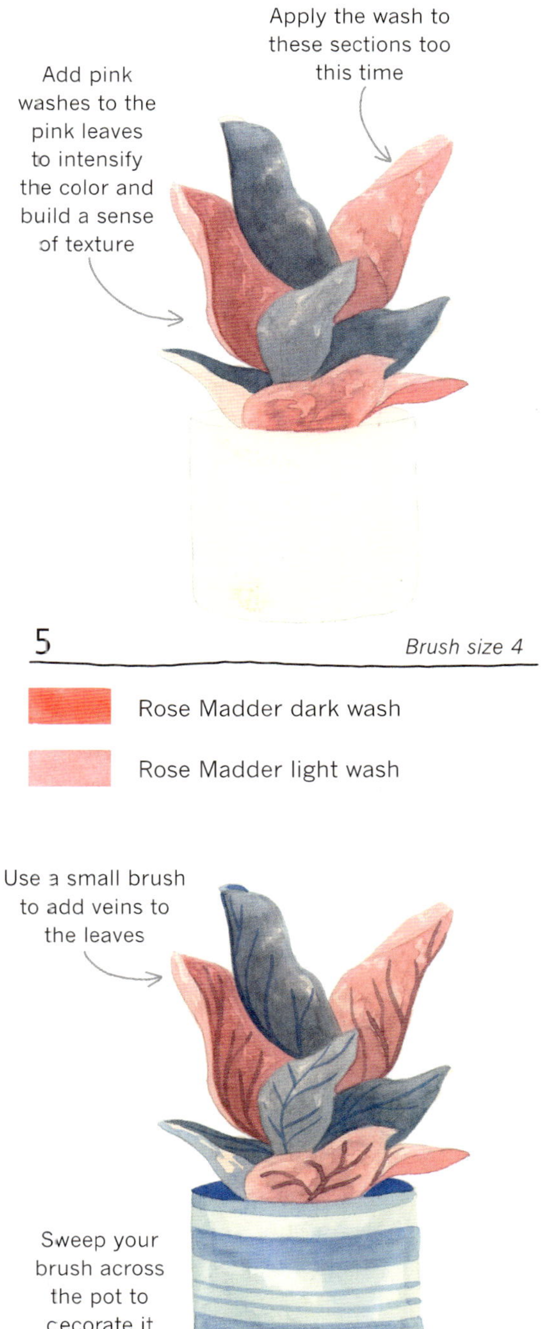

5 *Brush size 4*

Rose Madder dark wash

Rose Madder light wash

6 *Brush size 4*

Delft Blue light wash

Tip

*For a mottled, dewy effect, apply a light
wash while the previous layer is still wet.*

7 *Brush size 1*

Delft Blue dark wash

Beach Spirit

This three-color palette brings sun-soaked hues and calming blues—colors that bring to mind holidays and happiness. It is a cheering, versatile mix.

THE COLORS

Manganese Blue

Permanent Red Orange

Naples Yellow

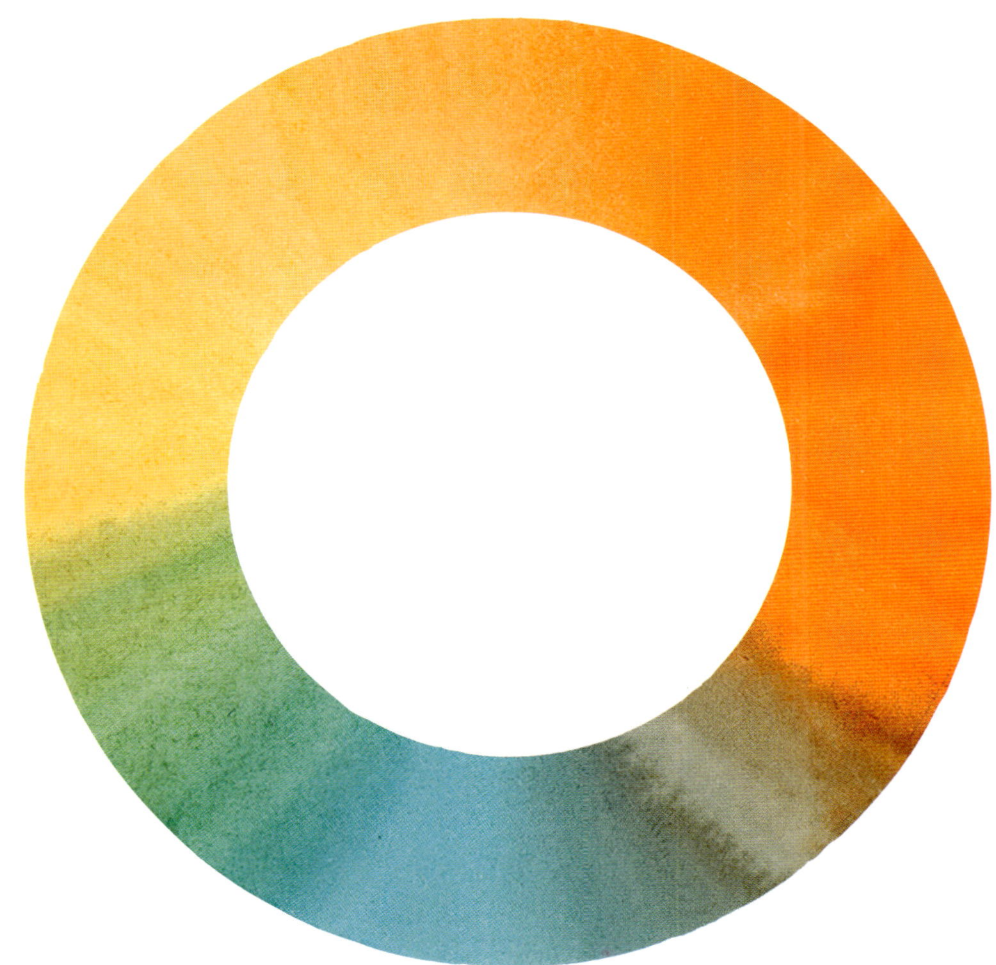

Mixing

The above shows the three colors on a simple
color wheel, each blending into its neighbor.
On the next page, you will see a chart showing
how the colors interact with each other.

COLOR CHART

Each color is shown at two strengths: a dark wash
and a light wash. See p. 19 for more on washes.

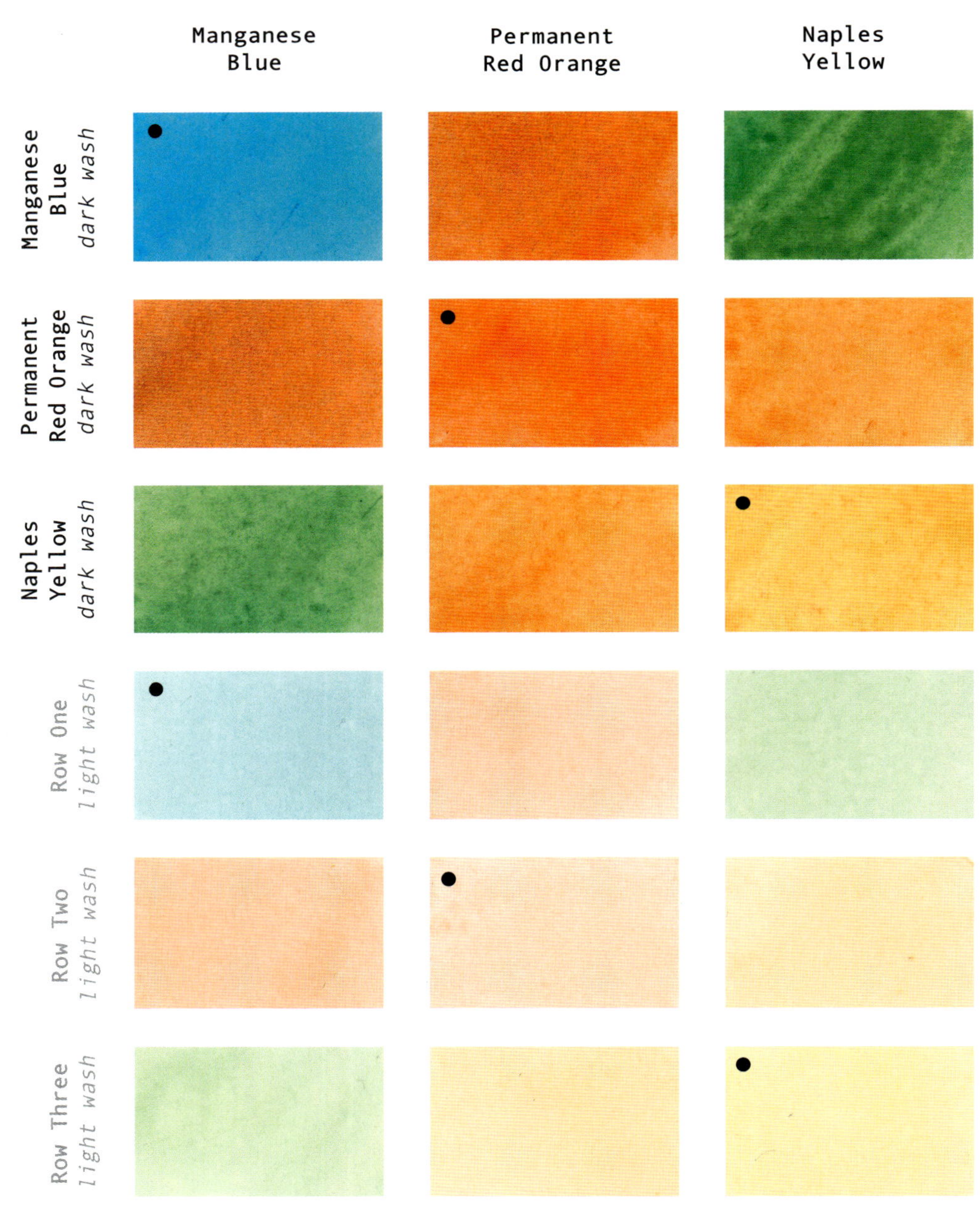

The Projects

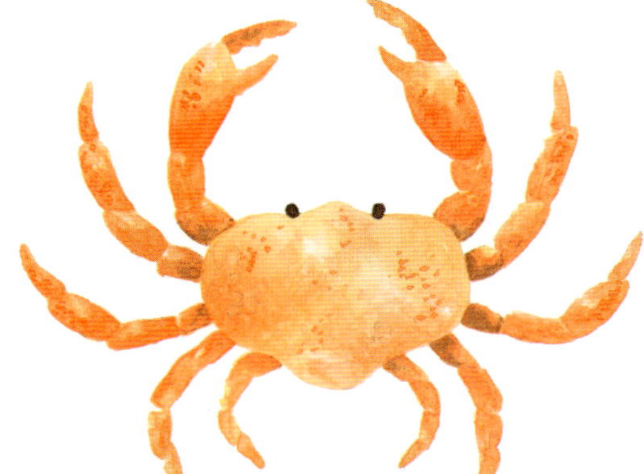

1. ROCKPOOL CRAB

2. COCKTAIL HOUR

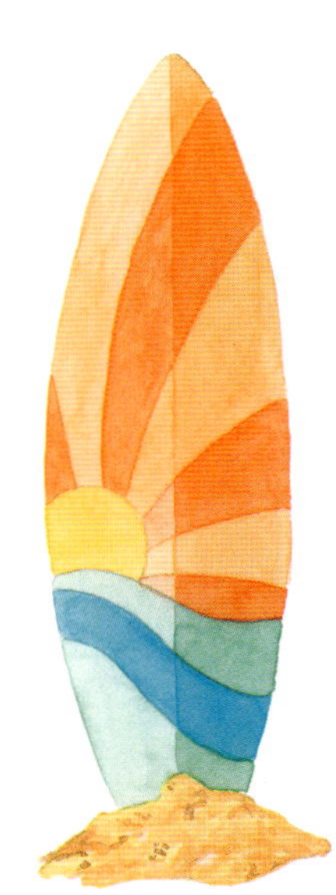

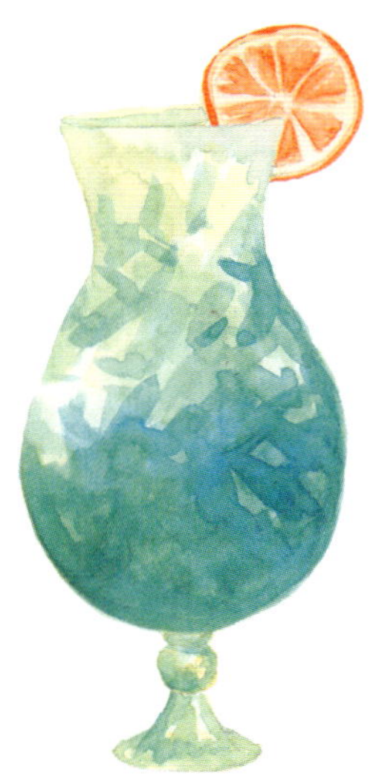

3. SURF'S UP

Rockpool Crab

Whether crustaceans bring to mind long afternoons rockpooling or seaside restaurants (shh!), there's no denying the beauty of their gleaming, orange shells.

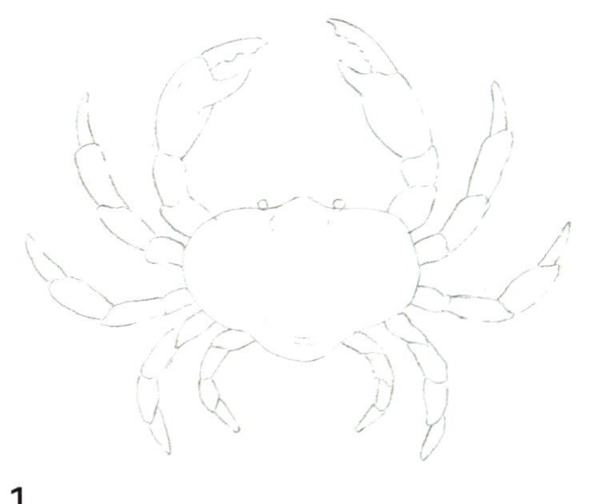

1

Begin with a simple pencil sketch.

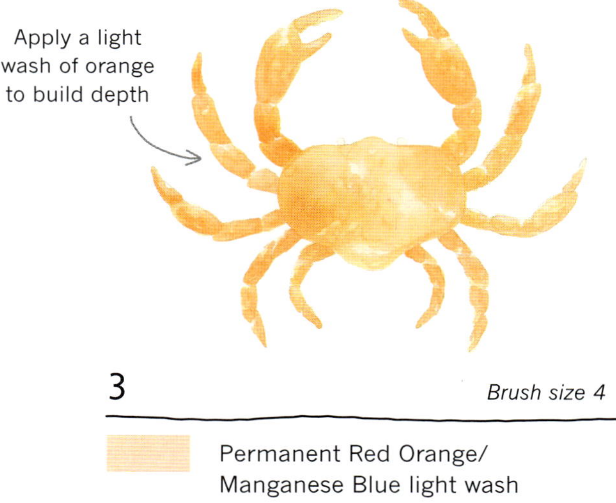

2 *Brush size 7*

Naples Yellow light wash

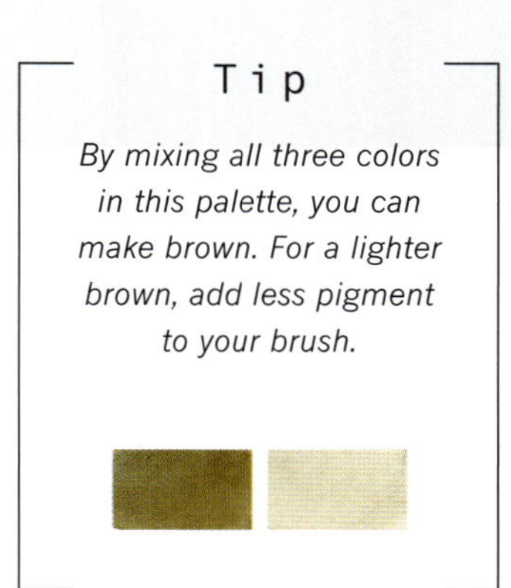

Tip

By mixing all three colors in this palette, you can make brown. For a lighter brown, add less pigment to your brush.

3 *Brush size 4*

Permanent Red Orange/
Manganese Blue light wash

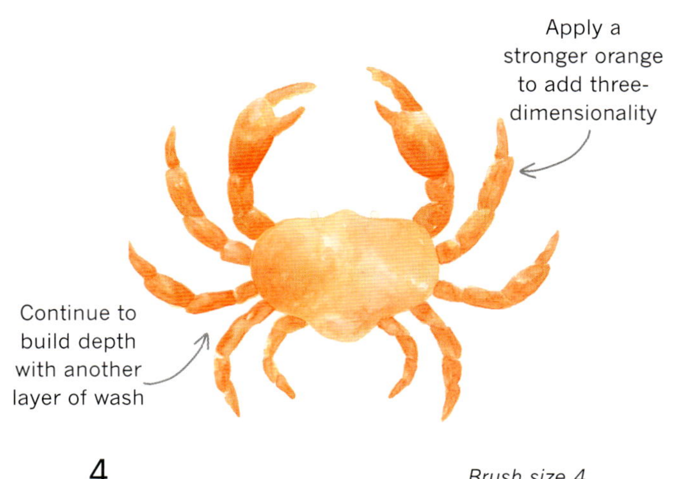

4 *Brush size 4*

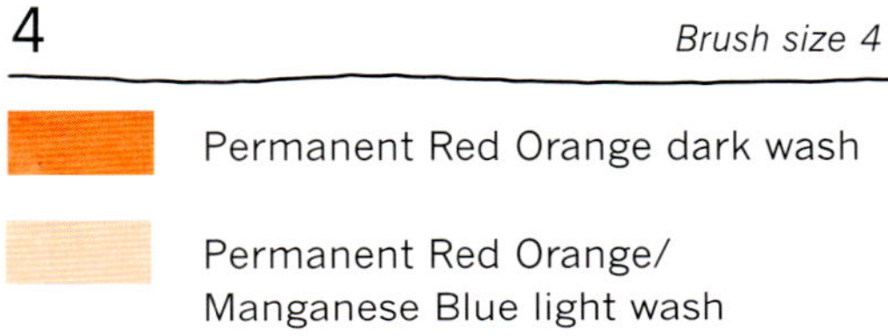

Permanent Red Orange dark wash

Permanent Red Orange/ Manganese Blue light wash

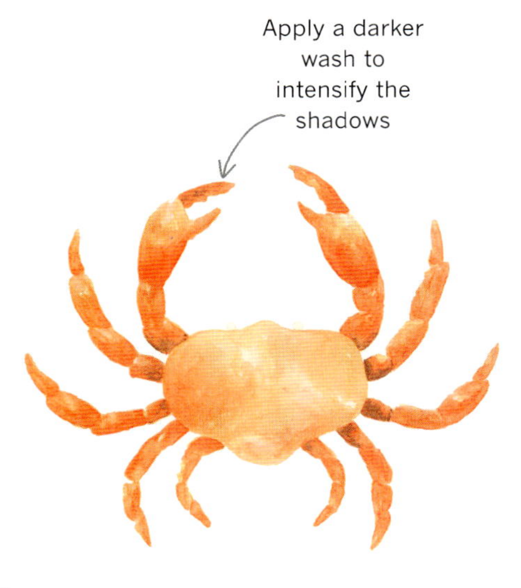

5 *Brush size 4*

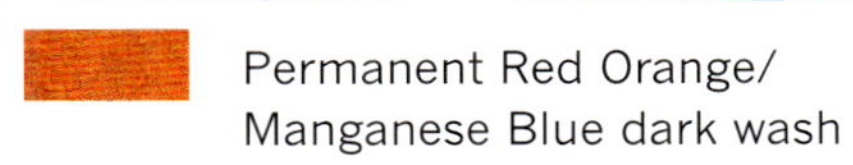

Permanent Red Orange/ Manganese Blue dark wash

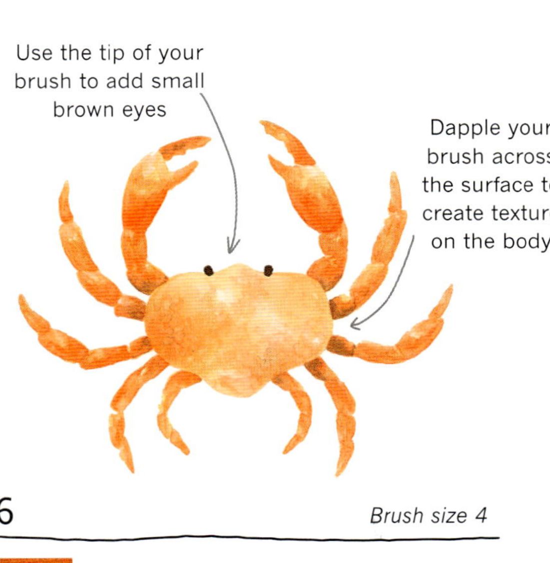

6 *Brush size 4*

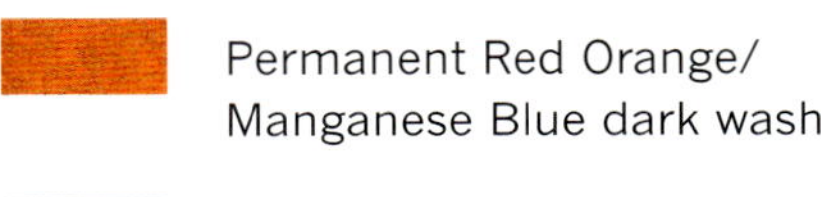

Permanent Red Orange/ Manganese Blue dark wash

All three colors, dark wash

> ### Tip
> *Let the previous layer dry before adding your fine details, or else the paint will bleed.*

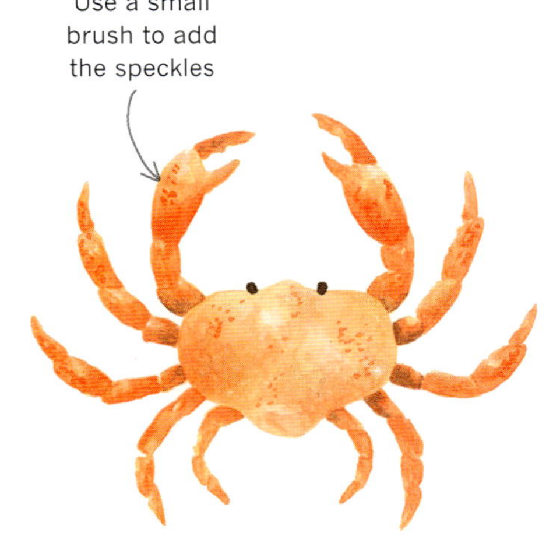

7 *Brush size 1*

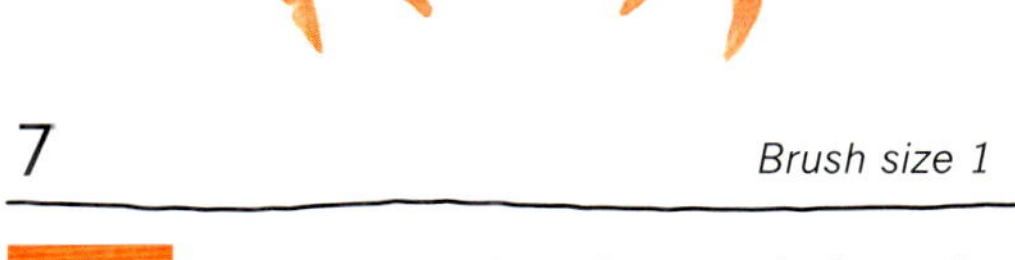

Permanent Red Orange dark wash

Cocktail Hour

Poolside or city slicking, cocktail or mocktail: this project is a treat at the end cf a day in the sun. The intensity of that blue, paired with a gleaming slice of orange . . . go on, take a sip.

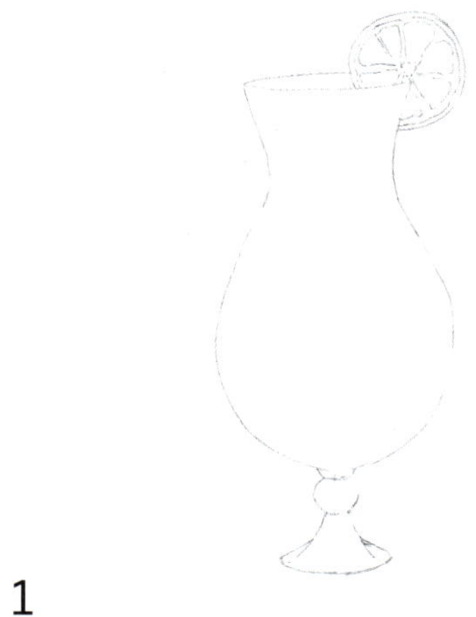

1

Begin with a simple pencil sketch.

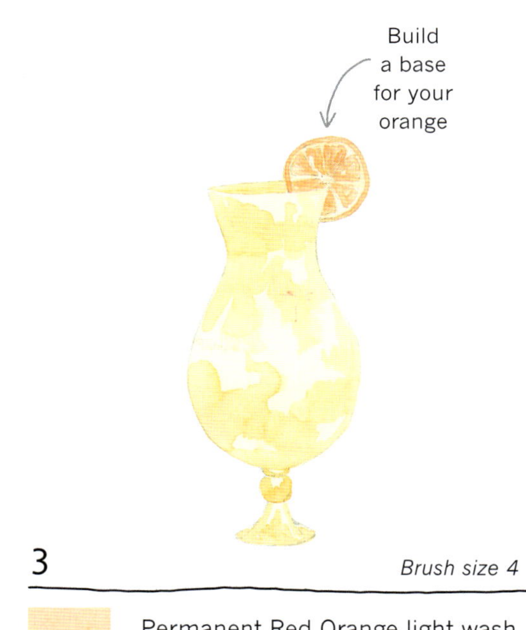

3

Brush size 4

Permanent Red Orange light wash

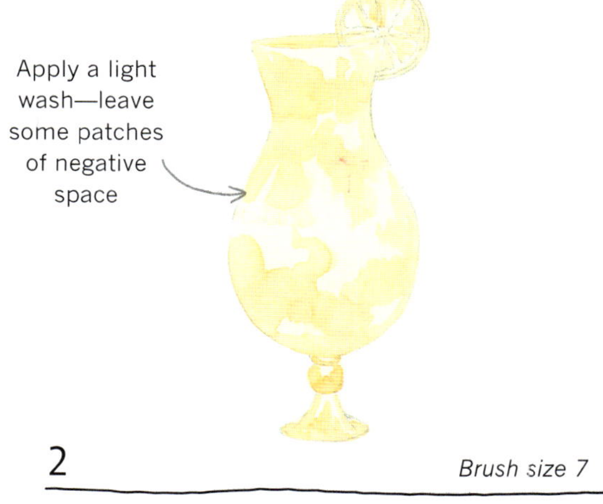

2

Brush size 7

Naples Yellow light wash

> **Tip**
>
> *Use the side of your paintbrush to create different brushstrokes.*

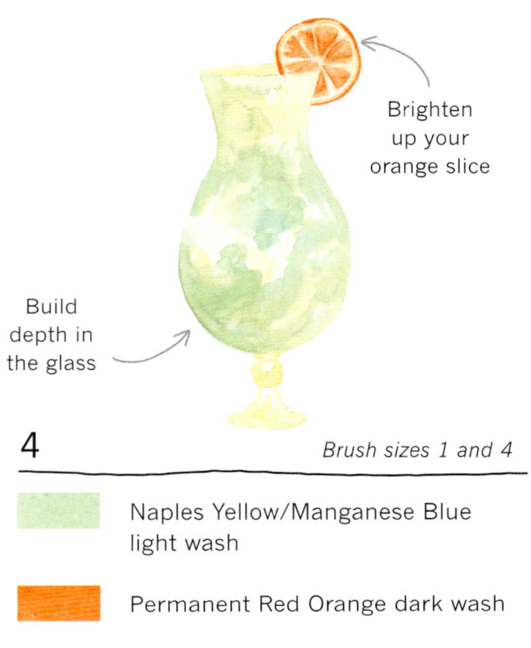

Brighten
up your
orange slice

Build
depth in
the glass

4   *Brush sizes 1 and 4*

Naples Yellow/Manganese Blue
light wash

Permanent Red Orange dark wash

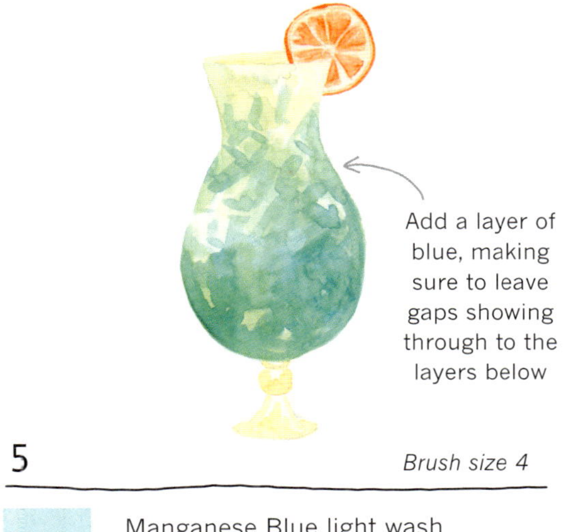

Add a layer of
blue, making
sure to leave
gaps showing
through to the
layers below

5   *Brush size 4*

Manganese Blue light wash

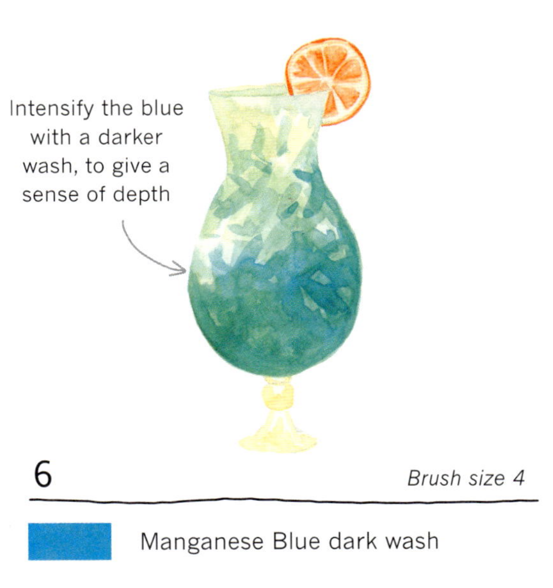

Intensify the blue
with a darker
wash, to give a
sense of depth

6   *Brush size 4*

Manganese Blue dark wash

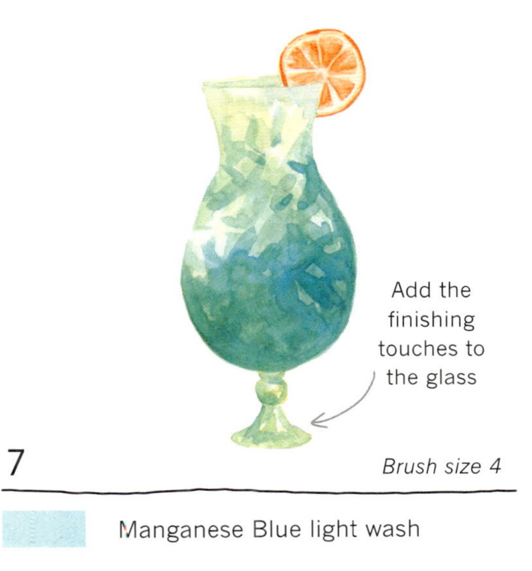

Add the
finishing
touches to
the glass

7   *Brush size 4*

Manganese Blue light wash

Surf's Up

This project is beach spirit in a nutshell. Build your own surfboard with a three-color palette—as the Hawaiian proverb goes, "You can't stop the waves, but you can learn how to surf."

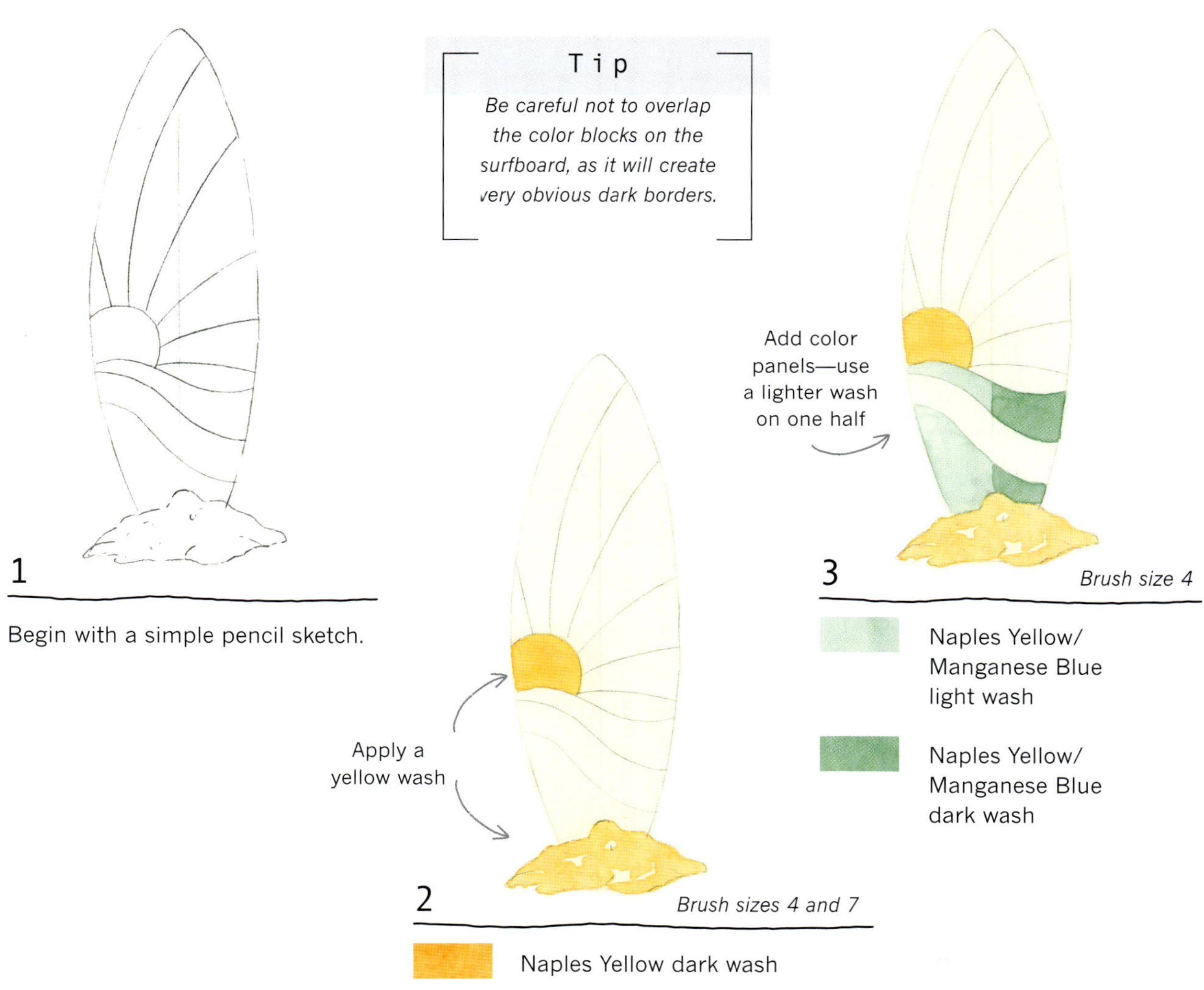

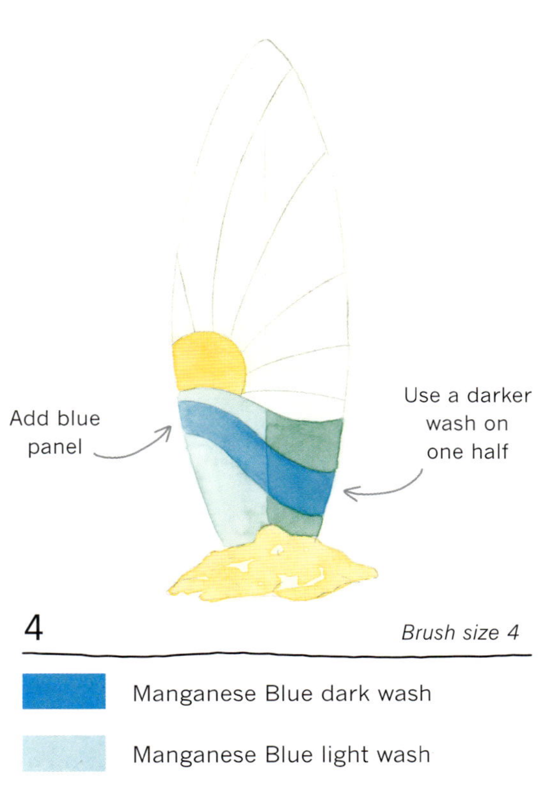

4 *Brush size 4*

Manganese Blue dark wash

Manganese Blue light wash

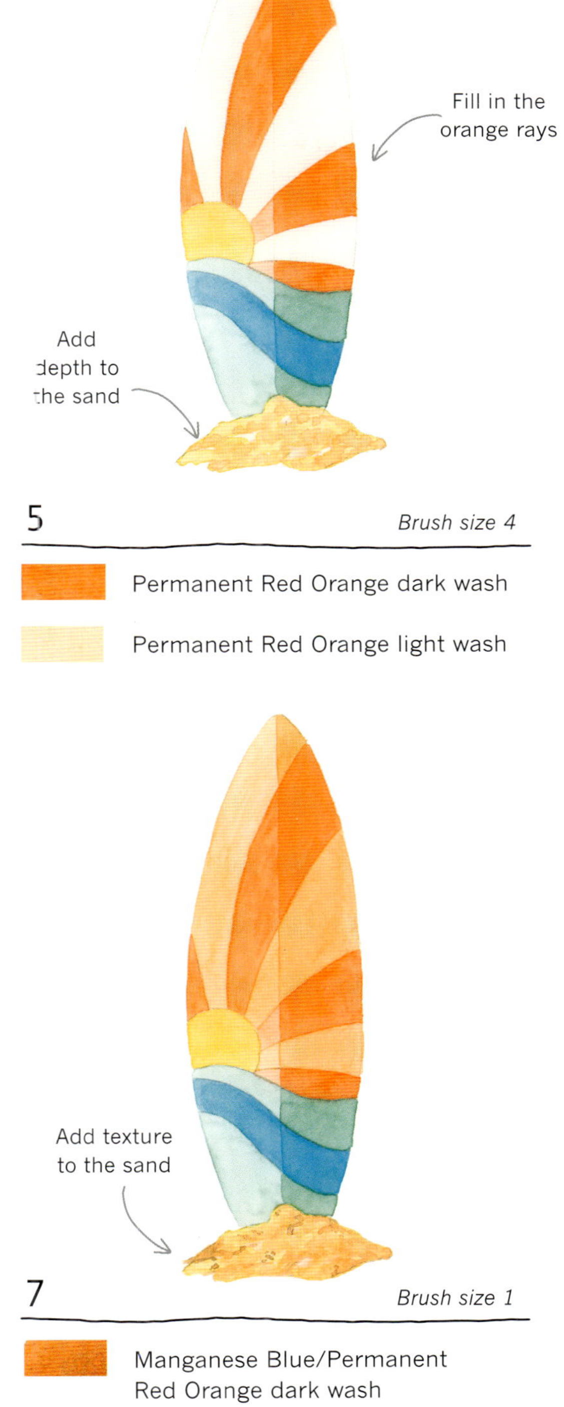

5 *Brush size 4*

Permanent Red Orange dark wash

Permanent Red Orange light wash

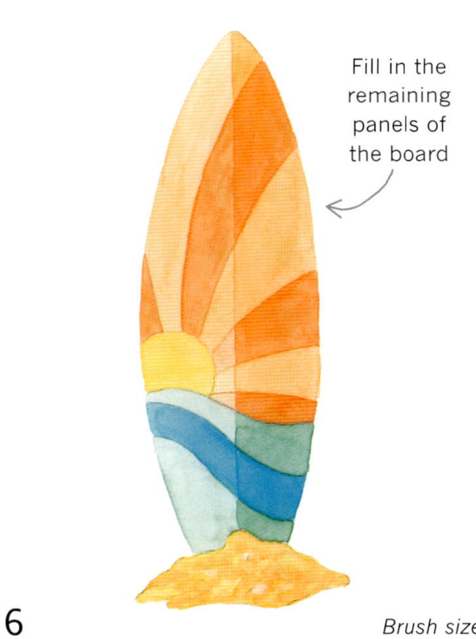

6 *Brush size 4*

Naples Yellow/Permanent Red Orange dark wash

Naples Yellow/Permanent Red Orange light wash

7 *Brush size 1*

Manganese Blue/Permanent Red Orange dark wash

Scandi Calm

This three-color palette is classy, restrained, and oh-so-calming. It is a grown-up mix that lends itself well to the natural world—and encourages you to breathe deeply.

THE COLORS

Buff Titanium

Pompeii Red

Perylene Green

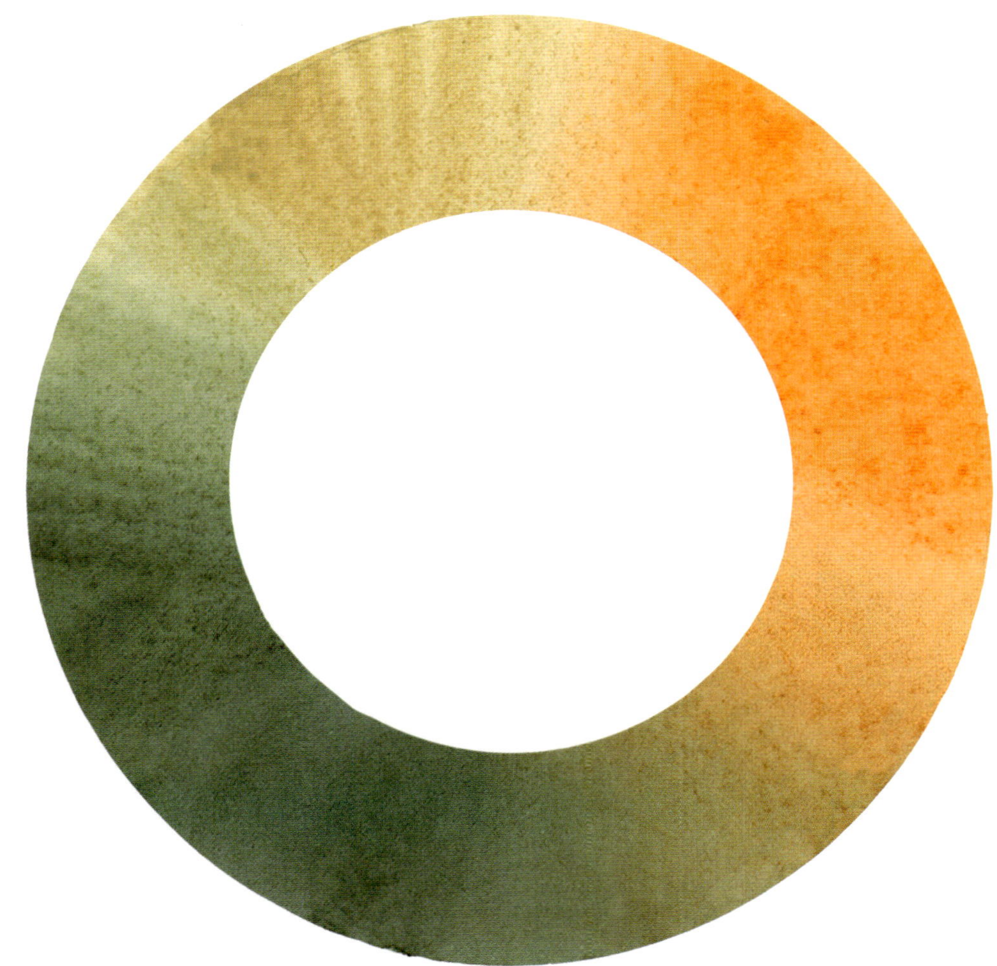

Mixing

The above shows the three colors on a simple
color wheel, each blending into its neighbor.
On the next page, you will see a chart showing
how the colors interact with each other.

COLOR CHART

Each color is shown at two strengths: a dark wash
and a light wash. See p. 19 for more on washes.

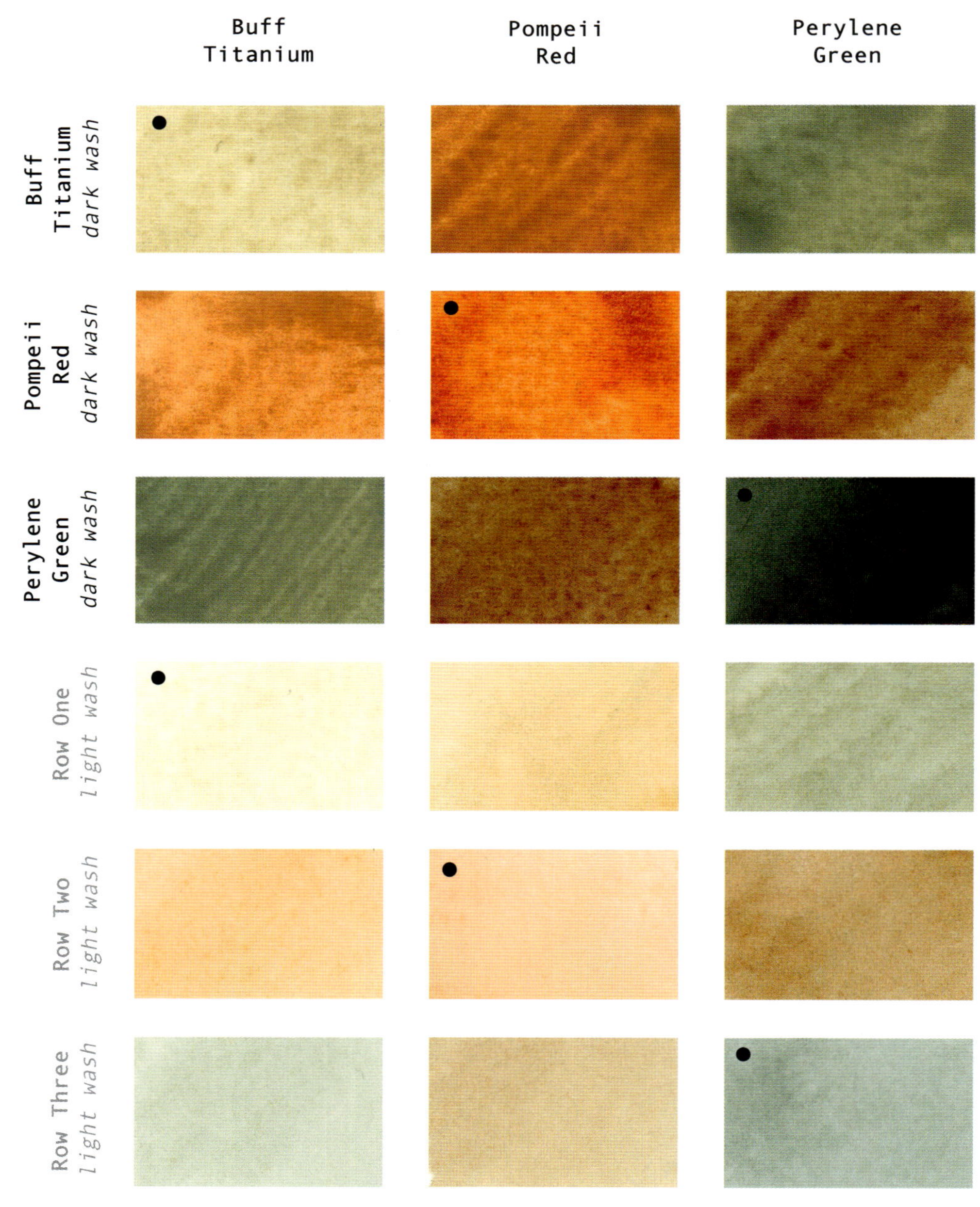

The Projects

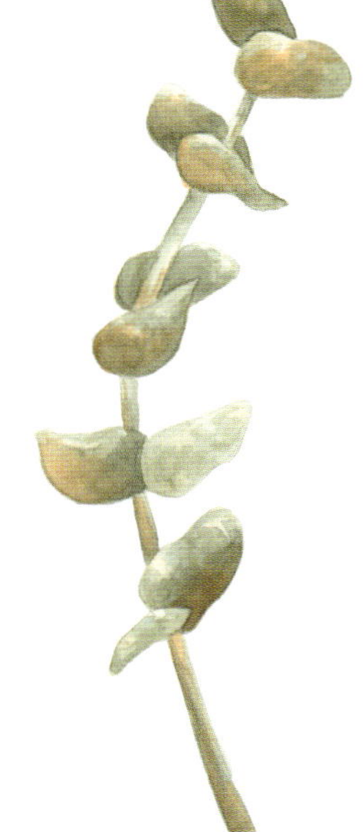

1. EUCALYPTUS

2. WICKER BASKET

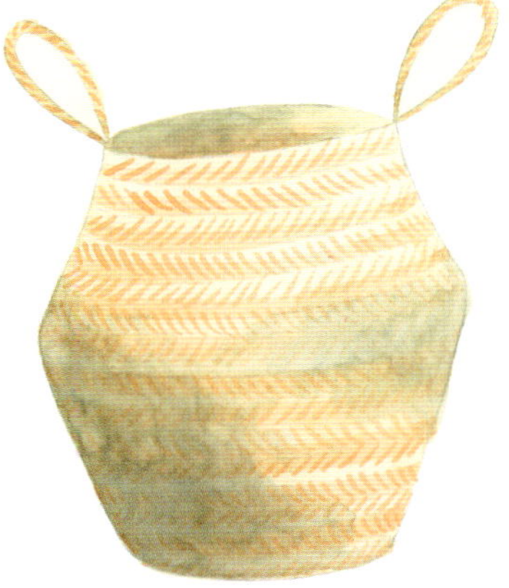

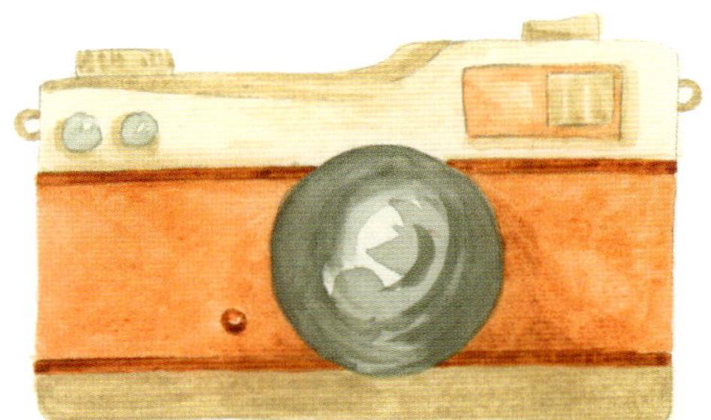

3. PHOTO TIME

Eucalyptus

If mindfulness was a plant, it would be eucalyptus. Find your inner calm by painting its silver-green leaves and you'll feel the benefits.

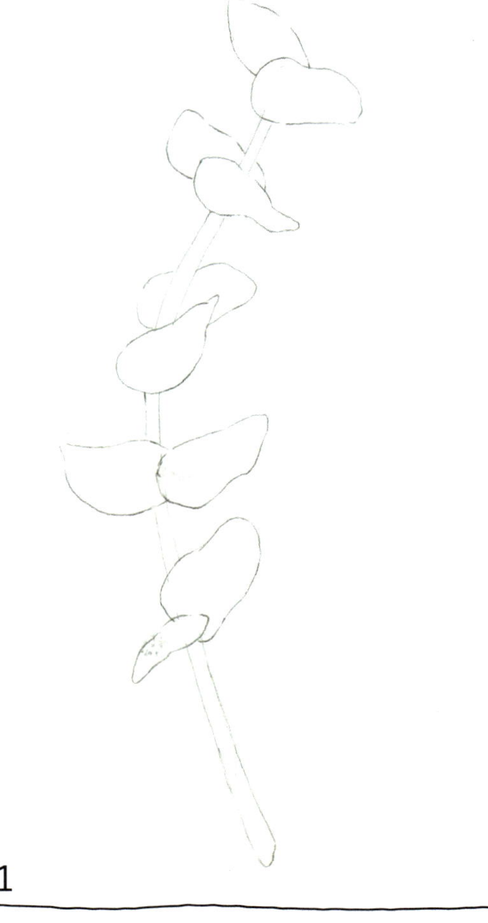

1

Begin with a simple pencil sketch.

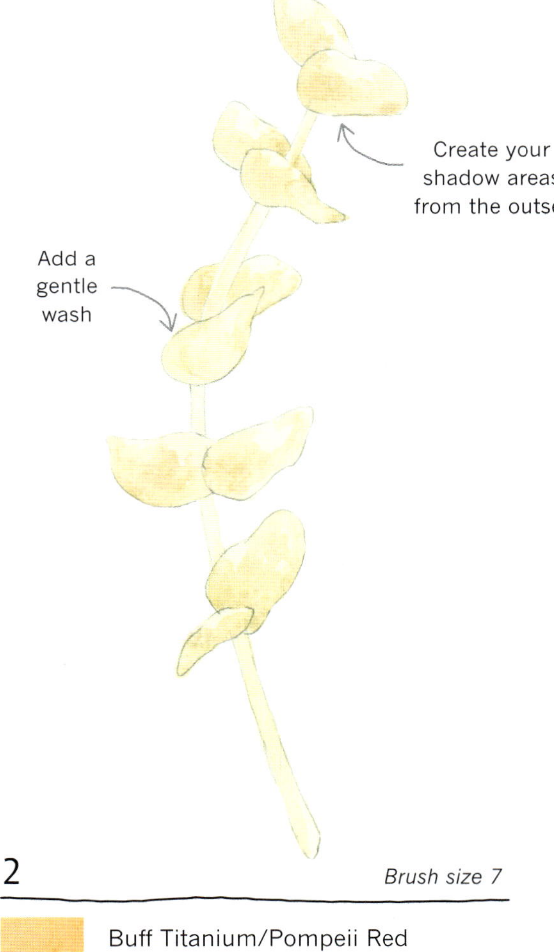

2

Brush size 7

Buff Titanium/Pompeii Red
light wash

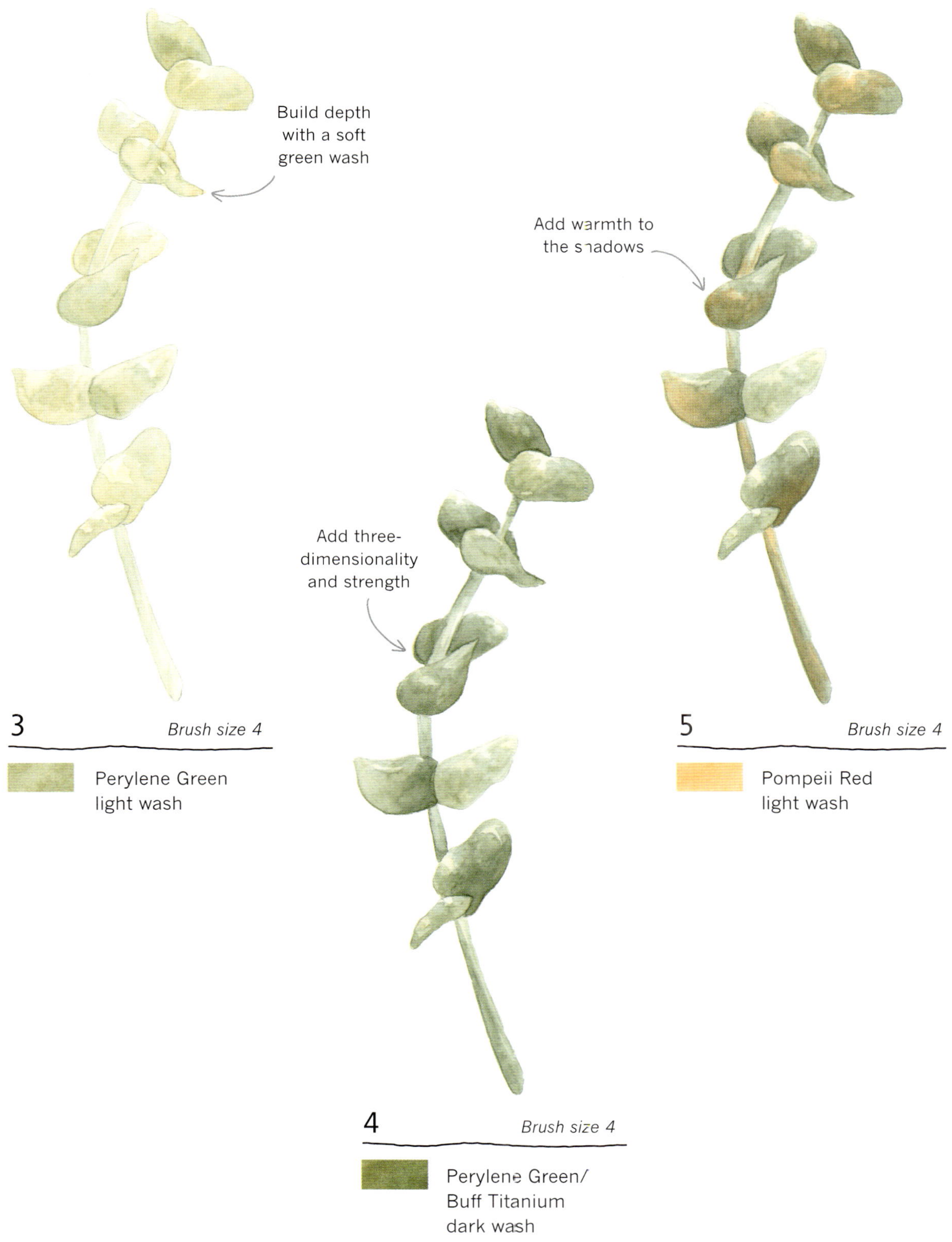

Build depth
with a soft
green wash

Add warmth to
the shadows

Add three-
dimensionality
and strength

3   Brush size 4
Perylene Green
light wash

5   Brush size 4
Pompeii Red
light wash

4   Brush size 4
Perylene Green/
Buff Titanium
dark wash

Wicker Basket

Sometimes simplicity is key: sunshine streaming through the window; a heavy, ceramic mug; a woven basket in the corner. Weave your own with this three-color palette.

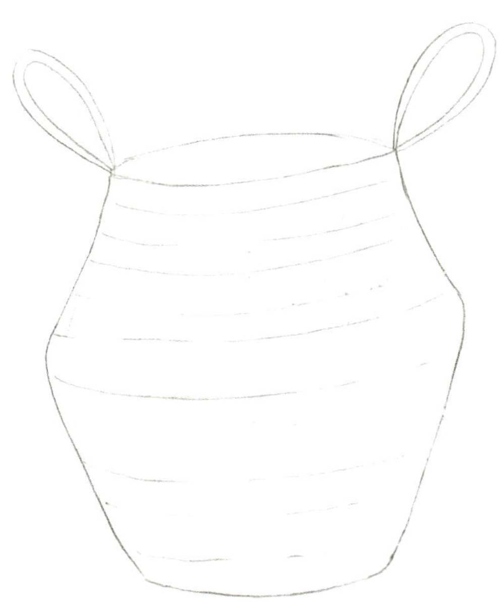

1

Begin with a simple pencil sketch.

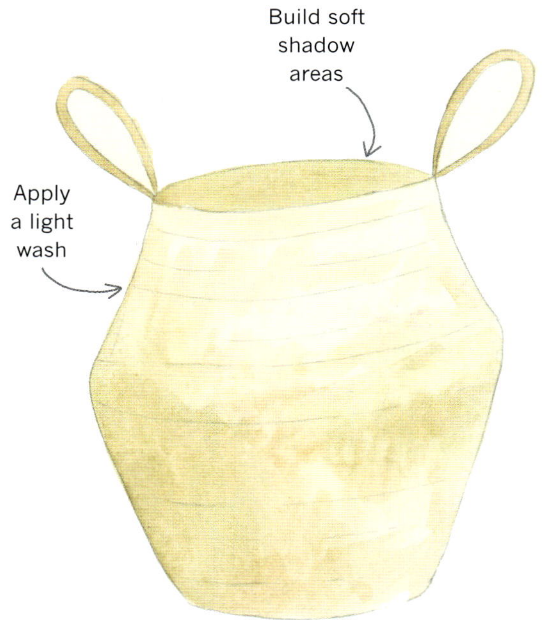

2

Brush size 7

Buff Titanium light wash

Buff Titanium/Perylene Green light wash

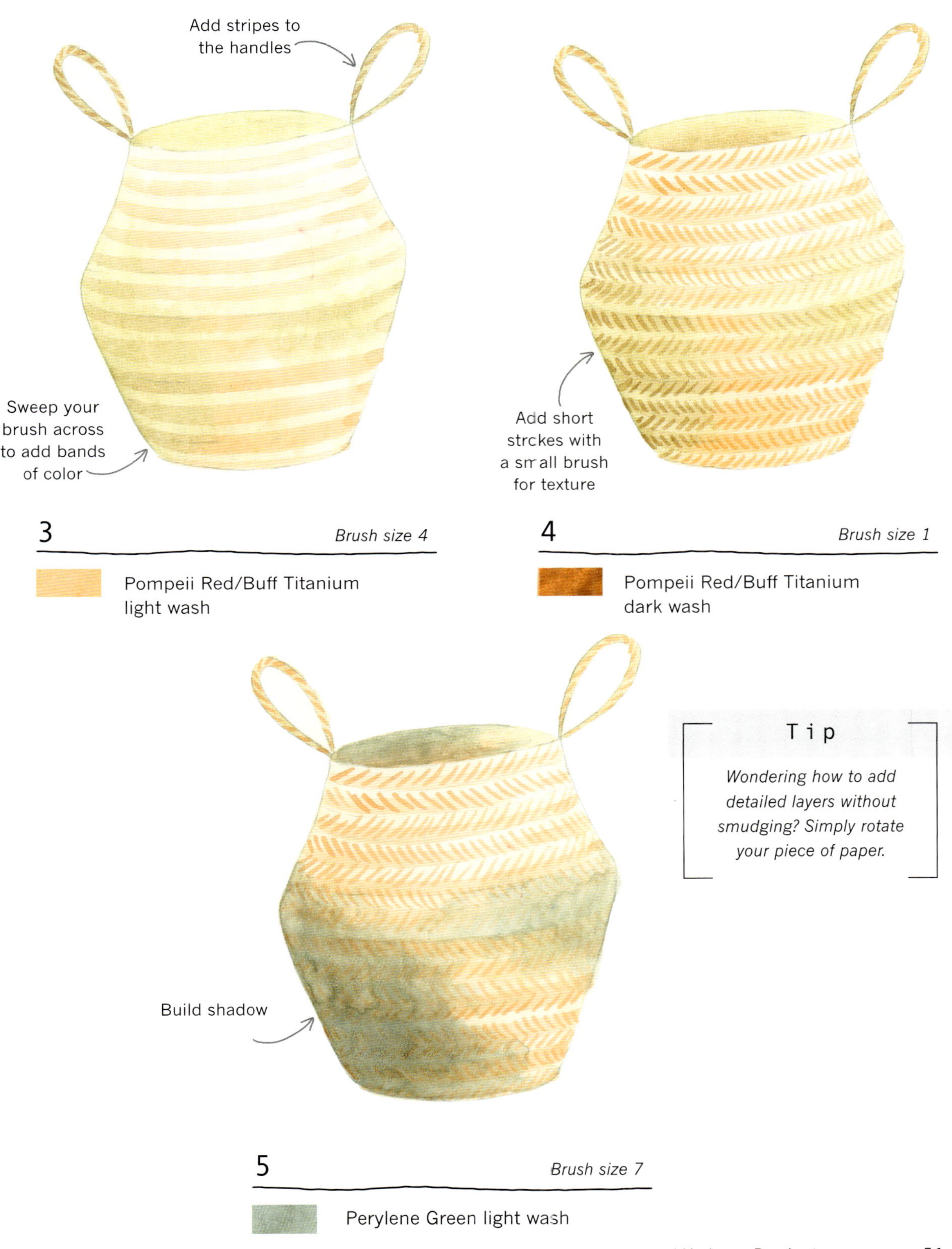

3   *Brush size 4*

Pompeii Red/Buff Titanium
light wash

4   *Brush size 1*

Pompeii Red/Buff Titanium
dark wash

Tip

*Wondering how to add
detailed layers without
smudging? Simply rotate
your piece of paper.*

5   *Brush size 7*

Perylene Green light wash

Photo Time

There's something nostalgic about the retro aesthetic of a film camera. Build your own with a three-color palette, and look at life through its romantic lens.

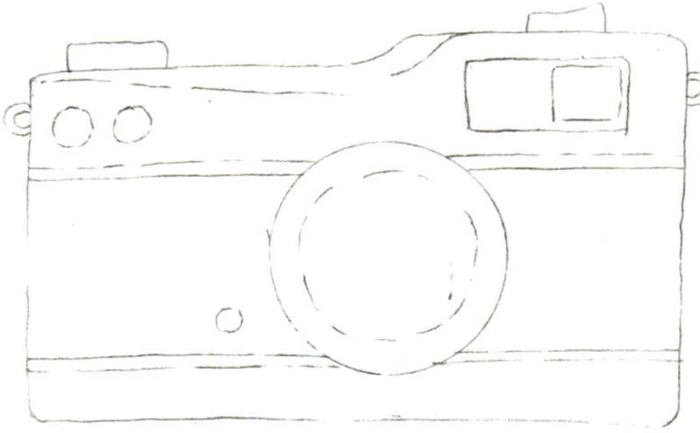

1

Begin with a simple pencil sketch.

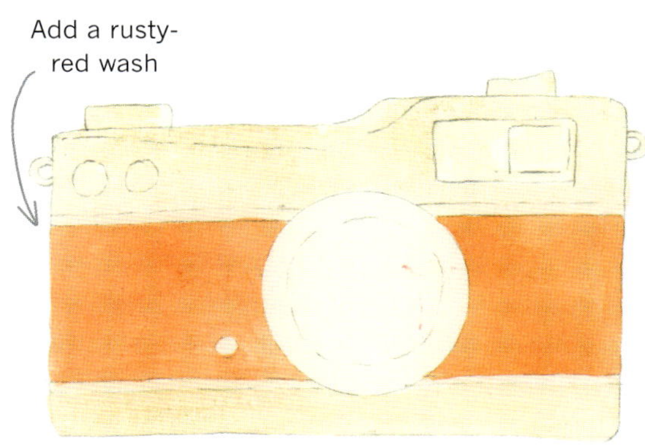

3 *Brush size 4*

Pompeii Red light wash

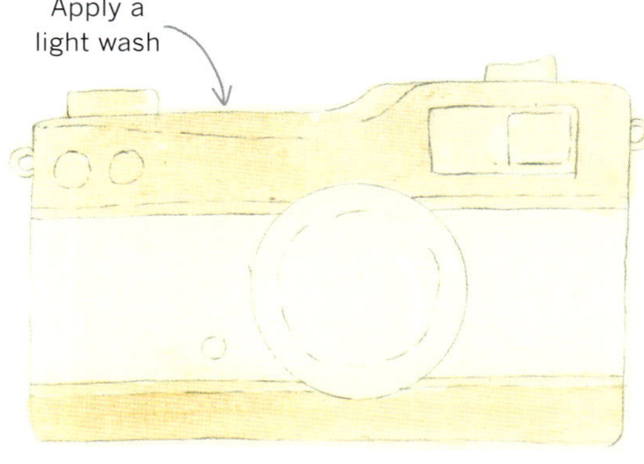

2 *Brush size 7*

Buff Titanium light wash

> ## Tip
>
> *Apply less water and more pigment to the brush for a deeper concentration of color.*

Build light washes and
add shadow for three-
dimensionality

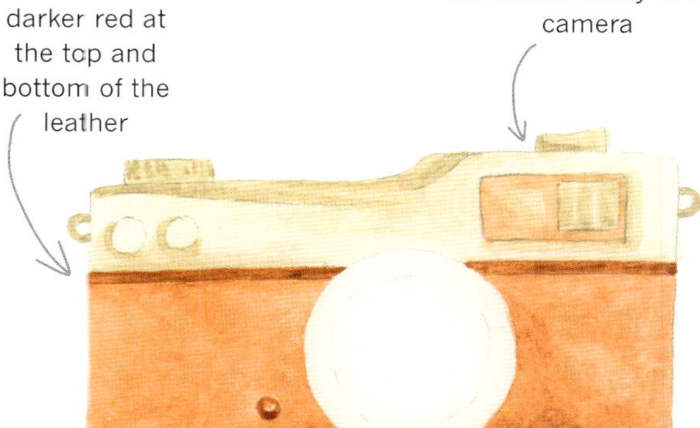

Add a line of
darker red at
the top and
bottom of the
leather

Intensify the reds: apply
a light wash here and on
the leather body of the
camera

4

Brush size 4

 Pompeii Red/Buff Titanium
light wash

Pompeii Red/Perylene Green
light wash

5

Brush size 4

Pomeii Red light wash

Pompeii Red dark wash

Use a light wash
of green for the
lens and details

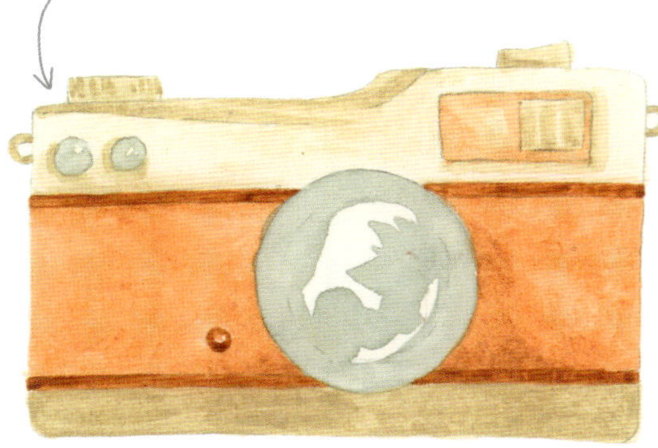

Intensify the green
of the lens, leaving
negative space for
the reflection

6

Brush size 4

 Perylene Green light wash

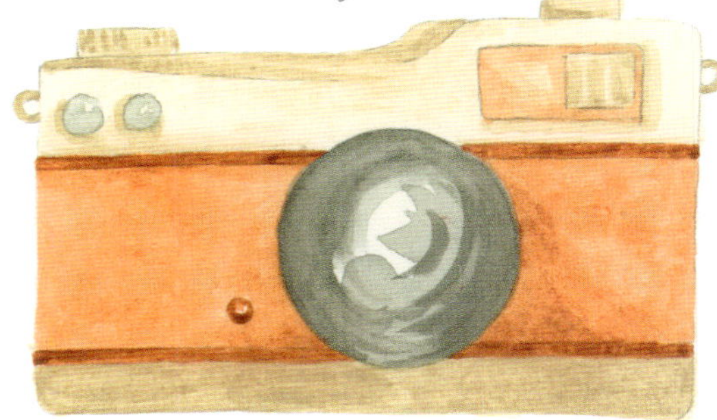

7

Brush size 4

Perylene Green dark wash

True Romance

This three-color palette is all about love and celebration.
It has a hopeful feel—romantic while still feeling urban.
It brings to mind sunsets and sunrises, watched
from a rooftop.

THE COLORS

Yellow Ocher

Rose Madder

Paynes Gray

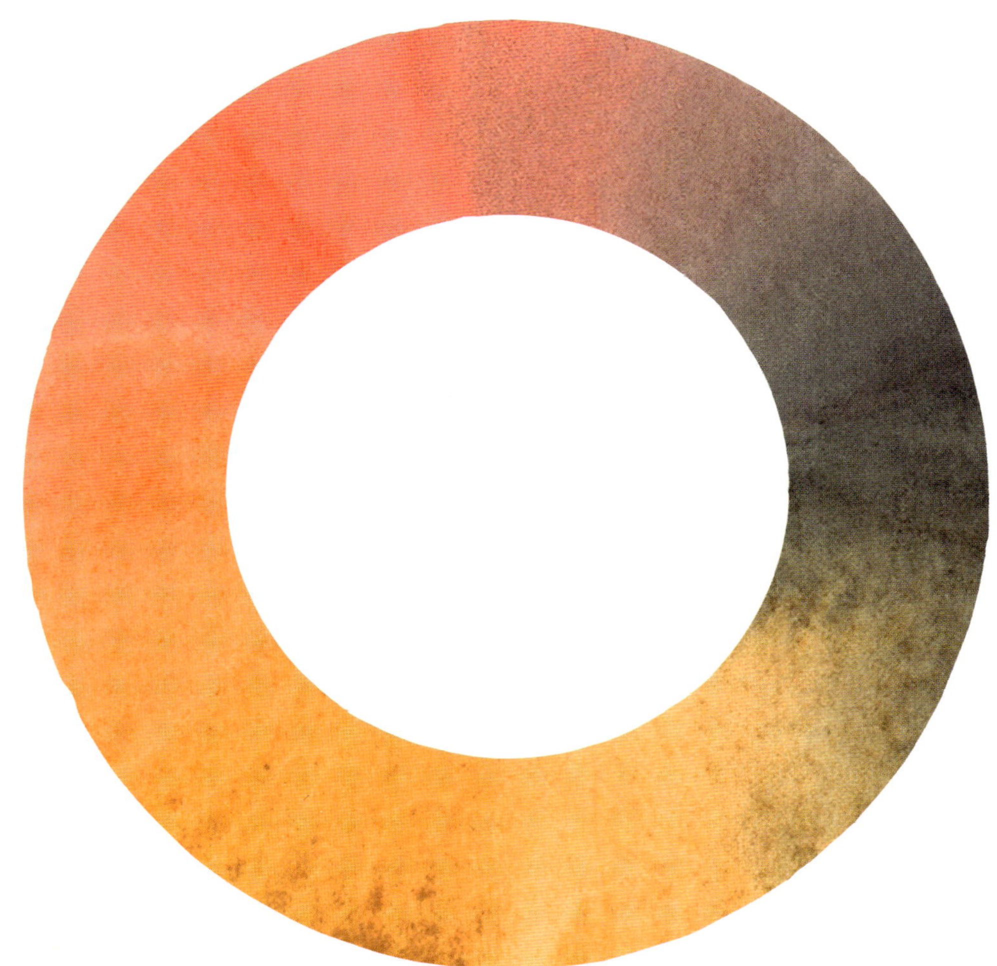

Mixing

The above shows the three colors on a simple
color wheel, each blending into its neighbor.
On the next page, you will see a chart showing
how the colors interact with each other.

COLOR CHART

Each color is shown at two strengths: a dark wash and a light wash. See p. 19 for more on washes.

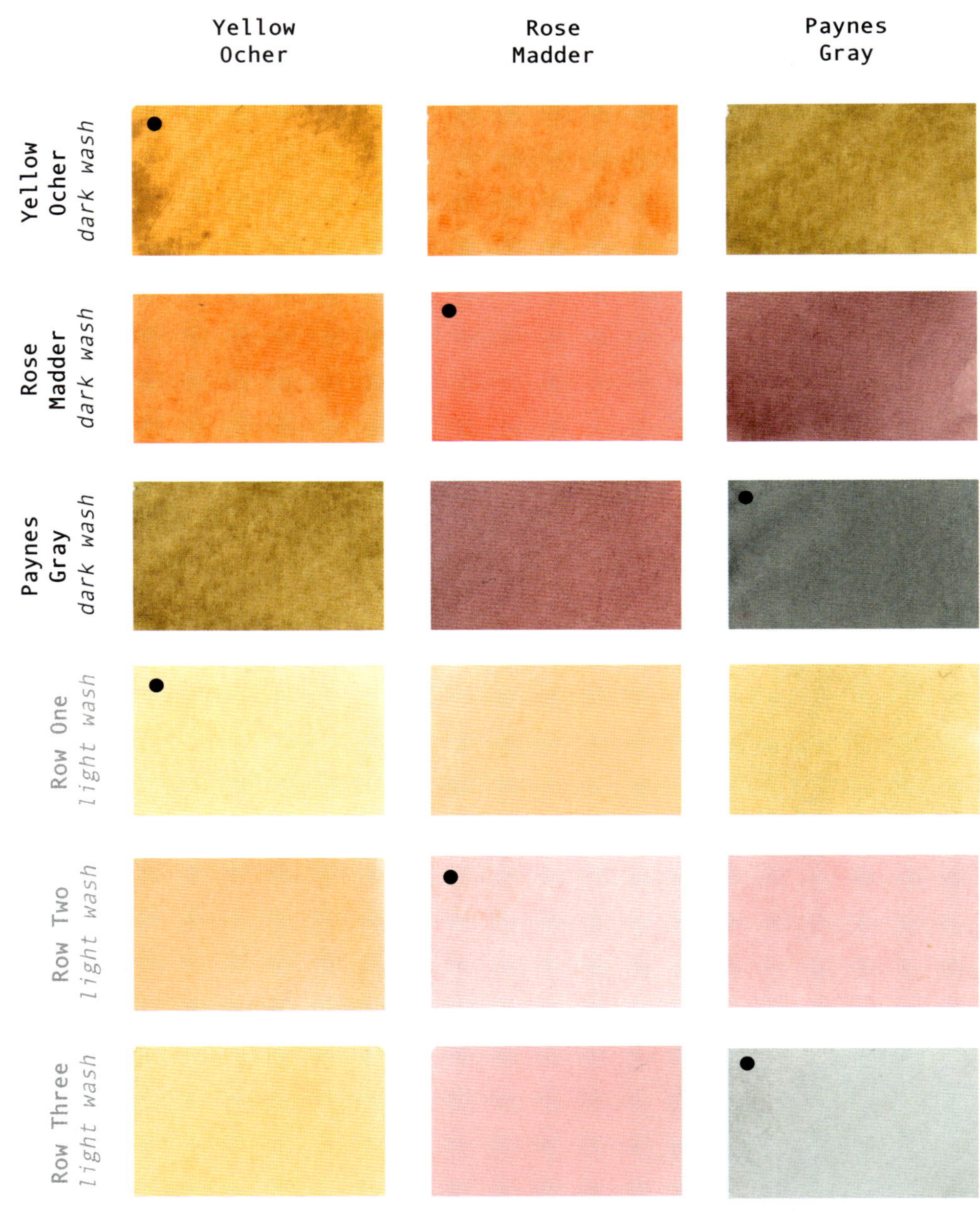

The Projects

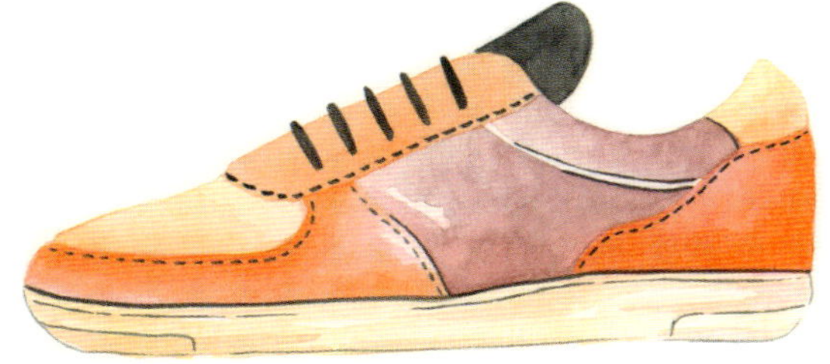

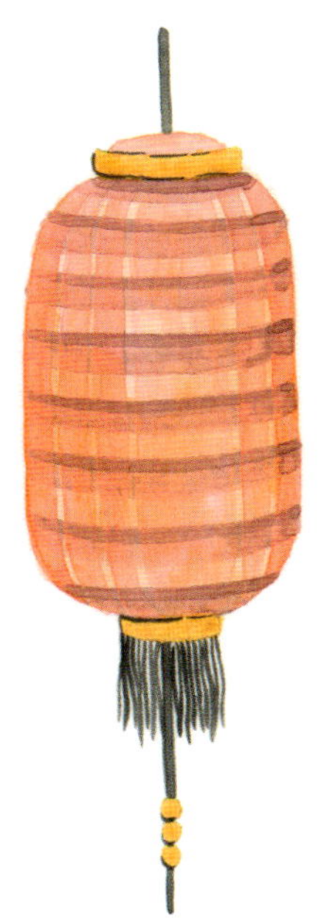

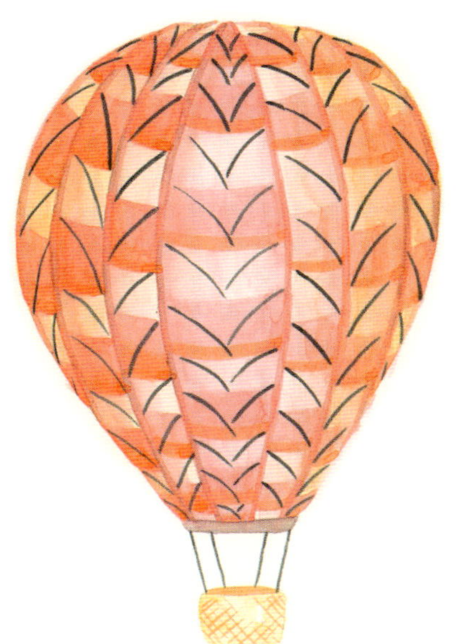

Sneaker

Put your cobbler skills to the test by adding washes to bold color panels in this sneaker, then use the tip of your brush to add the dark stitching and details in the final step.

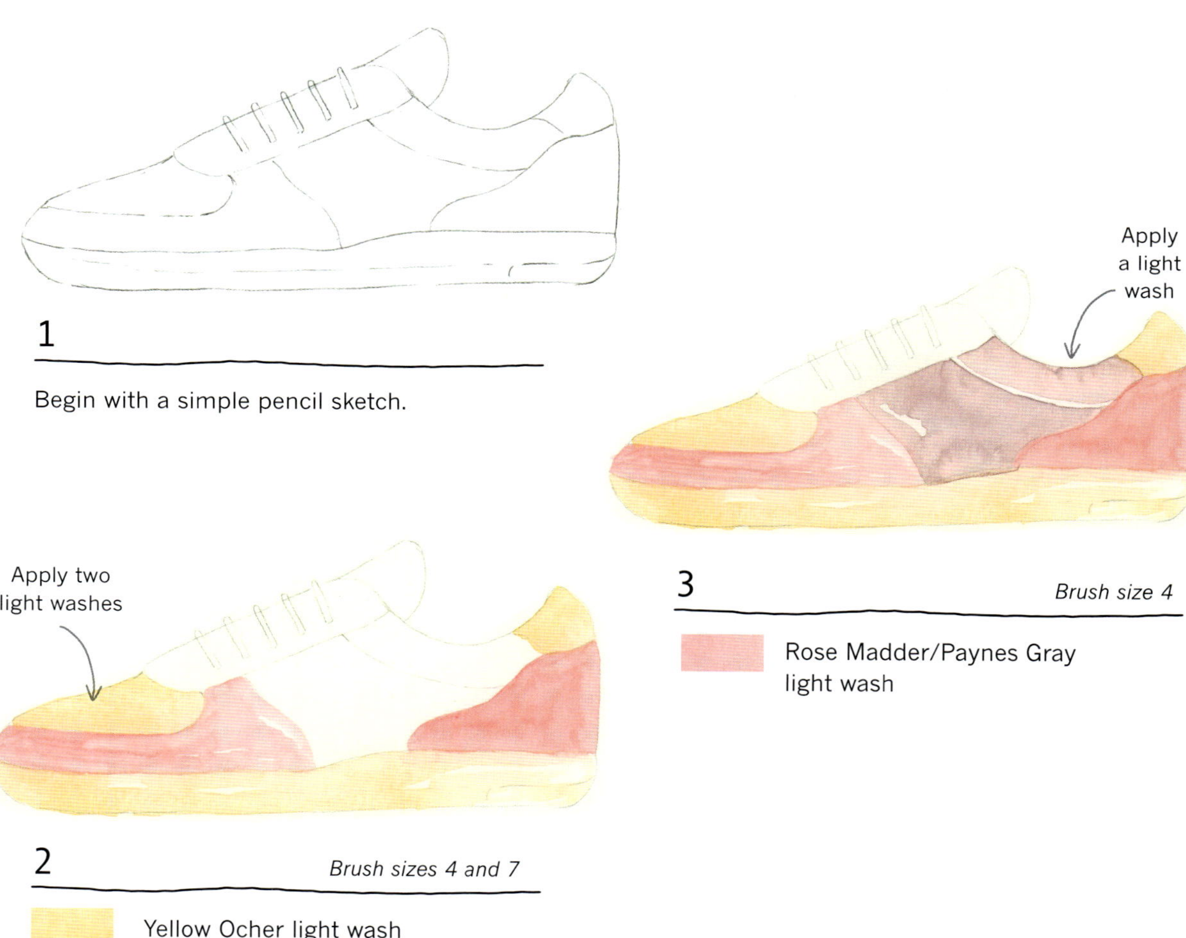

1

Begin with a simple pencil sketch.

2   *Brush sizes 4 and 7*

Yellow Ocher light wash

Rose Madder light wash

3   *Brush size 4*

Rose Madder/Paynes Gray light wash

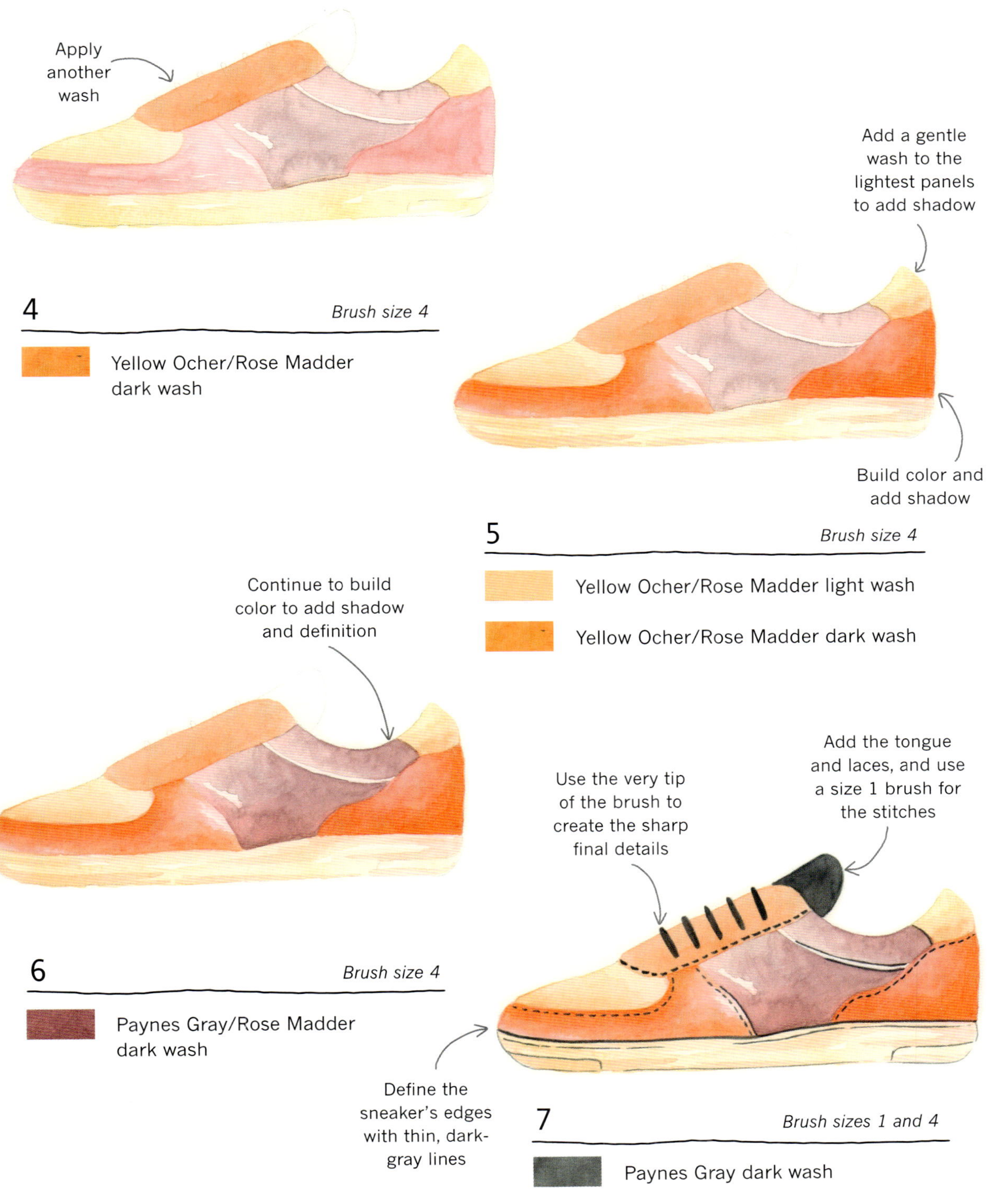

Apply another wash

Add a gentle wash to the lightest panels to add shadow

Build color and add shadow

Continue to build color to add shadow and definition

Use the very tip of the brush to create the sharp final details

Add the tongue and laces, and use a size 1 brush for the stitches

Define the sneaker's edges with thin, dark-gray lines

4   Brush size 4
Yellow Ocher/Rose Madder dark wash

5   Brush size 4
Yellow Ocher/Rose Madder light wash
Yellow Ocher/Rose Madder dark wash

6   Brush size 4
Paynes Gray/Rose Madder dark wash

7   Brush sizes 1 and 4
Paynes Gray dark wash

2 Lantern

Play with sweeping, curved, vertical, and horizontal bands of color to create the delicate texture of this paper lantern. Think warm summer evenings and celebration.

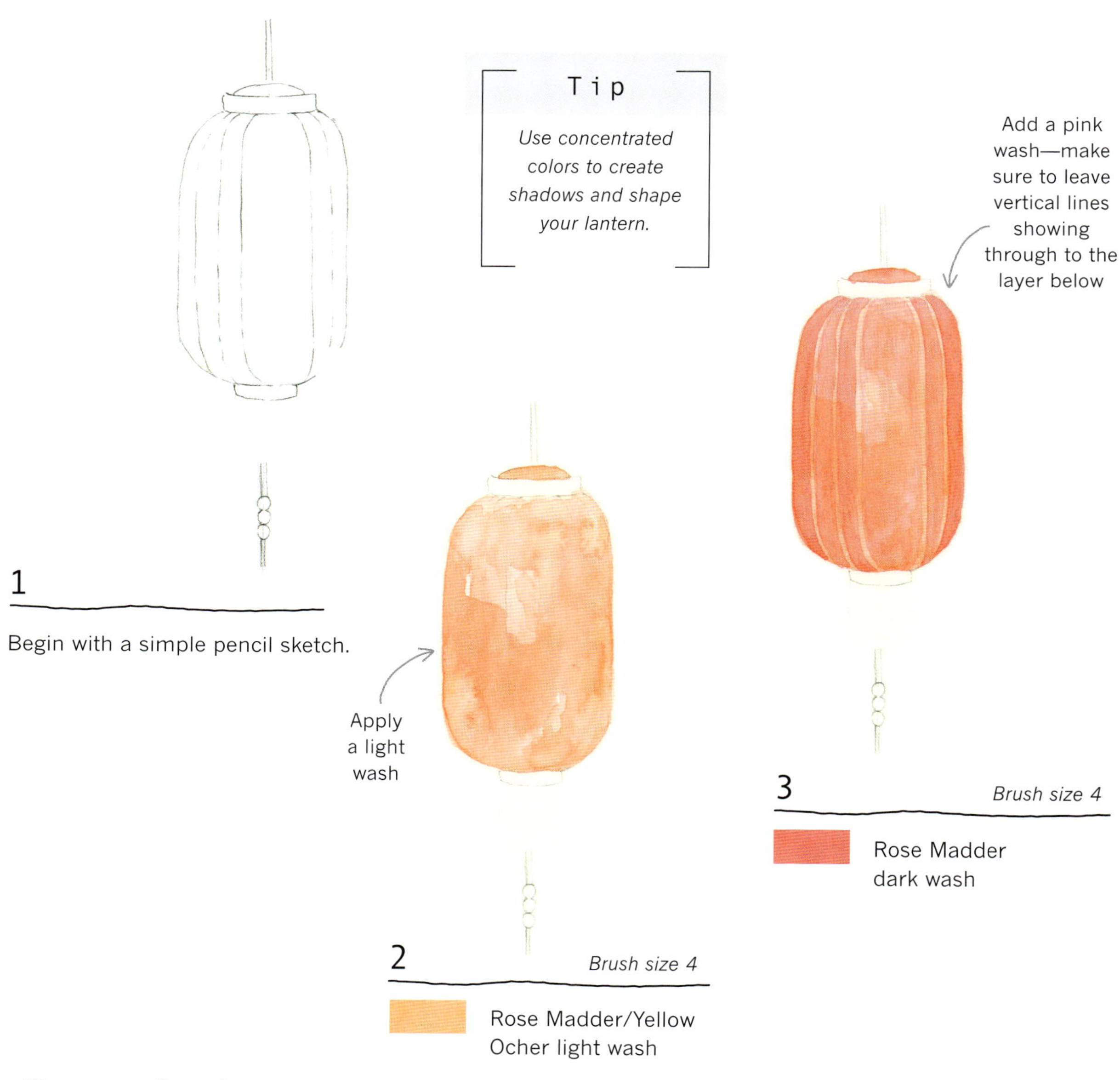

Tip

Use concentrated colors to create shadows and shape your lantern.

Add a pink wash—make sure to leave vertical lines showing through to the layer below

1

Begin with a simple pencil sketch.

Apply a light wash

2 *Brush size 4*

Rose Madder/Yellow Ocher light wash

3 *Brush size 4*

Rose Madder dark wash

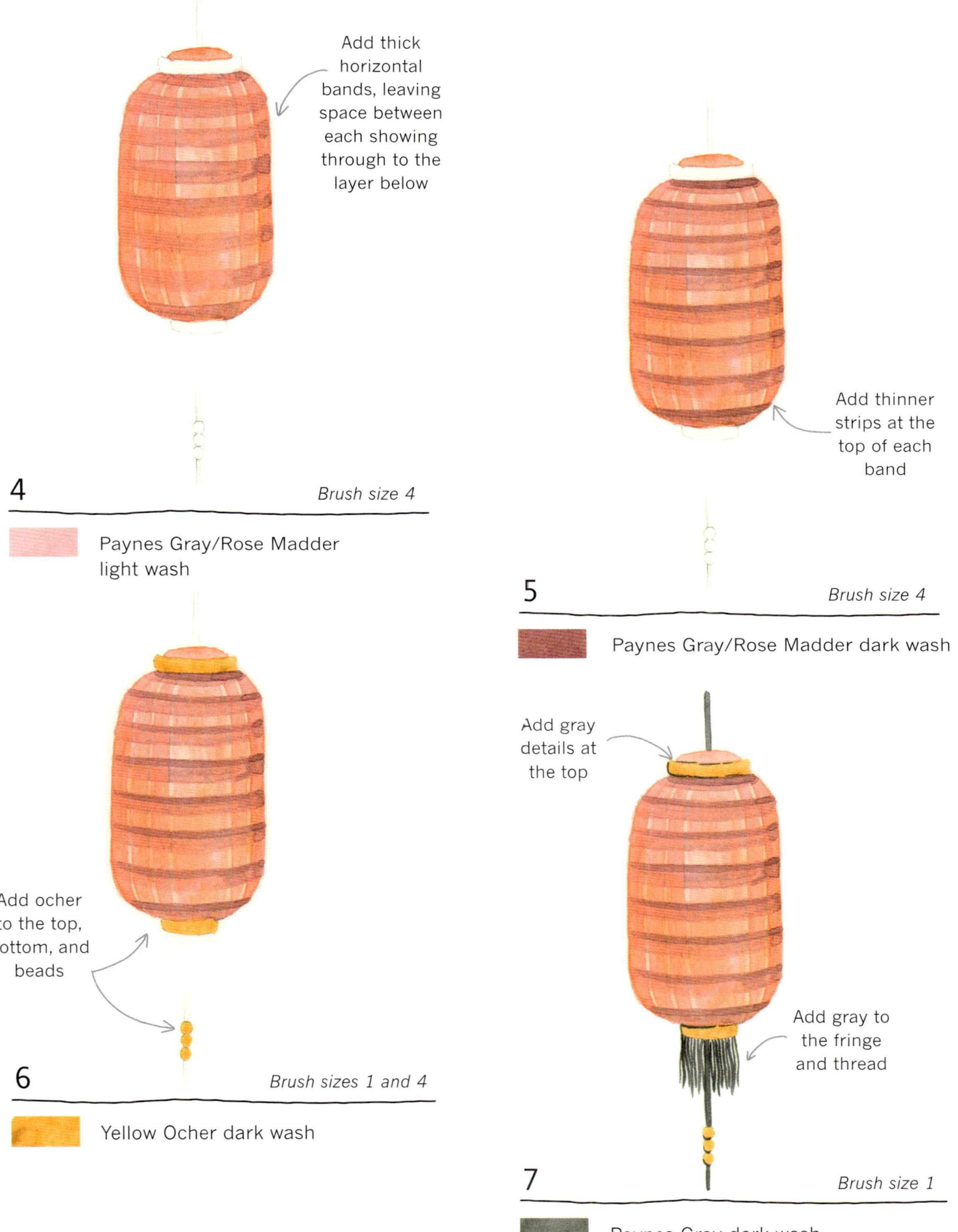

4   *Brush size 4*

Paynes Gray/Rose Madder light wash

5   *Brush size 4*

Paynes Gray/Rose Madder dark wash

6   *Brush sizes 1 and 4*

Yellow Ocher dark wash

7   *Brush size 1*

Paynes Gray dark wash

Hot-Air Balloon

Up, up, and away! Float above your everyday worries and enjoy the view—this project will leave you feeling buoyant. Top tip: Paynes Gray is a great secret weapon for adding details in the final stages of a watercolor project.

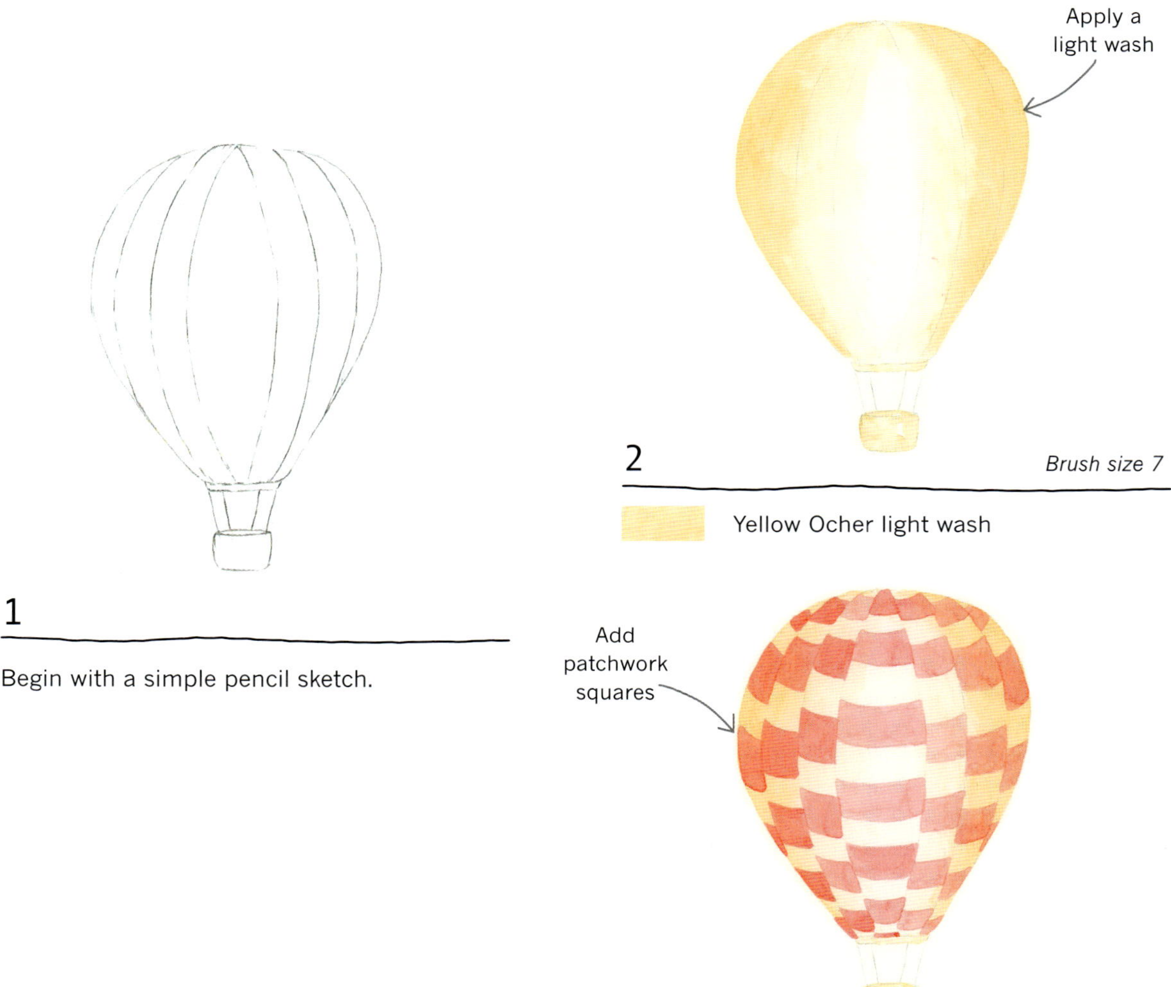

1

Begin with a simple pencil sketch.

2 *Brush size 7*

Yellow Ocher light wash

3 *Brush size 4*

Rose Madder/Paynes Gray dark wash

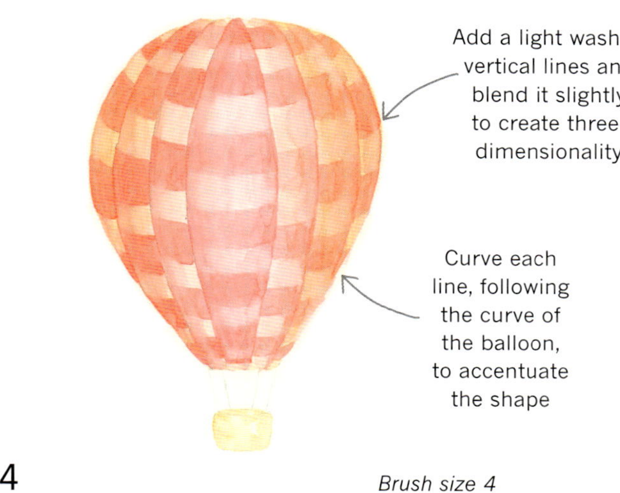

4   *Brush size 4*

Rose Madder light wash

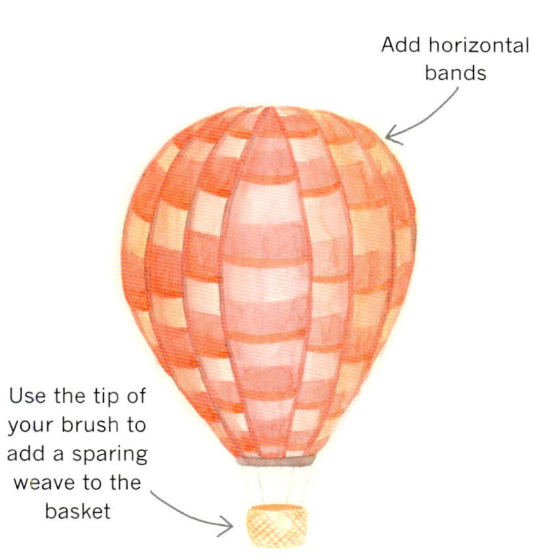

6   *Brush sizes 1 and 4*

Yellow Ocher/Paynes Gray dark wash

Rose Madder/Paynes Gray dark wash

5   *Brush size 4*

Rose Madder dark wash

Rose Madder/Paynes Gray light wash

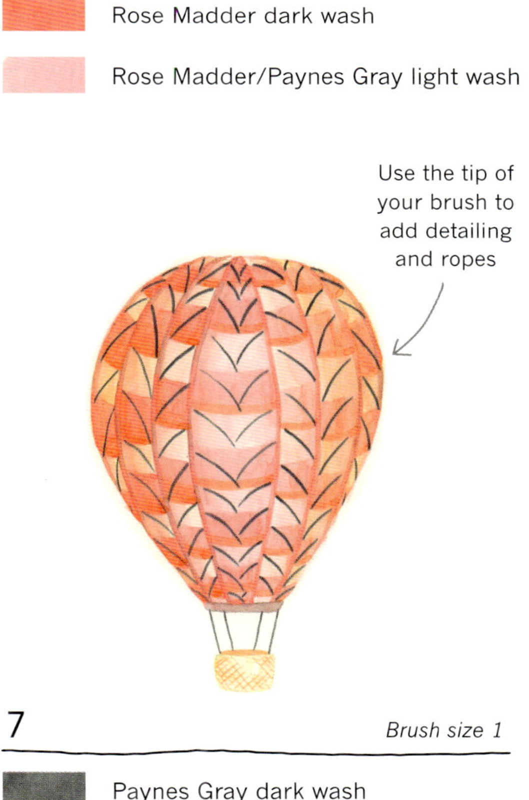

7   *Brush size 1*

Paynes Gray dark wash

Tropical Sun

This three-color palette is all about tropical vibes. Think warm sunshine, gleaming green leaves, fruit and flowers . . . It's a mix that will have you packing your bags for your next adventure.

THE COLORS

Cadmium Yellow

Italian Deep Ocher

Cobalt Turquoise

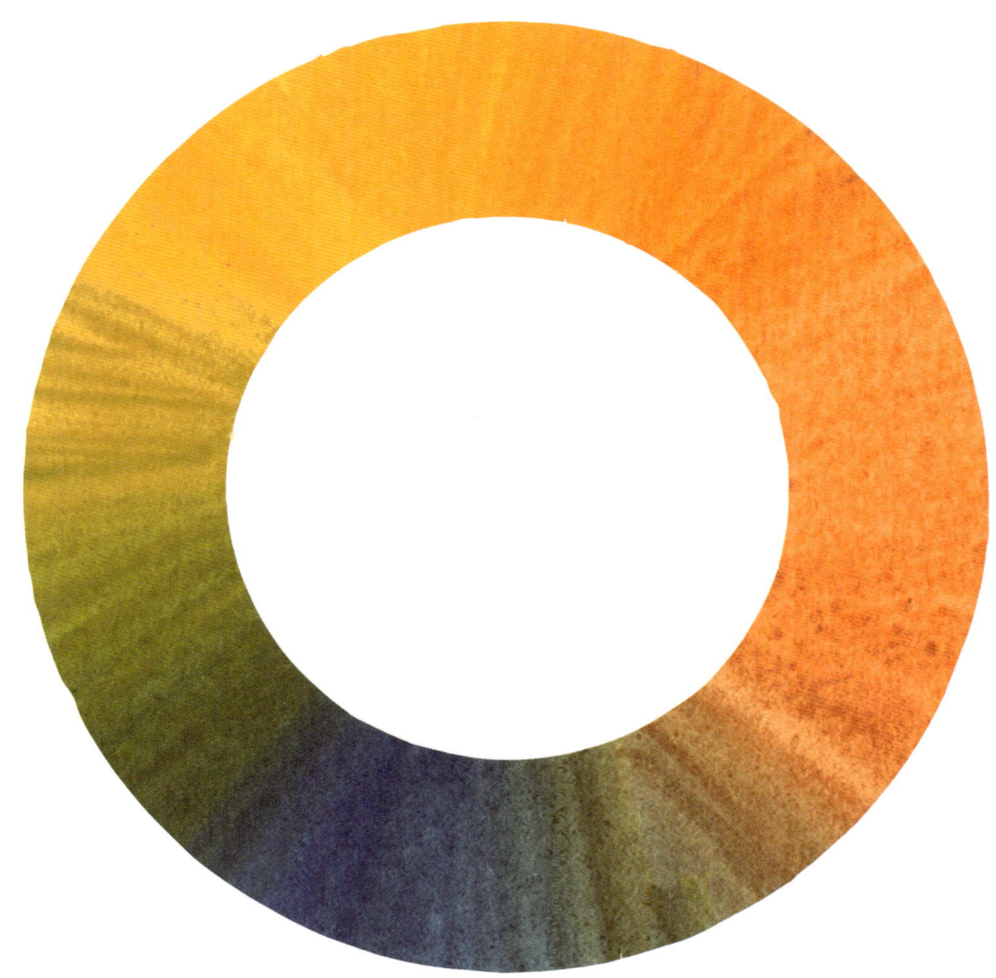

Mixing

The above shows the three colors on a simple
color wheel, each blending into its neighbor.
On the next page, you will see a chart showing
how the colors interact with each other.

COLOR CHART

Each color is shown at two strengths: a dark wash and a light wash. See p. 19 for more on washes.

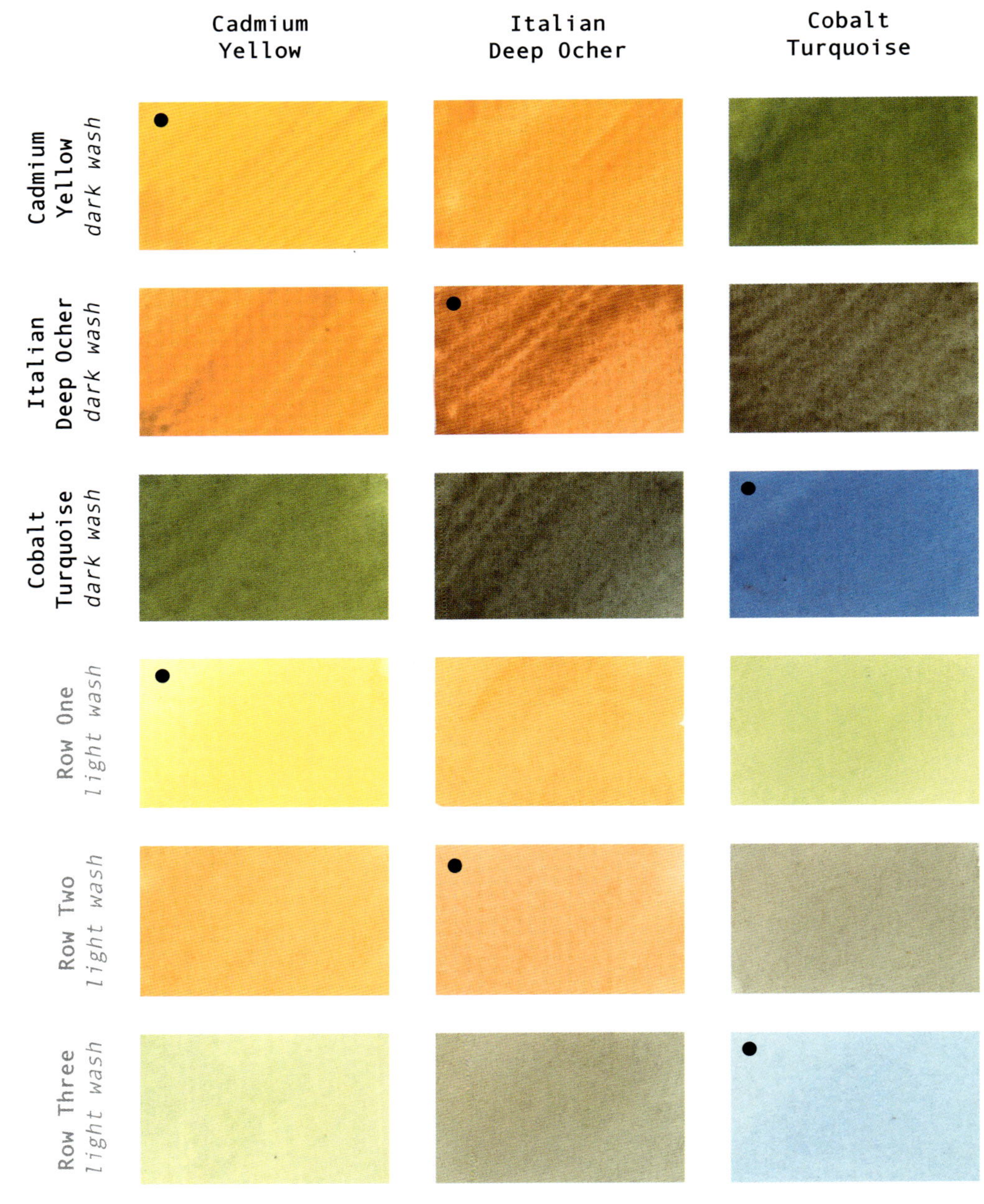

The Projects

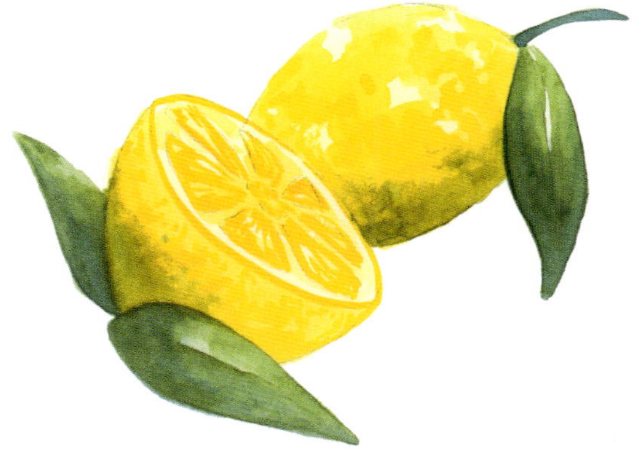

1. LEMONS

2. TIGER

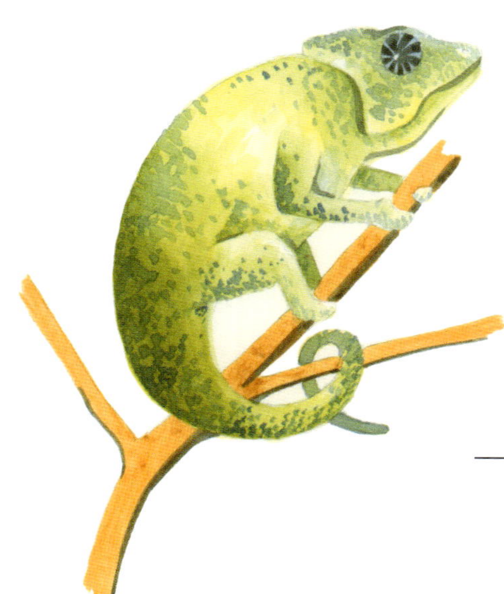

3. CHAMELEON

Lemons

Fresh and zesty, this project will bring a squeeze of sunshine to your watercolor practice. Make sure to leave negative space on the fruit to capture that textured lemon skin.

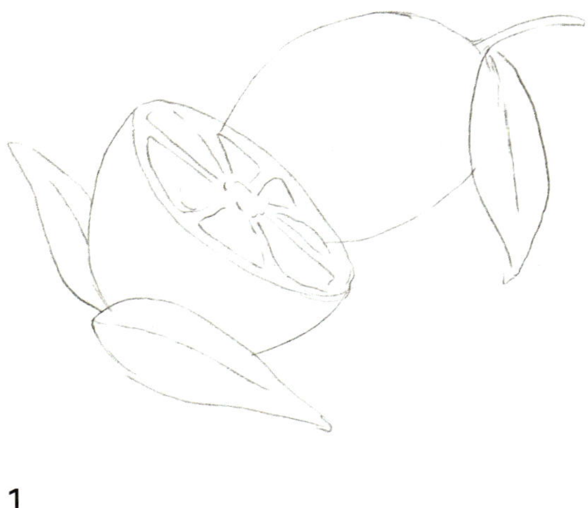

1

Begin with a simple pencil sketch.

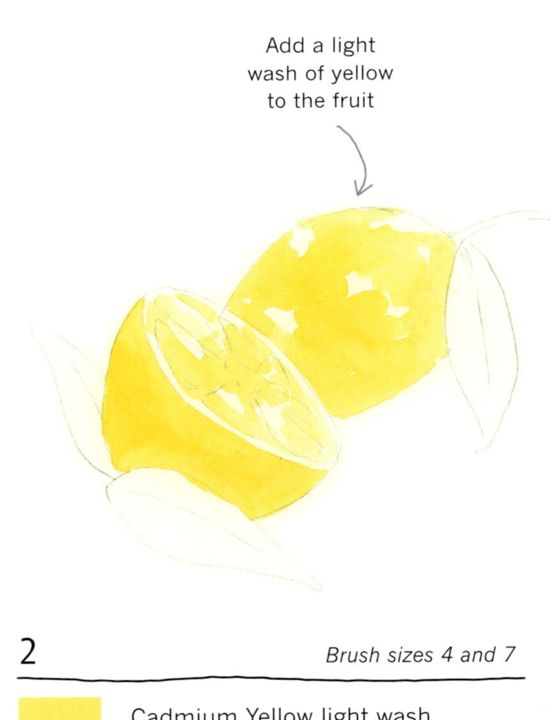

2   *Brush sizes 4 and 7*

Cadmium Yellow light wash

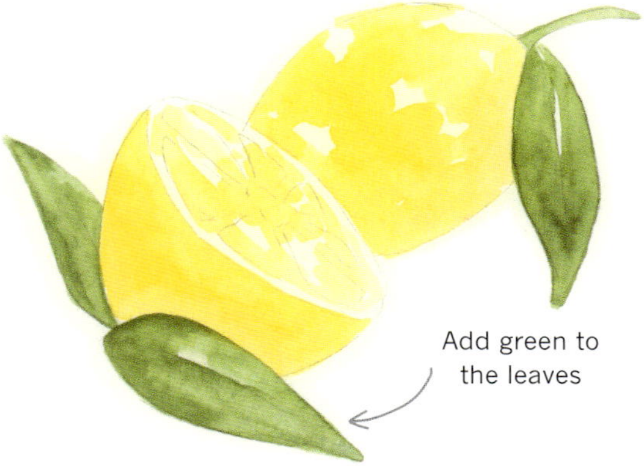

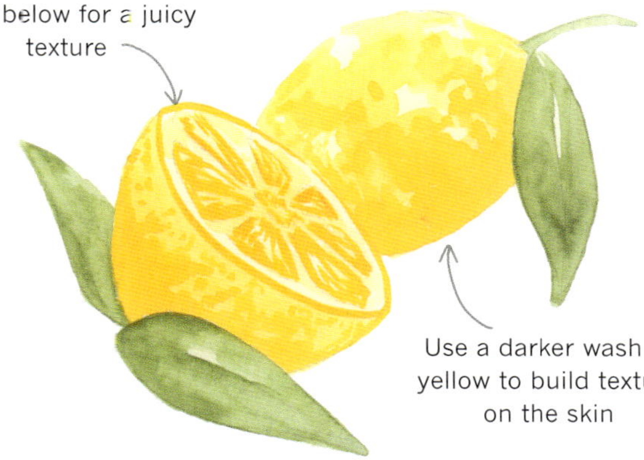

3 *Brush size 4*

Cobalt Turquoise/Cadmium Yellow
dark wash

4 *Brush sizes 1 and 4*

Italian Deep Ocher/Cadmium Yellow
dark wash

Cadmium Yellow dark wash

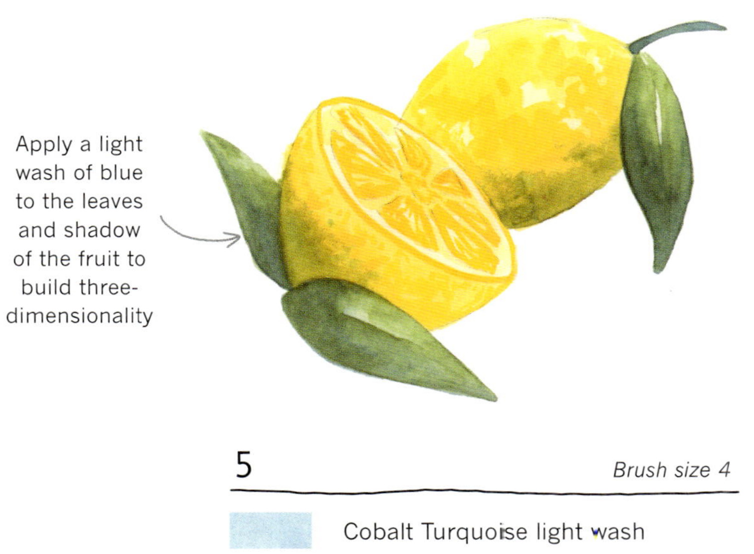

5 *Brush size 4*

Cobalt Turquoise light wash

Tiger

You can use the tiger's distinctive stripes to create a beautiful sense of three-dimensionality. Imagine where the tiger's spine would run from tail to neck, and arch your stripes accordingly.

> **Tip**
>
> *Use subtle shading to establish three-dimensionality, and reinforce the tiger's shape through its stripes.*

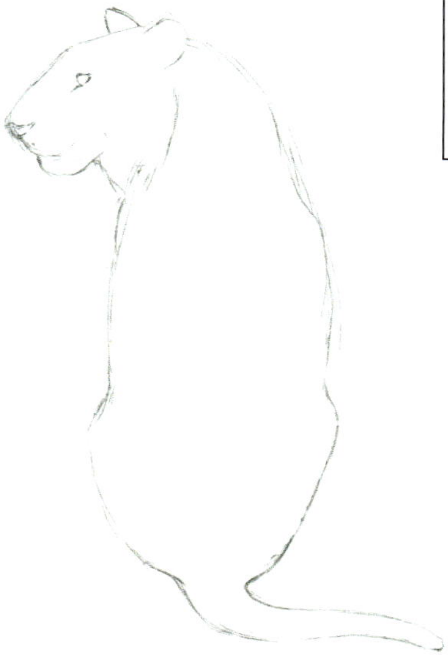

1

Begin with a simple pencil sketch.

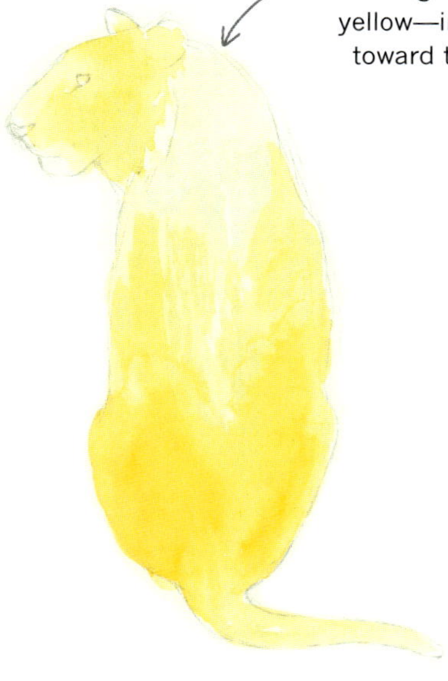

Add a light wash of yellow—intensify toward the tail

2

Brush sizes 4 and 7

Cadmium Yellow light wash

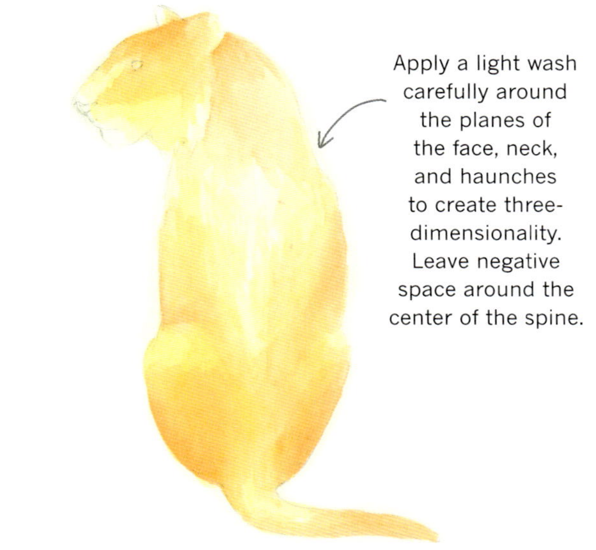

Apply a light wash carefully around the planes of the face, neck, and haunches to create three-dimensionality. Leave negative space around the center of the spine.

3 *Brush size 4*

Italian Deep Ocher light wash

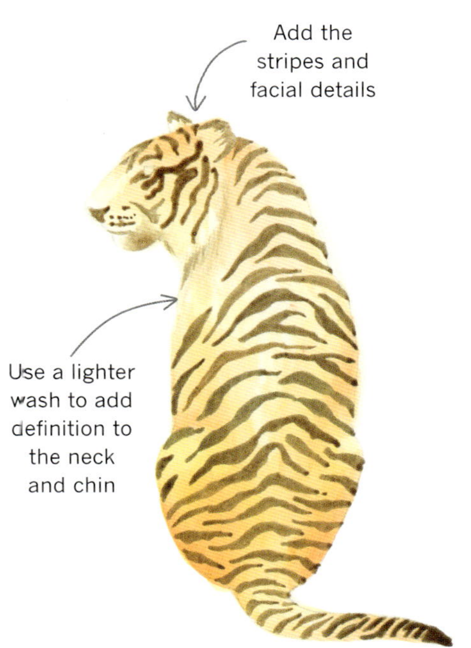

Add the stripes and facial details

Use a lighter wash to add definition to the neck and chin

4 *Brush size 1*

Cobalt Turquoise/Italian Deep Ocher dark wash

Cobalt Turquoise/Italian Deep Ocher light wash

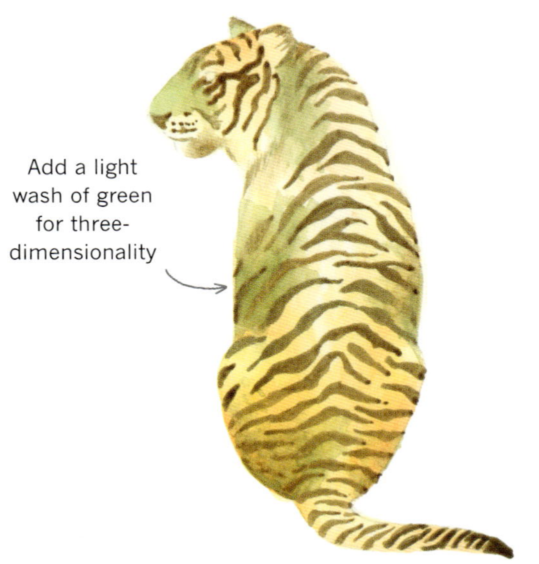

Add a light wash of green for three-dimensionality

5 *Brush size 4*

Cadmium Yellow/Cobalt Turquoise light wash

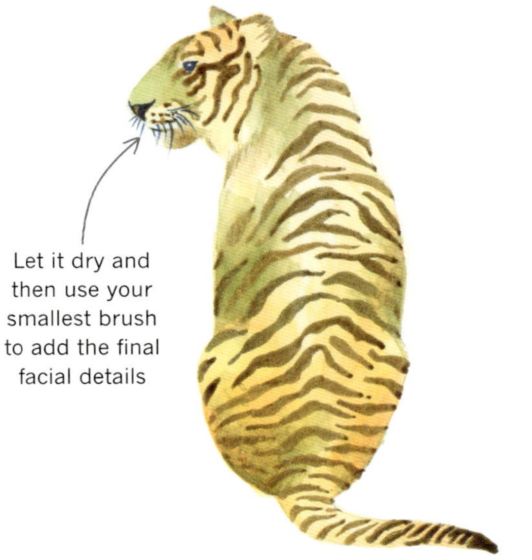

Let it dry and then use your smallest brush to add the final facial details

6 *Brush size 1*

Cobalt Turquoise dark wash

Chameleon

This chameleon is a pleasure to paint. Take time on the drawing for this one before you start painting, to get the position of the limbs and tail right in relation to the branch.

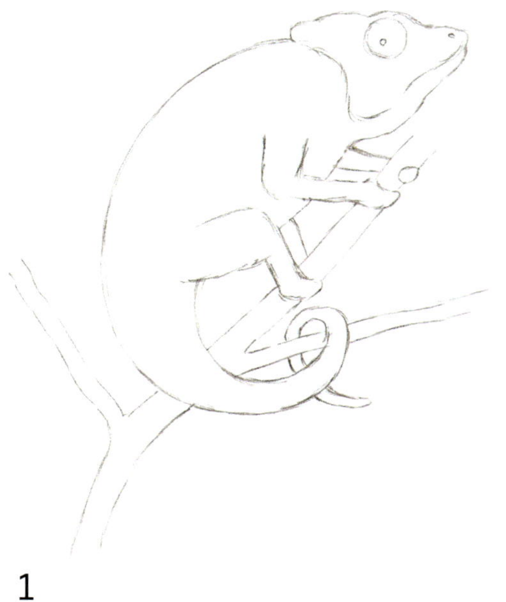

1

Begin with a simple pencil sketch.

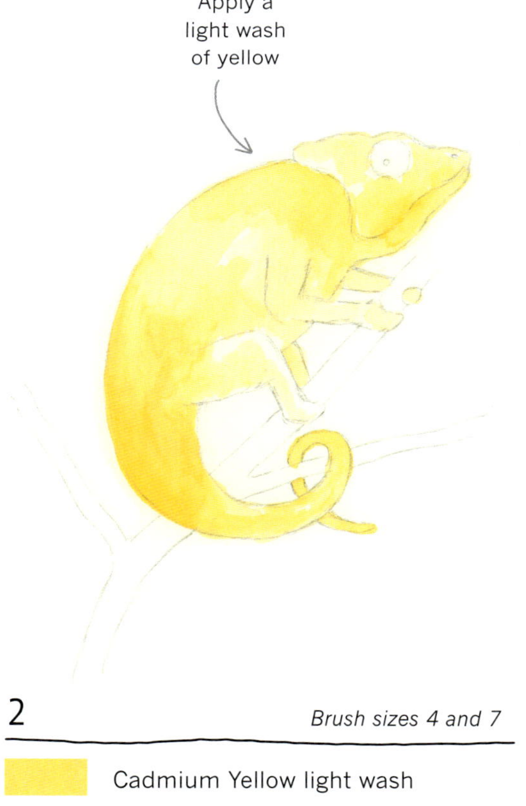

2
Brush sizes 4 and 7

Cadmium Yellow light wash

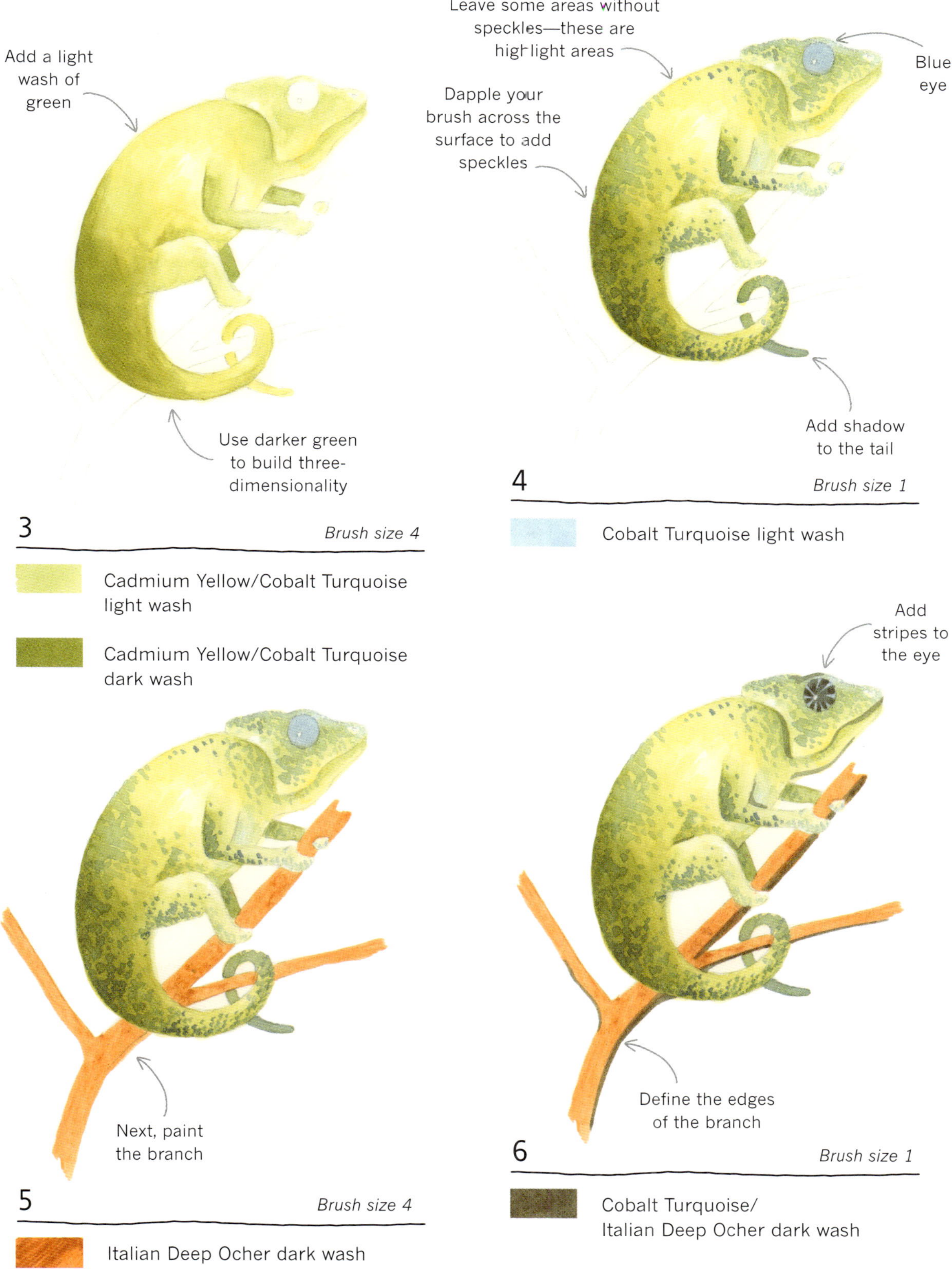

Add a light wash of green
Use darker green to build three-dimensionality

3
Brush size 4
Cadmium Yellow/Cobalt Turquoise light wash
Cadmium Yellow/Cobalt Turquoise dark wash

Leave some areas without speckles—these are highlight areas
Dapple your brush across the surface to add speckles
Blue eye
Add shadow to the tail

4
Brush size 1
Cobalt Turquoise light wash

Next, paint the branch

5
Brush size 4
Italian Deep Ocher dark wash

Add stripes to the eye
Define the edges of the branch

6
Brush size 1
Cobalt Turquoise/ Italian Deep Ocher dark wash

Magic Touch

This three-color palette will put a spell on you. Just read
the names of the colors: Green Gold, Alizarin Crimson,
Moonglow . . . This is a palette to charm, equally capable
of blushing sparkles and gleaming intensity.

THE COLORS

Green Gold

Alizarin Crimson

Moonglow

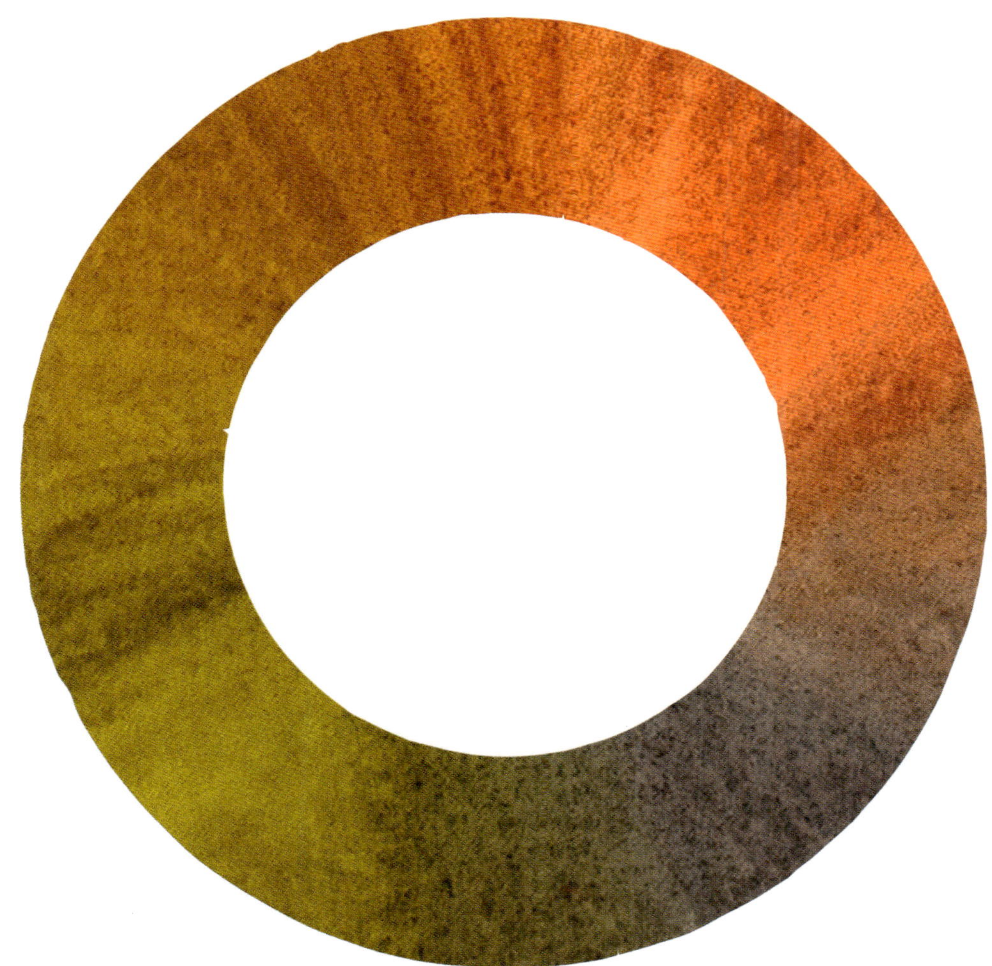

Mixing

The above shows the three colors on a simple
color wheel, each blending into its neighbor.
On the next page, you will see a chart showing
how the colors interact with each other.

COLOR CHART

Each color is shown at two strengths: a dark wash and a light wash. See p. 19 for more on washes.

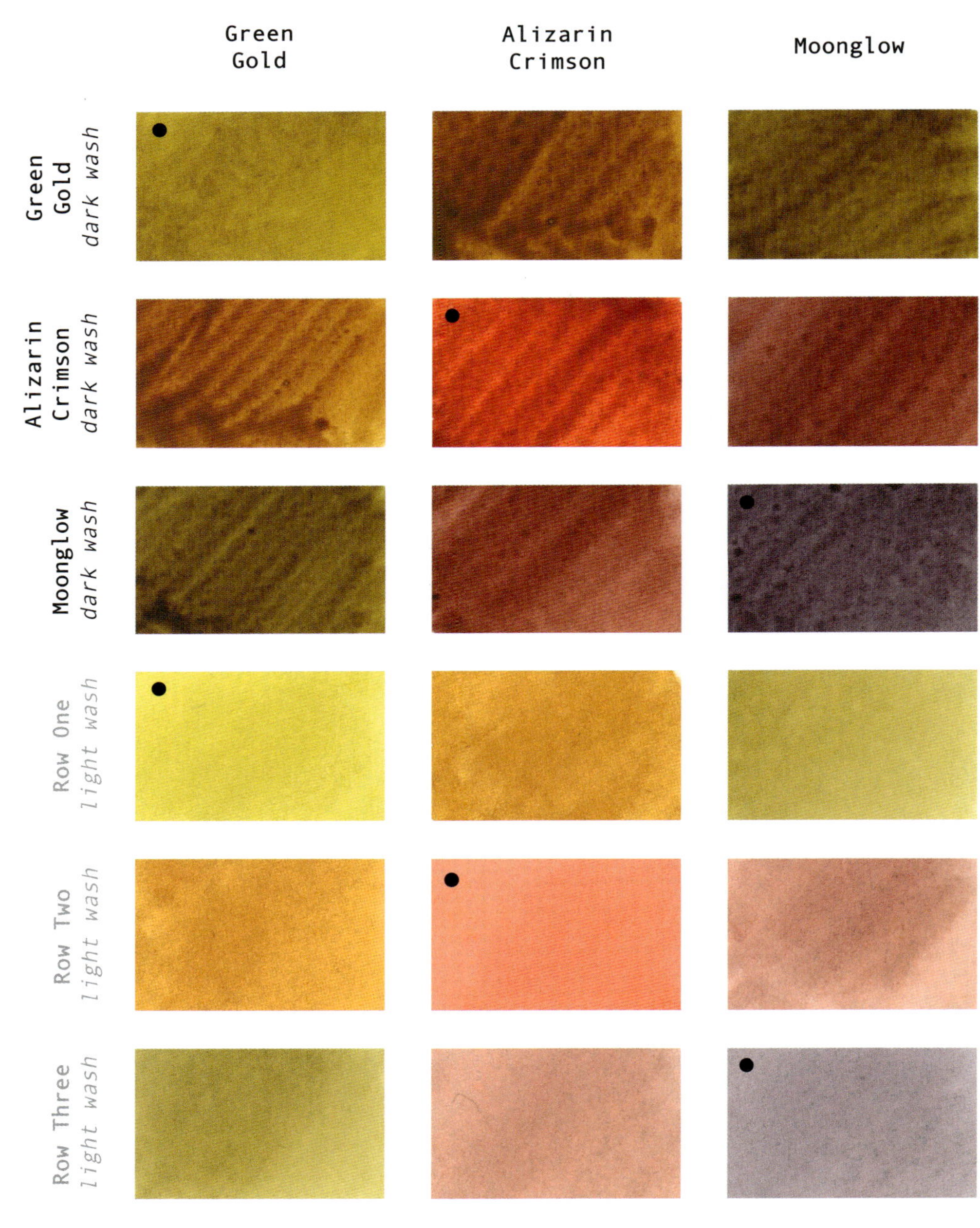

The Projects

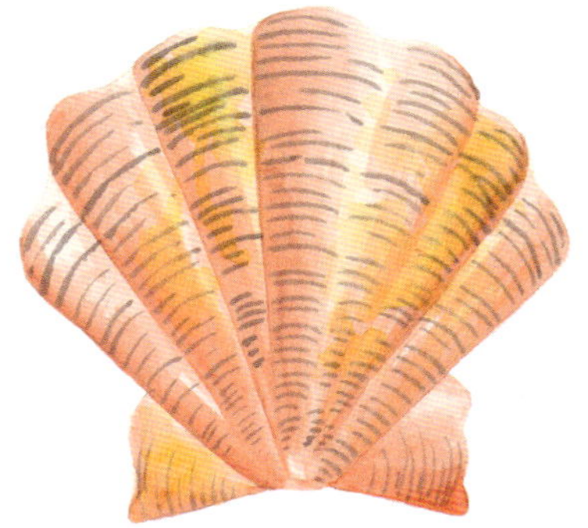

1. SHELL

2. POPSICLE

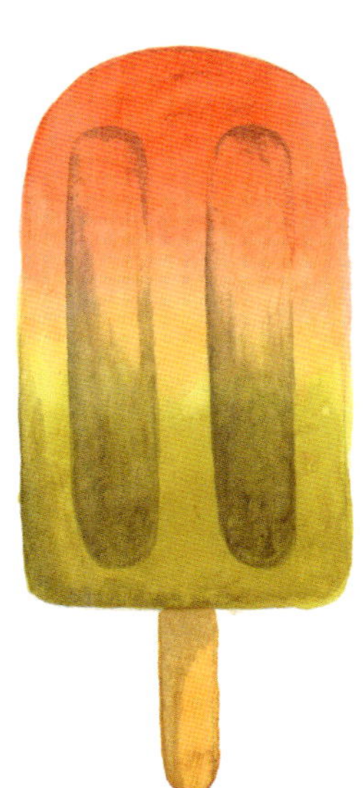

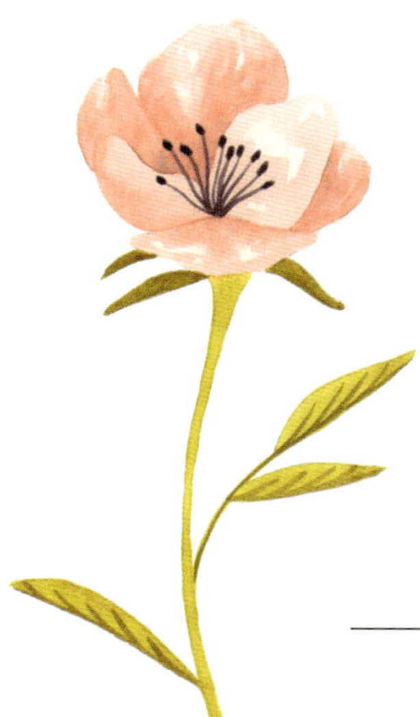

3. FLORA

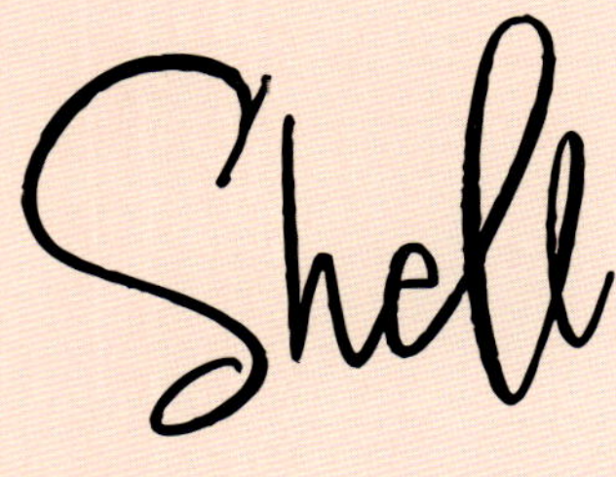

Shell

Have you ever spent a while studying a simple object like a shell? The longer you look, the more detail is revealed. Spend time on the shadows to achieve a sense of three-dimensionality.

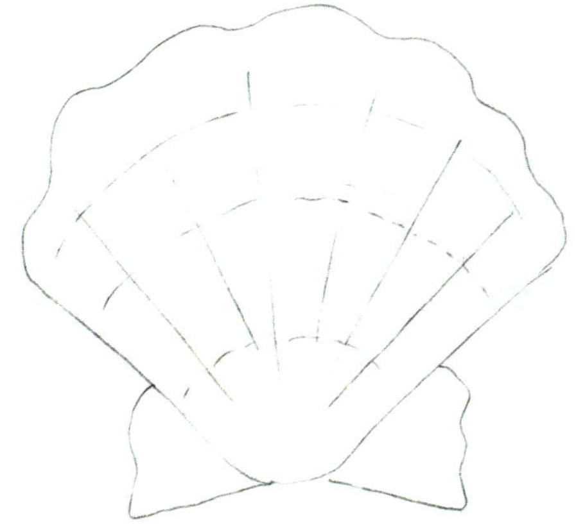

1

Begin with a simple pencil sketch.

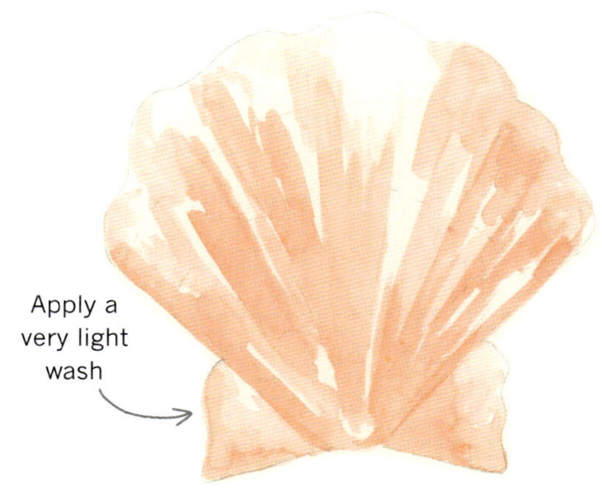

2

Brush sizes 4 and 7

 Alizarin Crimson light wash

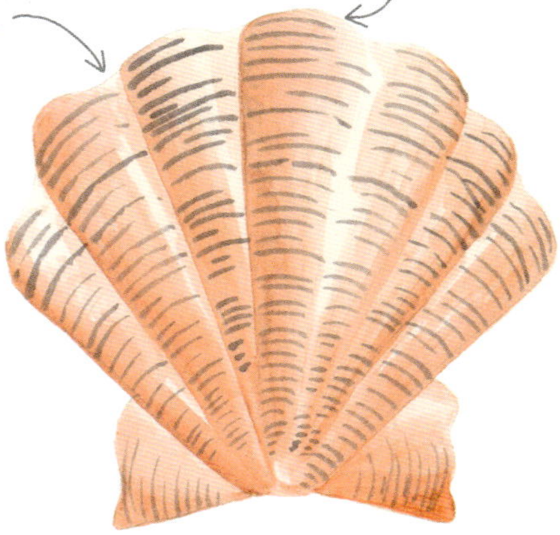

3

Brush size 4

Alizarin Crimson/Moonglow
light wash

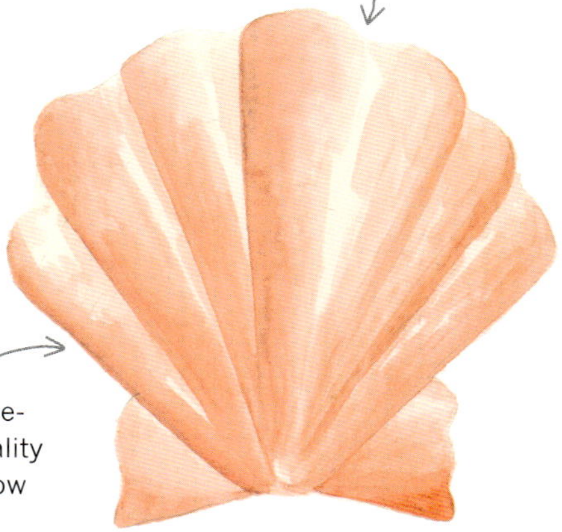

4

Brush size 1

Moonglow light wash

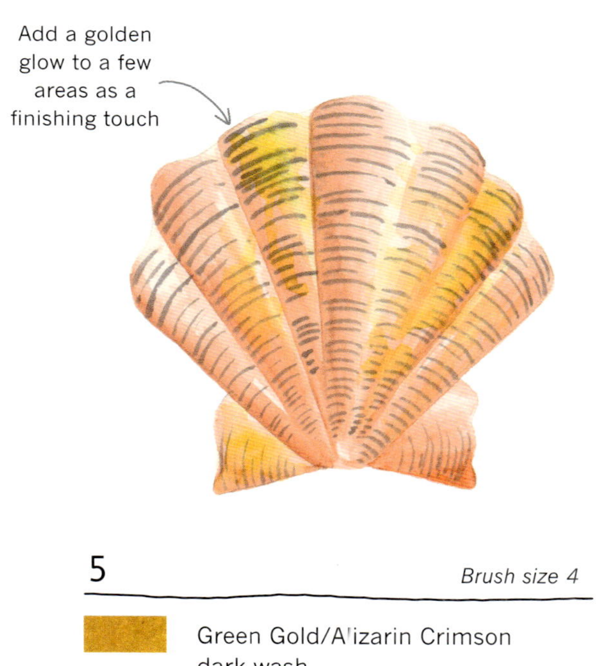

5

Brush size 4

Green Gold/Alizarin Crimson
dark wash

Popsicle

This project is cool satisfaction on a summer's day. Apply the Green Gold and the Alizarin Crimson wet-on-wet to achieve that seamless blend, then wait for it to dry before adding the final details.

1

Begin with a simple pencil sketch.

Apply a light wash to the stick

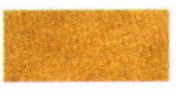

2   *Brush sizes 4 and 7*

Alizarin Crimson/Green Gold light wash

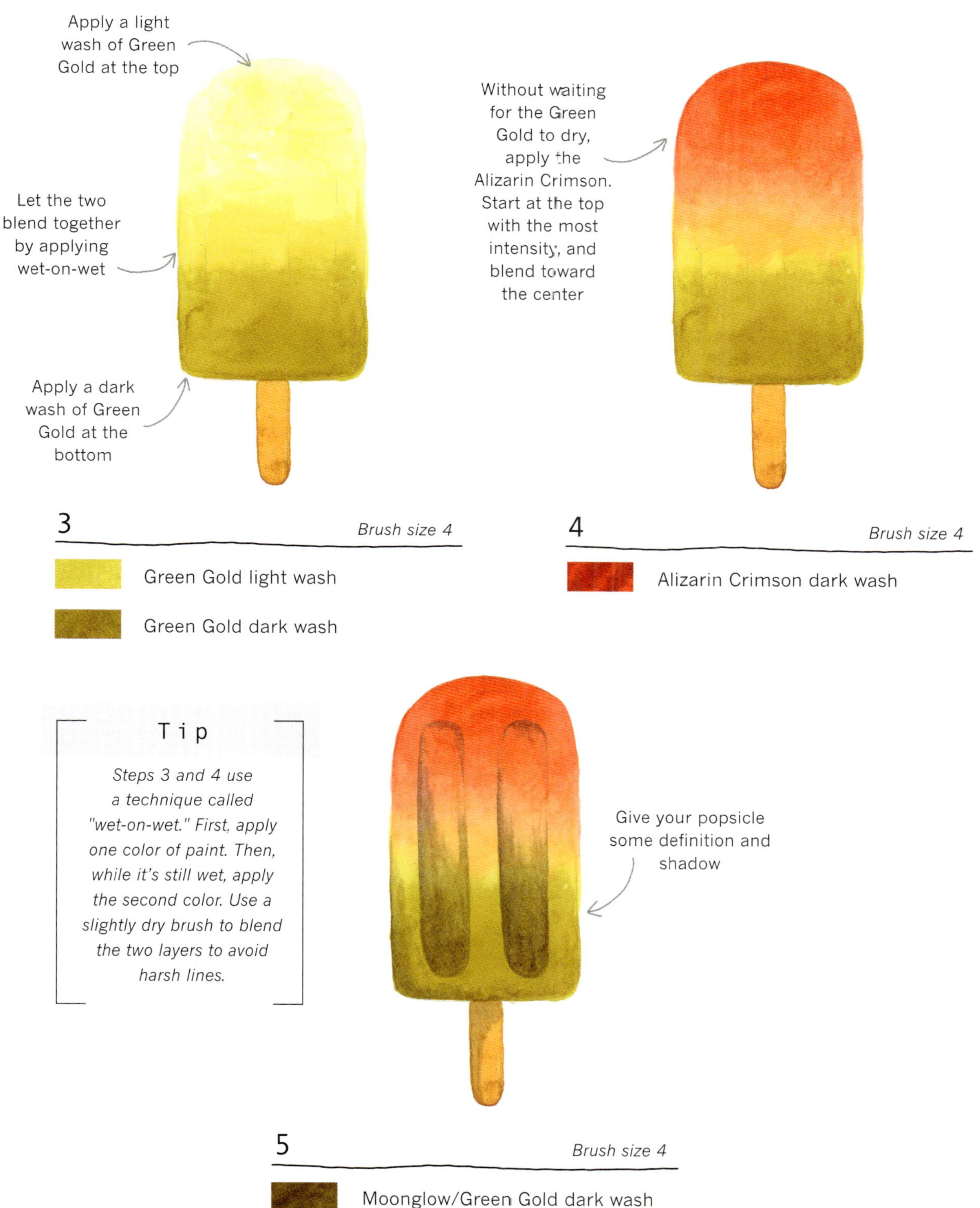

3   *Brush size 4*

Green Gold light wash

Green Gold dark wash

4   *Brush size 4*

Alizarin Crimson dark wash

Tip

Steps 3 and 4 use a technique called "wet-on-wet." First, apply one color of paint. Then, while it's still wet, apply the second color. Use a slightly dry brush to blend the two layers to avoid harsh lines.

5   *Brush size 4*

Moonglow/Green Gold dark wash

Flora

Keep things minimal in this elegant project: a single-stemmed flower is the very definition of natural beauty. Let each layer dry before adding the next for a crisp look.

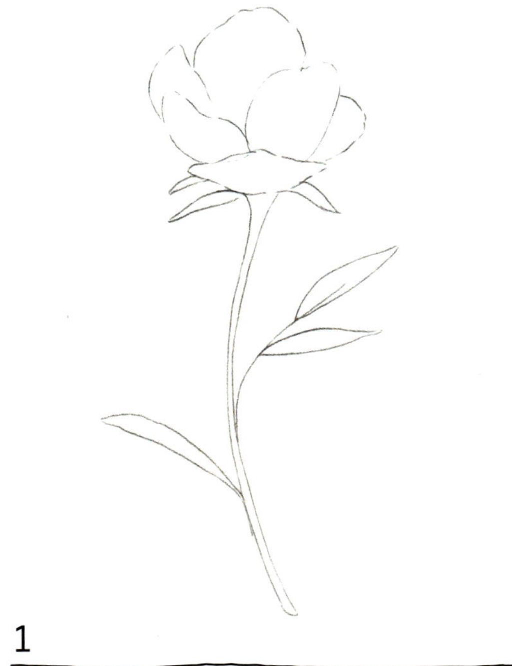

1

Begin with a simple pencil sketch.

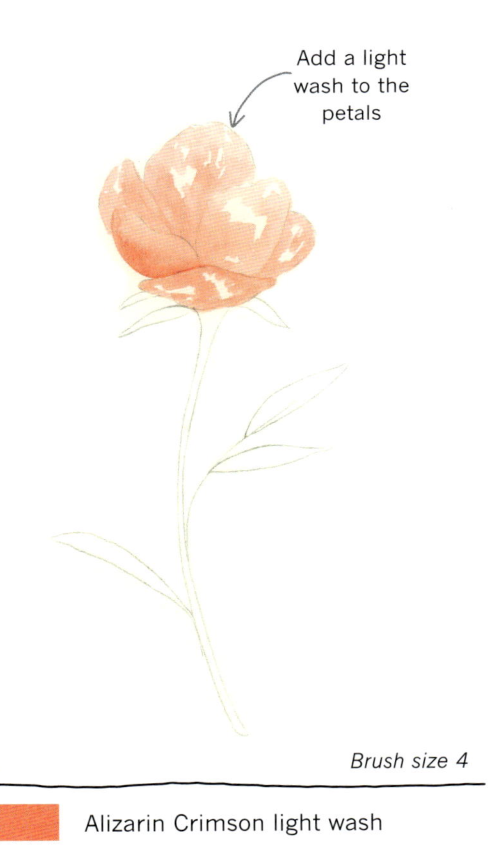

2

Brush size 4

Alizarin Crimson light wash

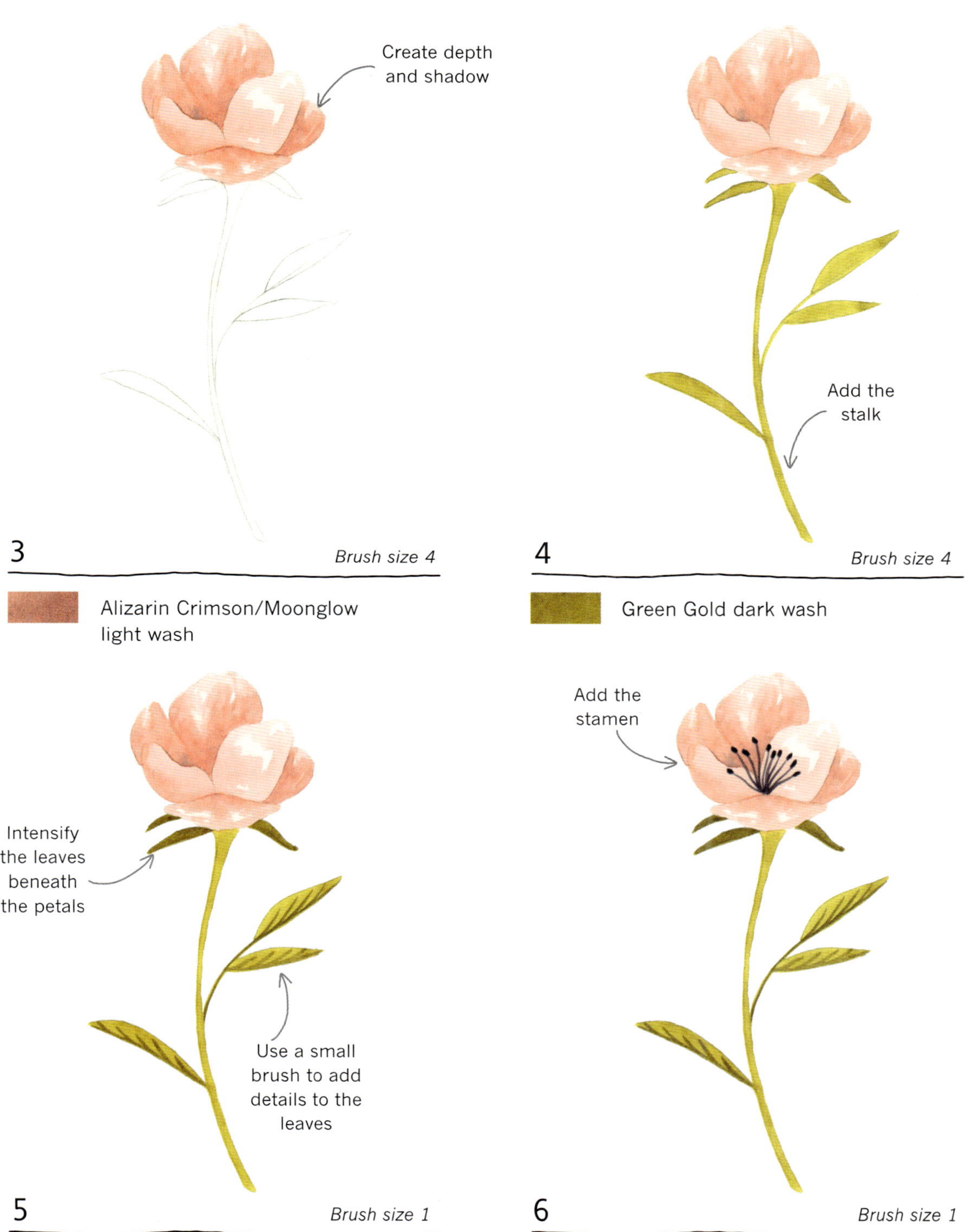

3   *Brush size 4*

Alizarin Crimson/Moonglow
light wash

4   *Brush size 4*

Green Gold dark wash

5   *Brush size 1*

Moonglow/Green Gold dark wash

6   *Brush size 1*

Moonglow dark wash

Spring Fresh

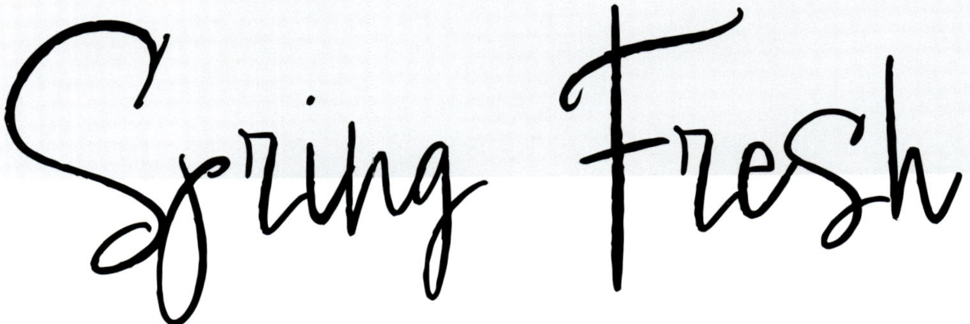

This three-color palette produces both optimistic brights and dreamy pastels—colors to boost your mood at the end of winter. It is a fresh, sunny mix that lends itself well to flowers and the natural world.

THE COLORS

Cadmium Yellow

Rose Madder

Phthalo Turquoise

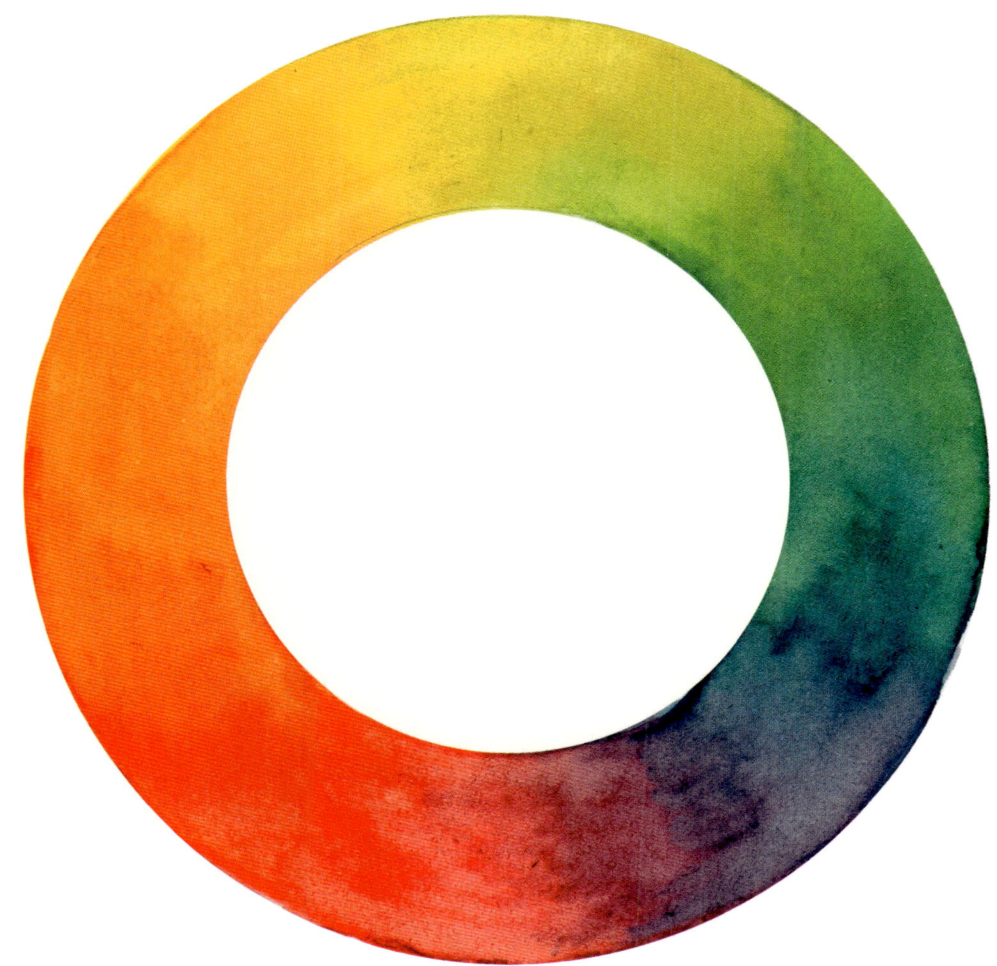

Mixing

The above shows the three colors on a simple
color wheel, each blending into its neighbor.
On the next page, you will see a chart showing
how the colors interact with each other.

COLOR CHART

Each color is shown at two strengths: a dark wash and a light wash. See p. 19 for more on washes.

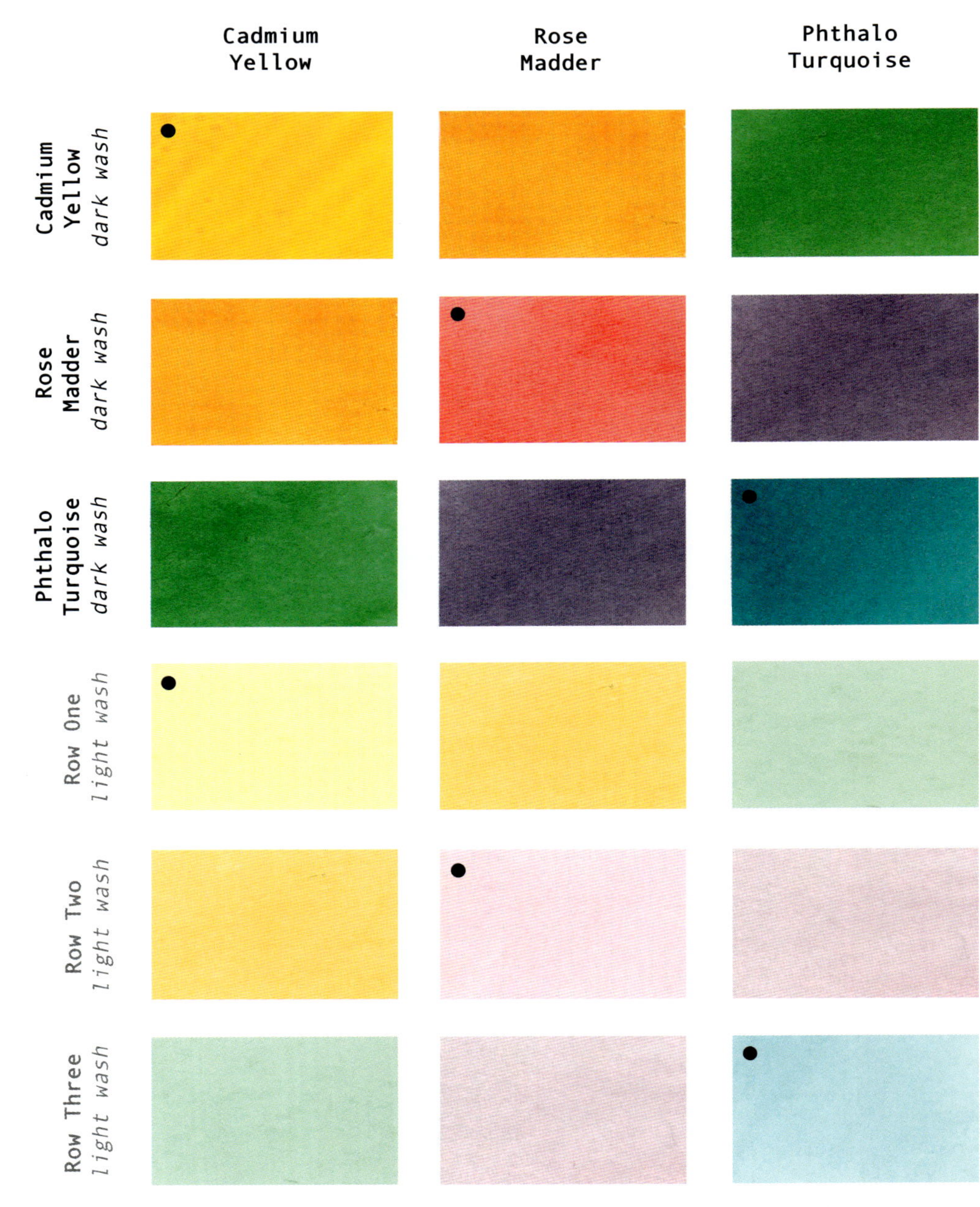

The Projects

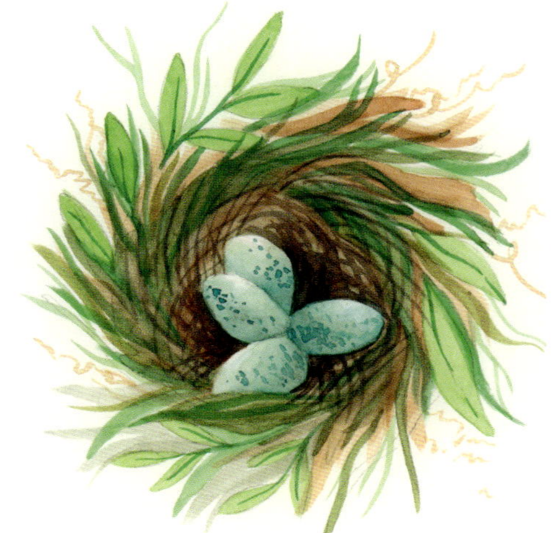

1. BIRD'S NEST

2. FLOWER POWER

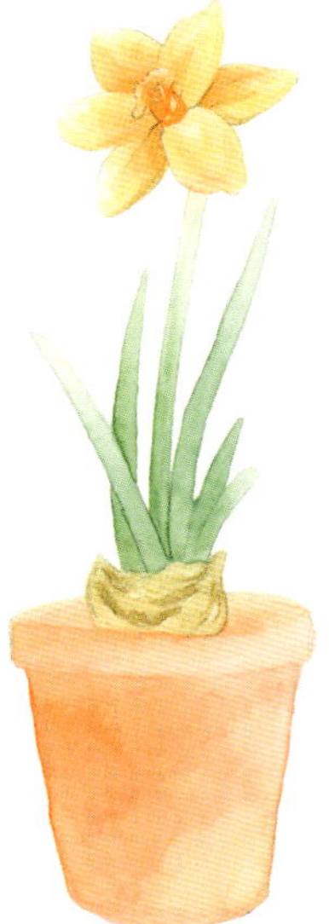

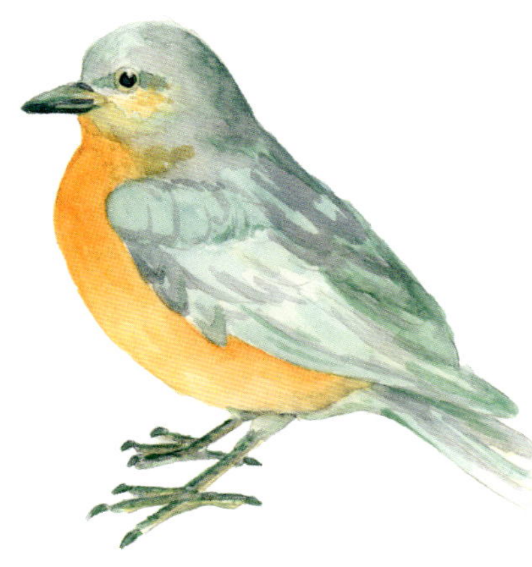

3. SPRINGTIME BIRD

Bird's Nest

Nothing captures spring vibes quite like speckled eggs, waiting to hatch.
Have fun mixing fresh greens and warm tones to build your own nest.

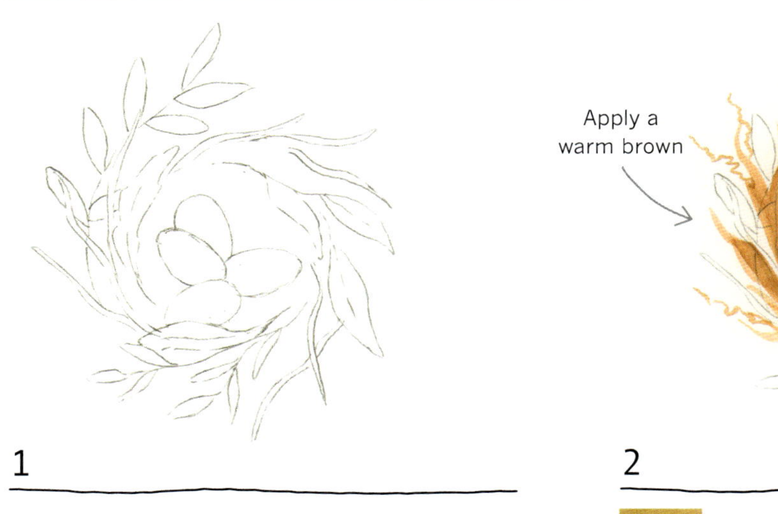

1

Begin with a simple pencil sketch.

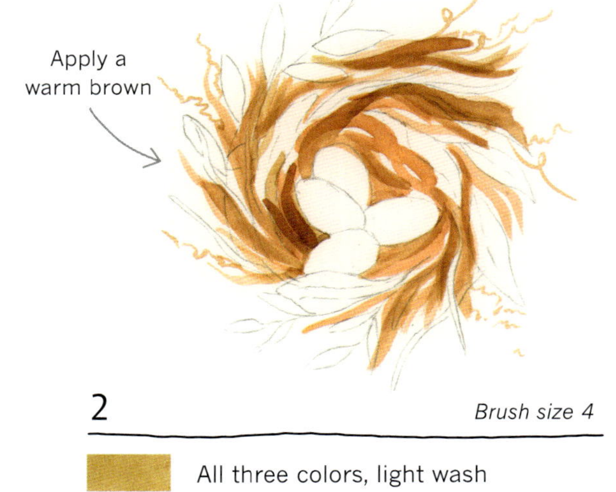

2

Brush size 4

All three colors, light wash

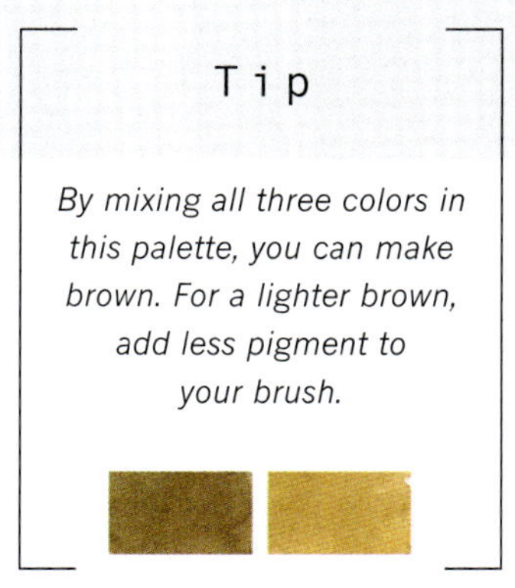

Tip

*By mixing all three colors in
this palette, you can make
brown. For a lighter brown,
add less pigment to
your brush.*

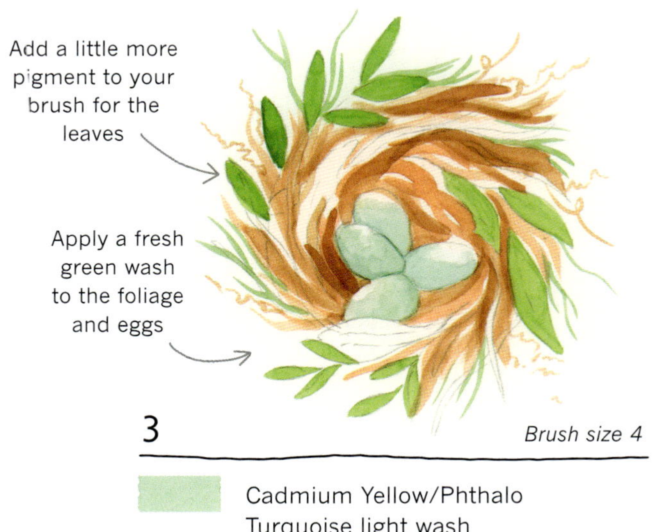

3

Brush size 4

Cadmium Yellow/Phthalo
Turquoise light wash

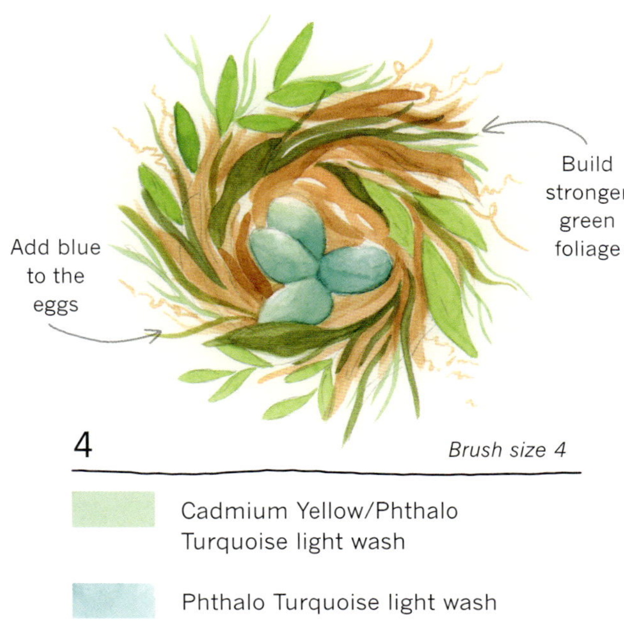

Add blue
to the
eggs

Build
stronger
green
foliage

4 *Brush size 4*

Cadmium Yellow/Phthalo Turquoise light wash

Phthalo Turquoise light wash

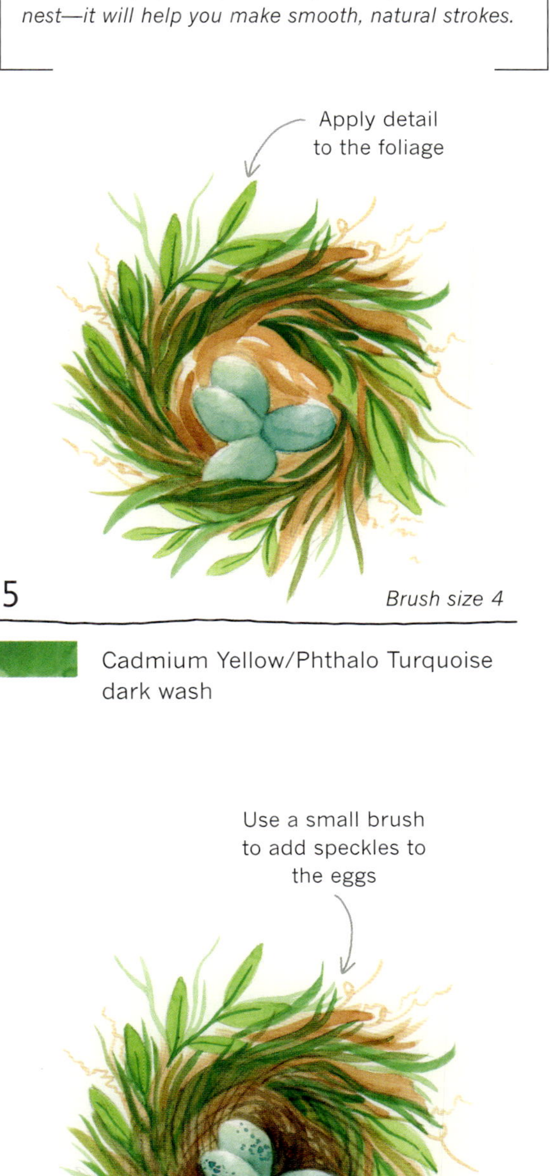

Apply detail
to the foliage

5 *Brush size 4*

Cadmium Yellow/Phthalo Turquoise dark wash

Use a small brush
to add speckles to
the eggs

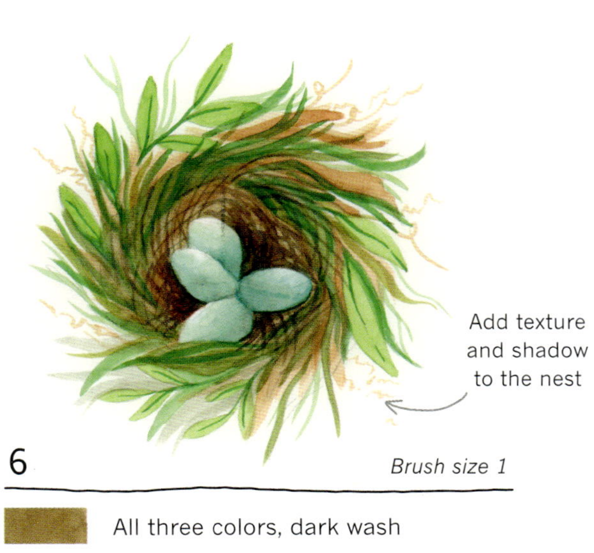

Add texture
and shadow
to the nest

6 *Brush size 1*

All three colors, dark wash

7 *Brush size 1*

Phthalo Turquoise dark wash

Flower Power

Say goodbye to winter with the blooming of the first daffodils of the year. Use simple layering to capture their sunny petals and trademark trumpet.

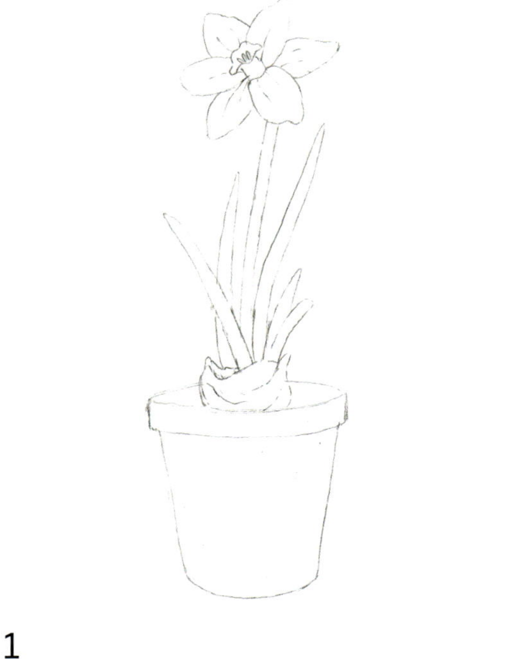

1

Begin with a simple pencil sketch.

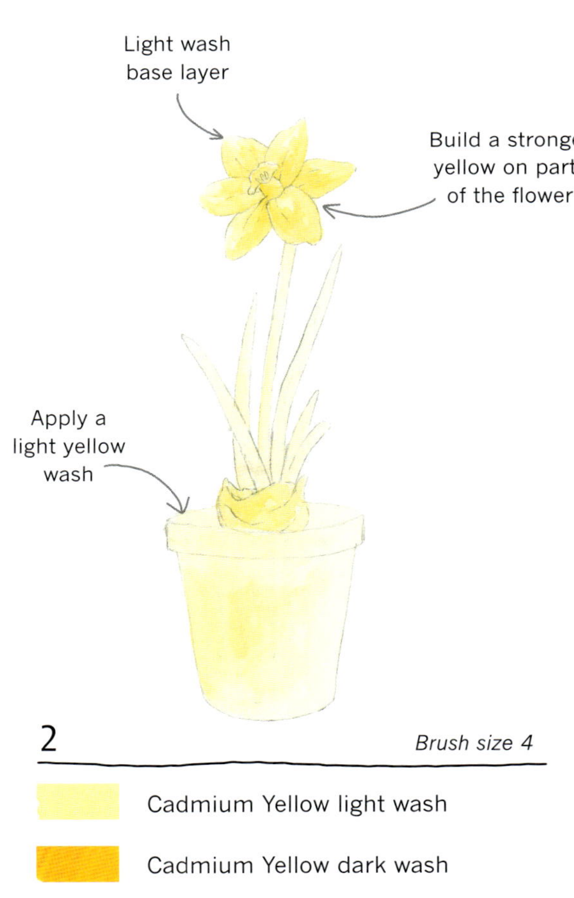

2

Brush size 4

Cadmium Yellow light wash

Cadmium Yellow dark wash

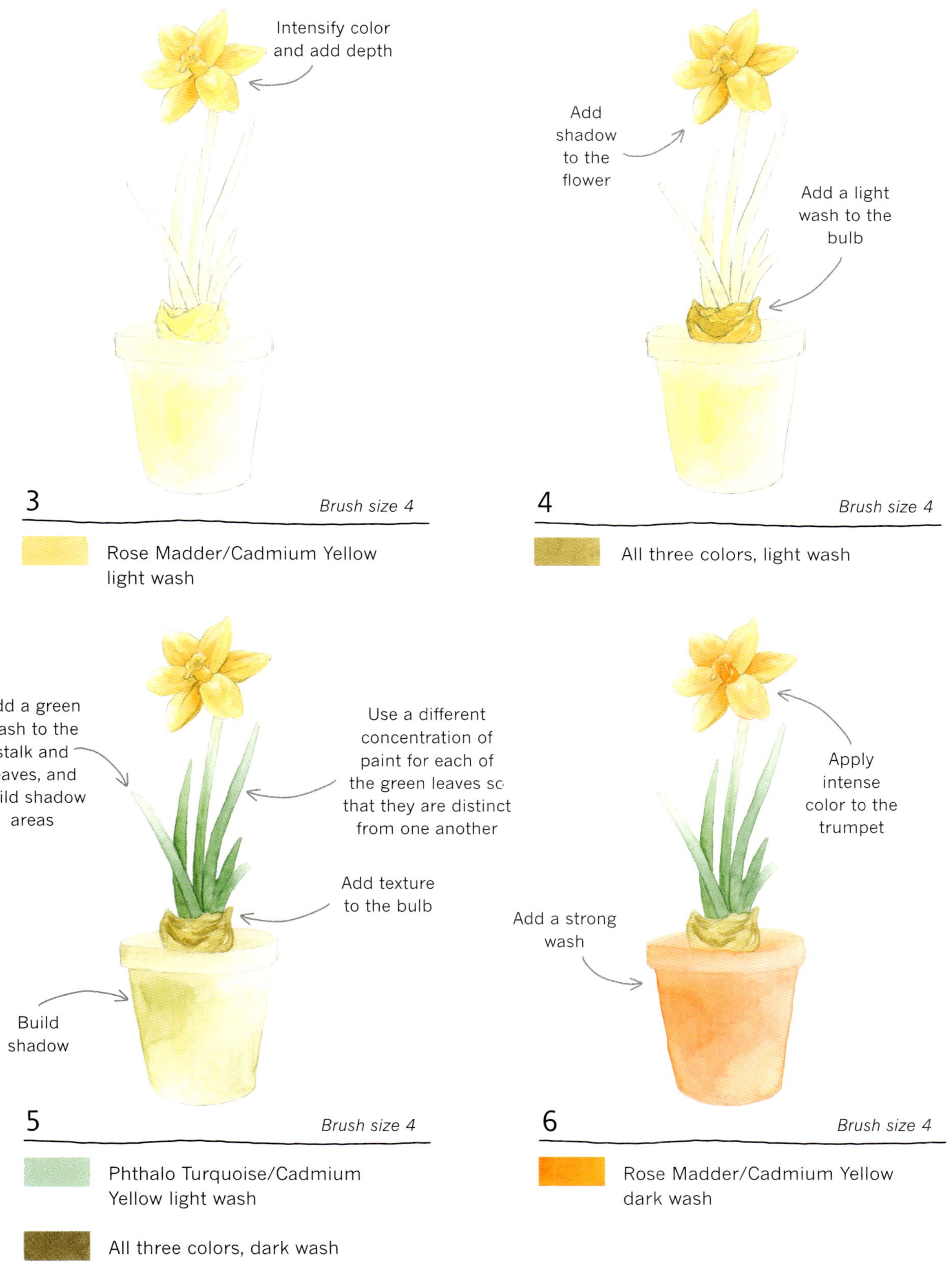

Intensify color
and add depth

3
Brush size 4

Rose Madder/Cadmium Yellow
light wash

Add
shadow
to the
flower

Add a light
wash to the
bulb

4
Brush size 4

All three colors, light wash

Add a green
wash to the
stalk and
leaves, and
build shadow
areas

Use a different
concentration of
paint for each of
the green leaves so
that they are distinct
from one another

Add texture
to the bulb

Build
shadow

5
Brush size 4

Phthalo Turquoise/Cadmium
Yellow light wash

All three colors, dark wash

Apply
intense
color to the
trumpet

Add a strong
wash

6
Brush size 4

Rose Madder/Cadmium Yellow
dark wash

Springtime Bird

If you're ever stuck for inspiration when it comes to color mixing, ask the birds! The vivid colors in their plumage complement each other perfectly.

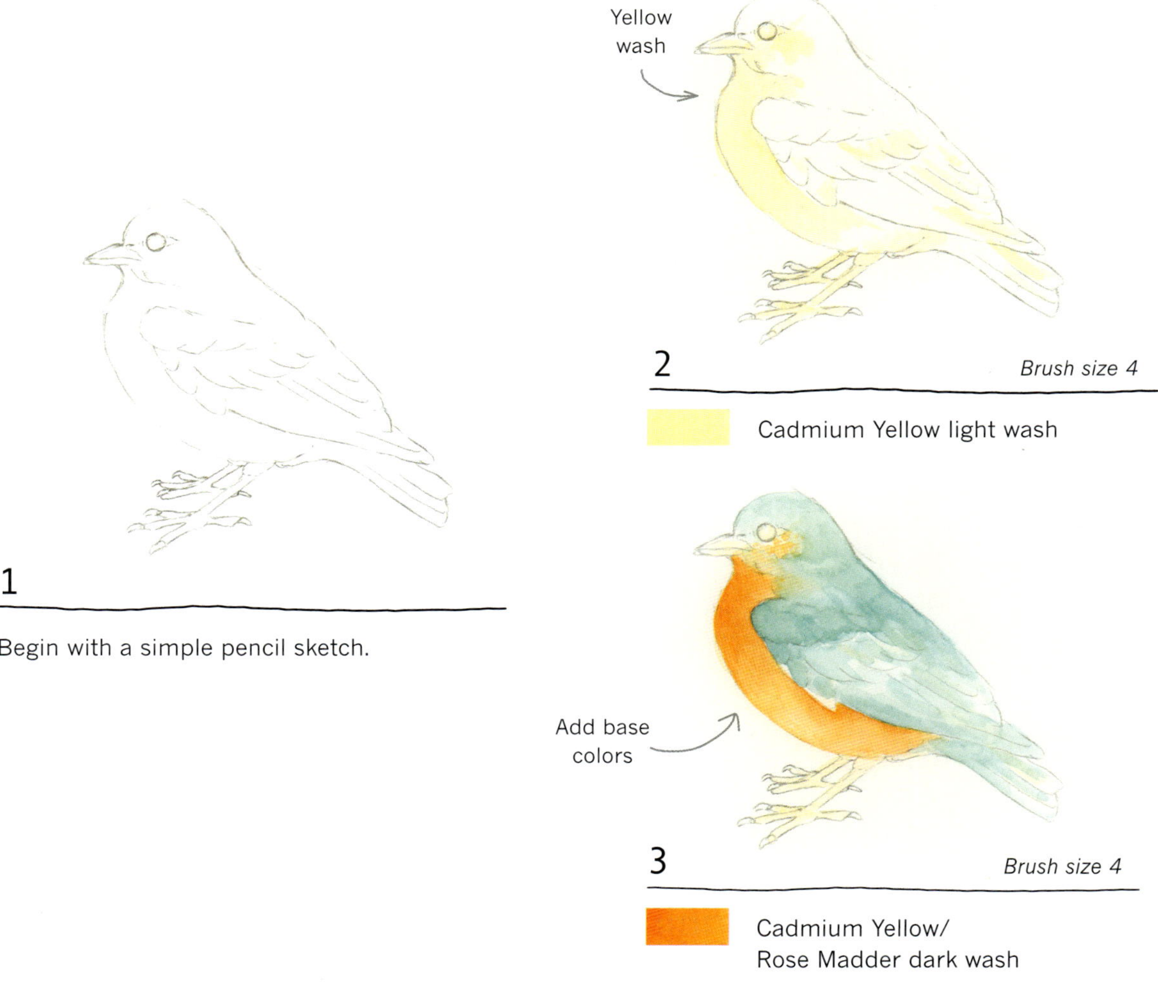

1

Begin with a simple pencil sketch.

2   *Brush size 4*

Cadmium Yellow light wash

3   *Brush size 4*

Cadmium Yellow/
Rose Madder dark wash

Phthalo Turquoise light wash

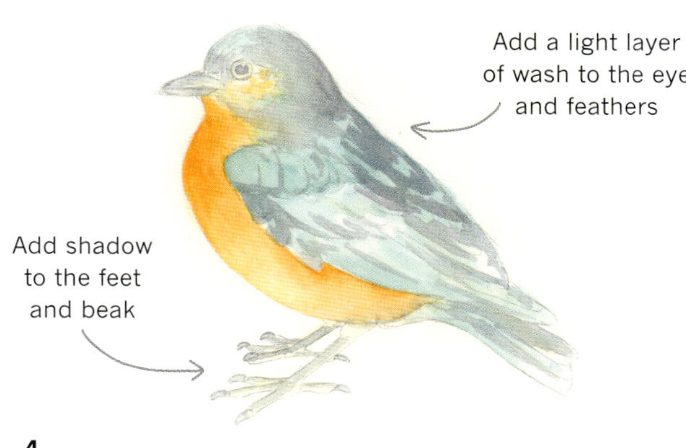

4   *Brush size 4*

Rose Madder/Phthalo Turquoise
light wash

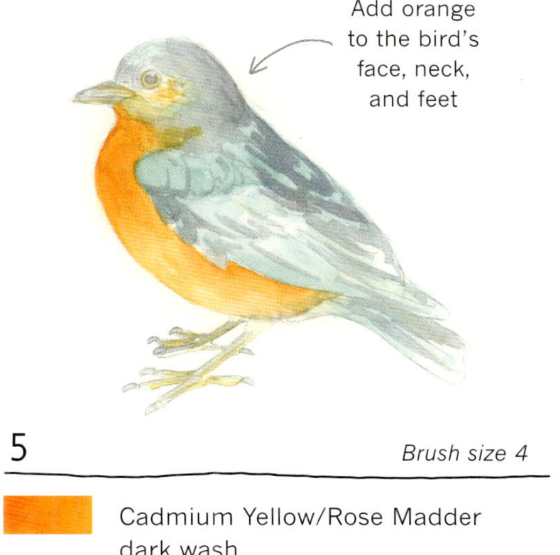

5   *Brush size 4*

Cadmium Yellow/Rose Madder
dark wash

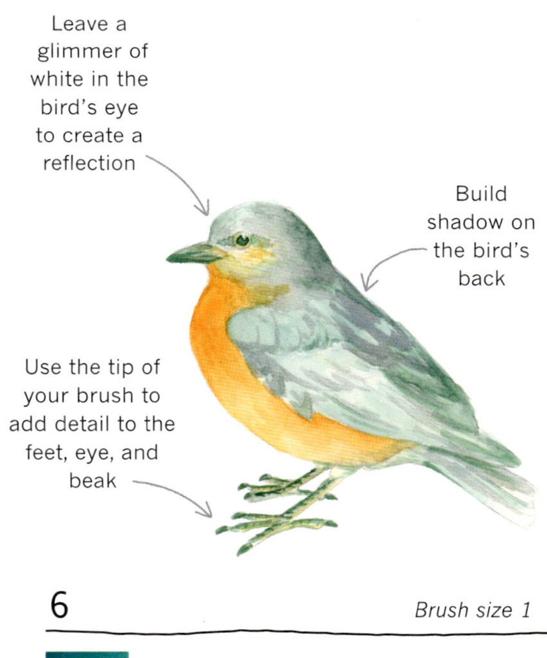

6   *Brush size 1*

Phthalo Turquoise dark wash

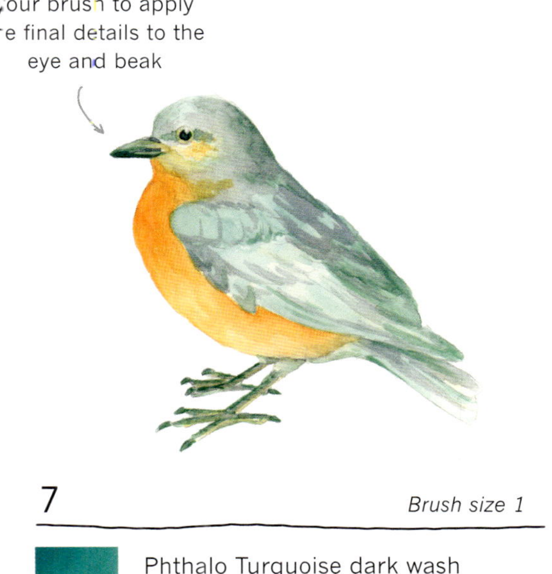

7   *Brush size 1*

Phthalo Turquoise dark wash

Summer Swoon

This three-color palette produces both hazy tones and dreamy blues—colors that feel like a long day in the sun. It is a laid-back, sultry mix that lends itself well to painting "en plein air," out in nature.

THE COLORS

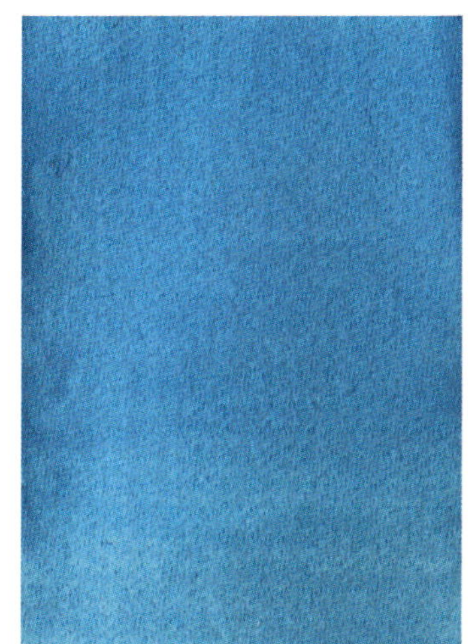

Cerulean Blue

Yellow Ocher

Phthalo Turquoise

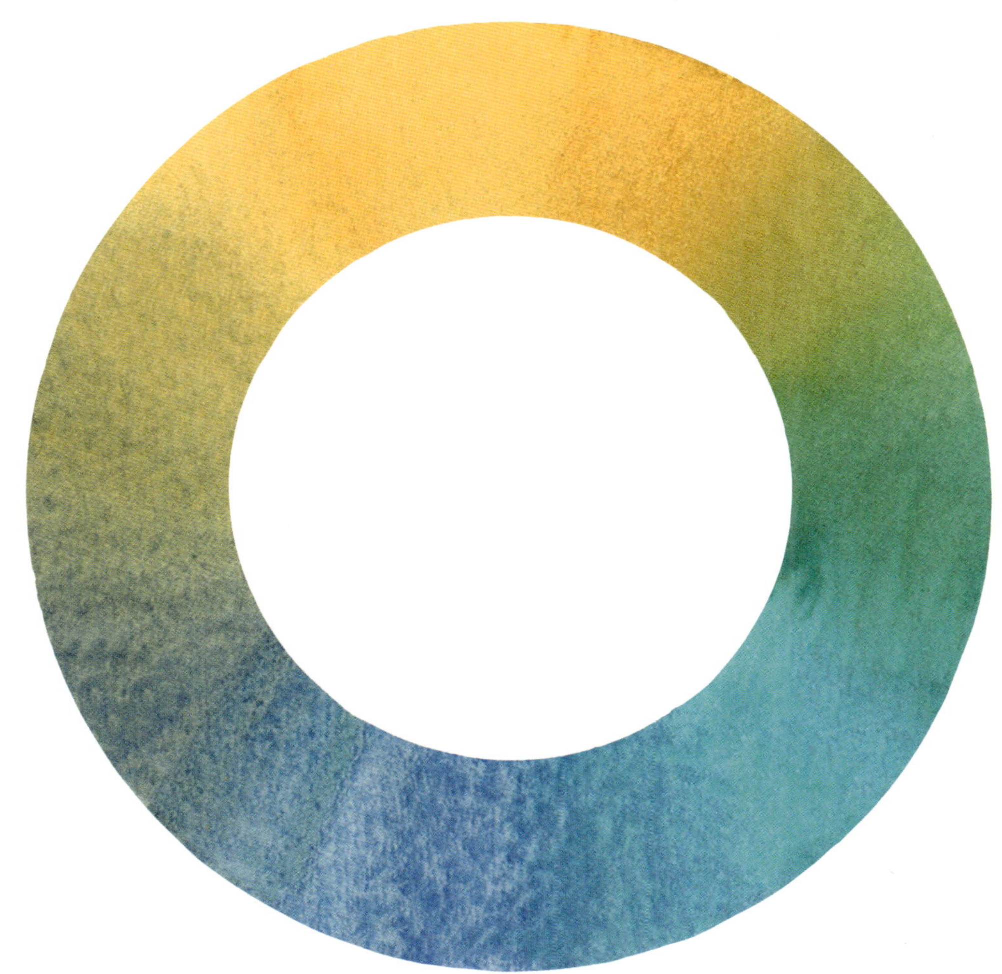

Mixing

The above shows the three colors on a simple
color wheel, each blending into its neighbor.
On the next page, you will see a chart showing
how the colors interact with each other.

COLOR CHART

Each color is shown at two strengths: a dark wash
and a light wash. See p. 19 for more on washes.

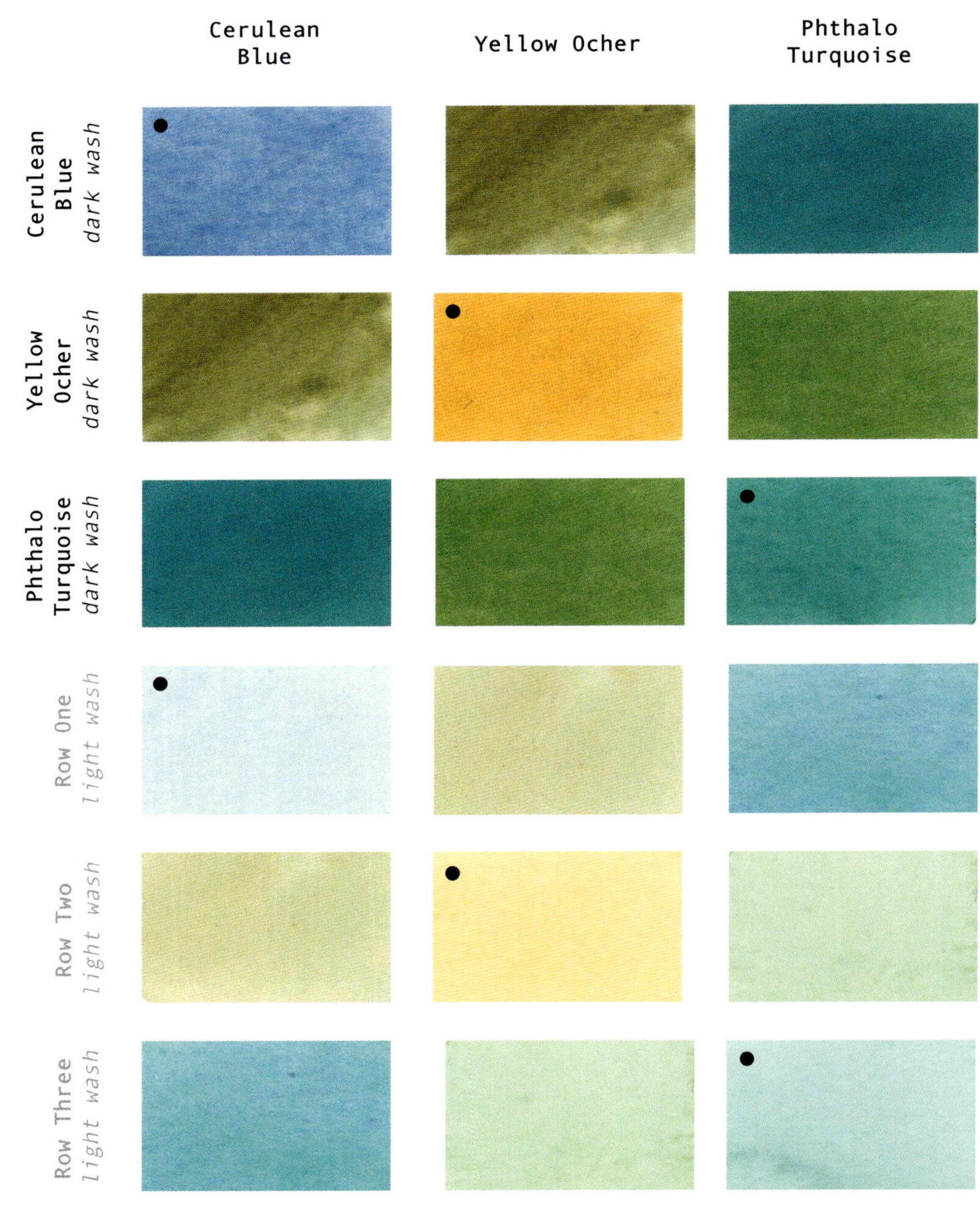

The Projects

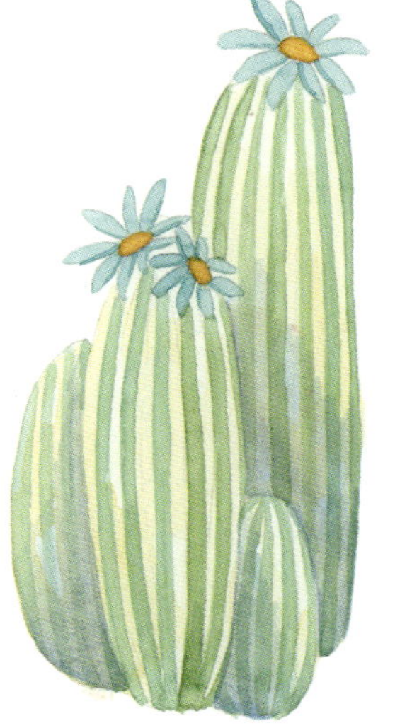

1. FLOWERING CACTUS

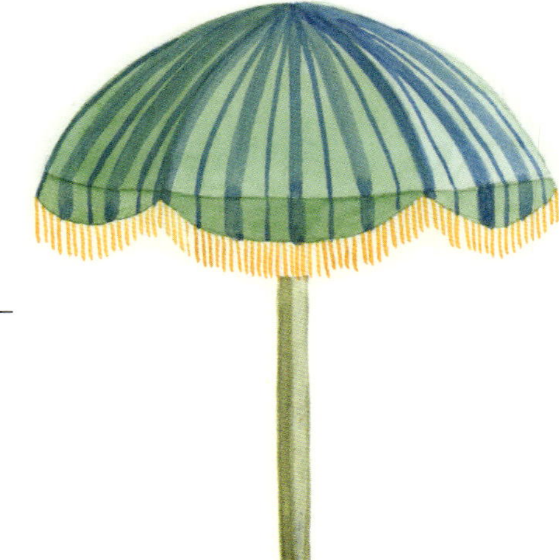

2. PARASOL

3. JOURNAL ENTRY

Flowering Cactus

Sweep your brush downward with long, smooth strokes to form the distinctive texture of this flowering cactus. Top tip: you might find it more comfortable to rotate the page when painting long lines like these.

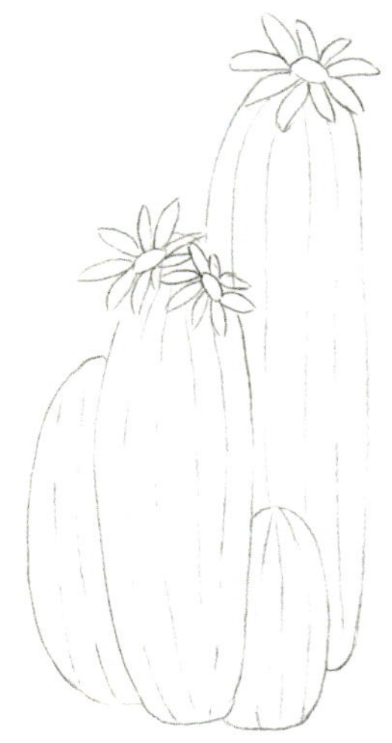

1

Begin with a simple pencil sketch.

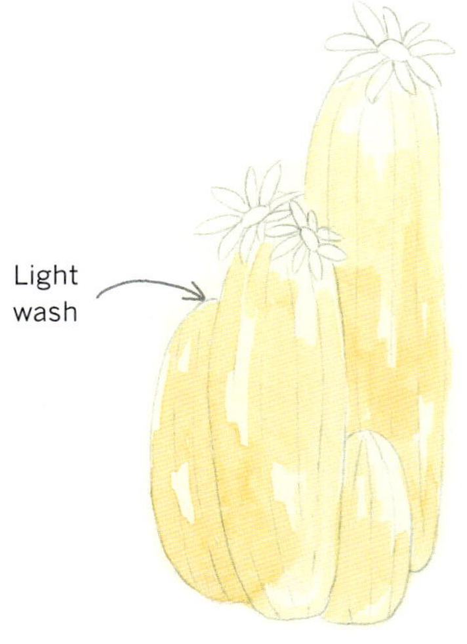

2   *Brush size 4*

Yellow Ocher light wash

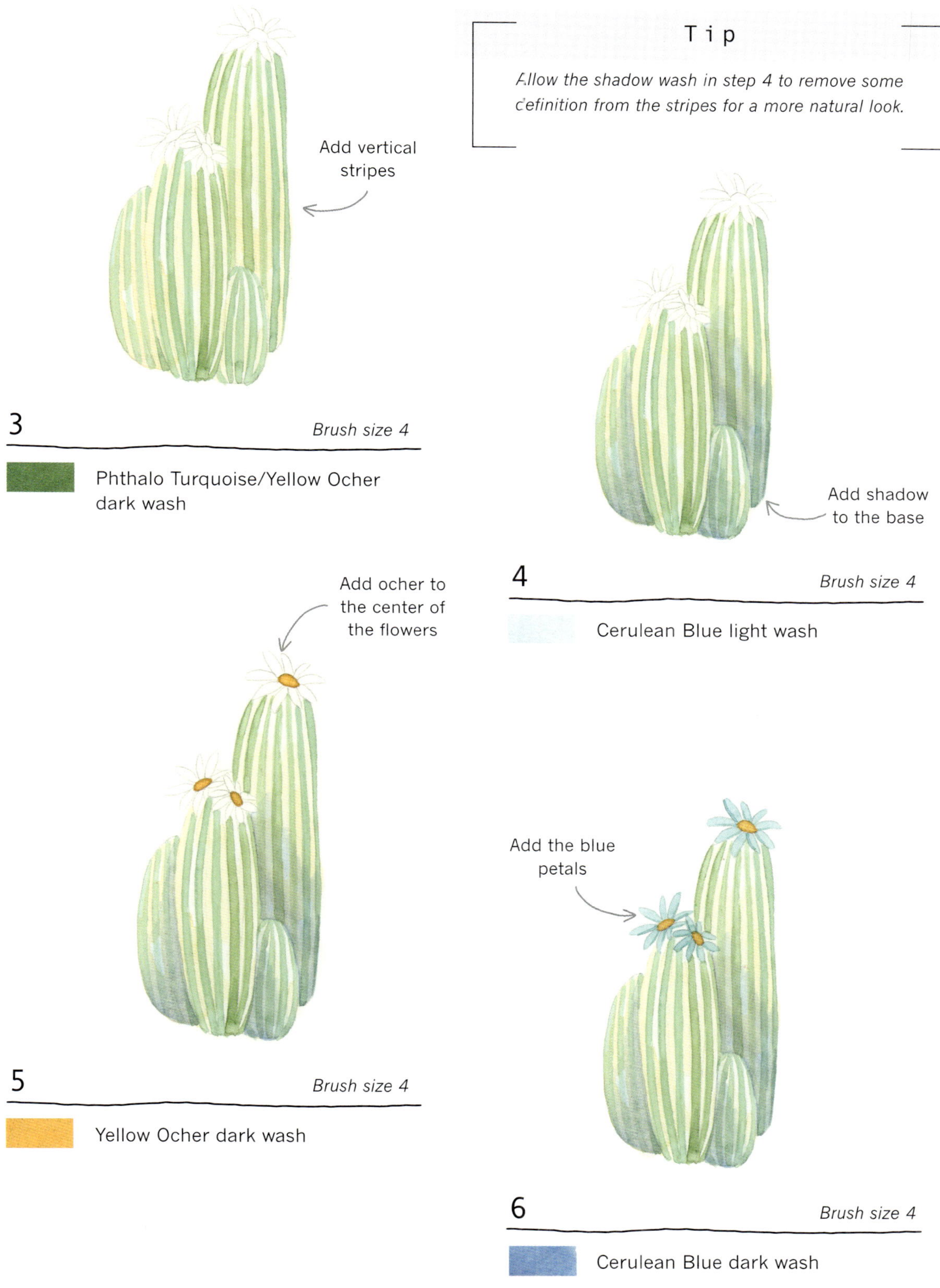

3   *Brush size 4*

Phthalo Turquoise/Yellow Ocher
dark wash

4   *Brush size 4*

Cerulean Blue light wash

5   *Brush size 4*

Yellow Ocher dark wash

6   *Brush size 4*

Cerulean Blue dark wash

Parasol

Kick back with a beach read, sip a cool drink, and keep the summer sun off your face with this jaunty parasol. Use the tip of your brush to add the fringe around its edge—guaranteed satisfaction.

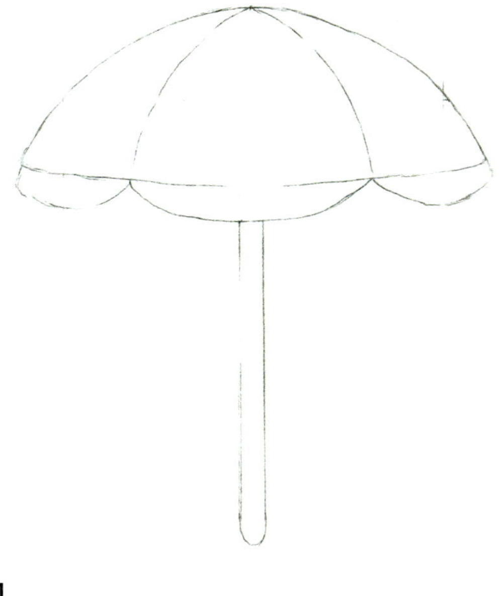

1

Begin with a simple pencil sketch.

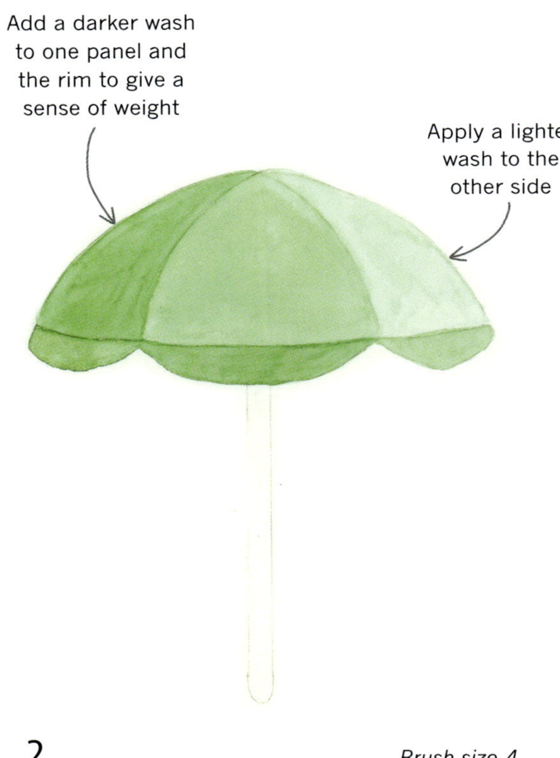

2 *Brush size 4*

Phthalo Turquoise/Yellow Ocher light wash

Phthalo Turquoise/Yellow Ocher dark wash

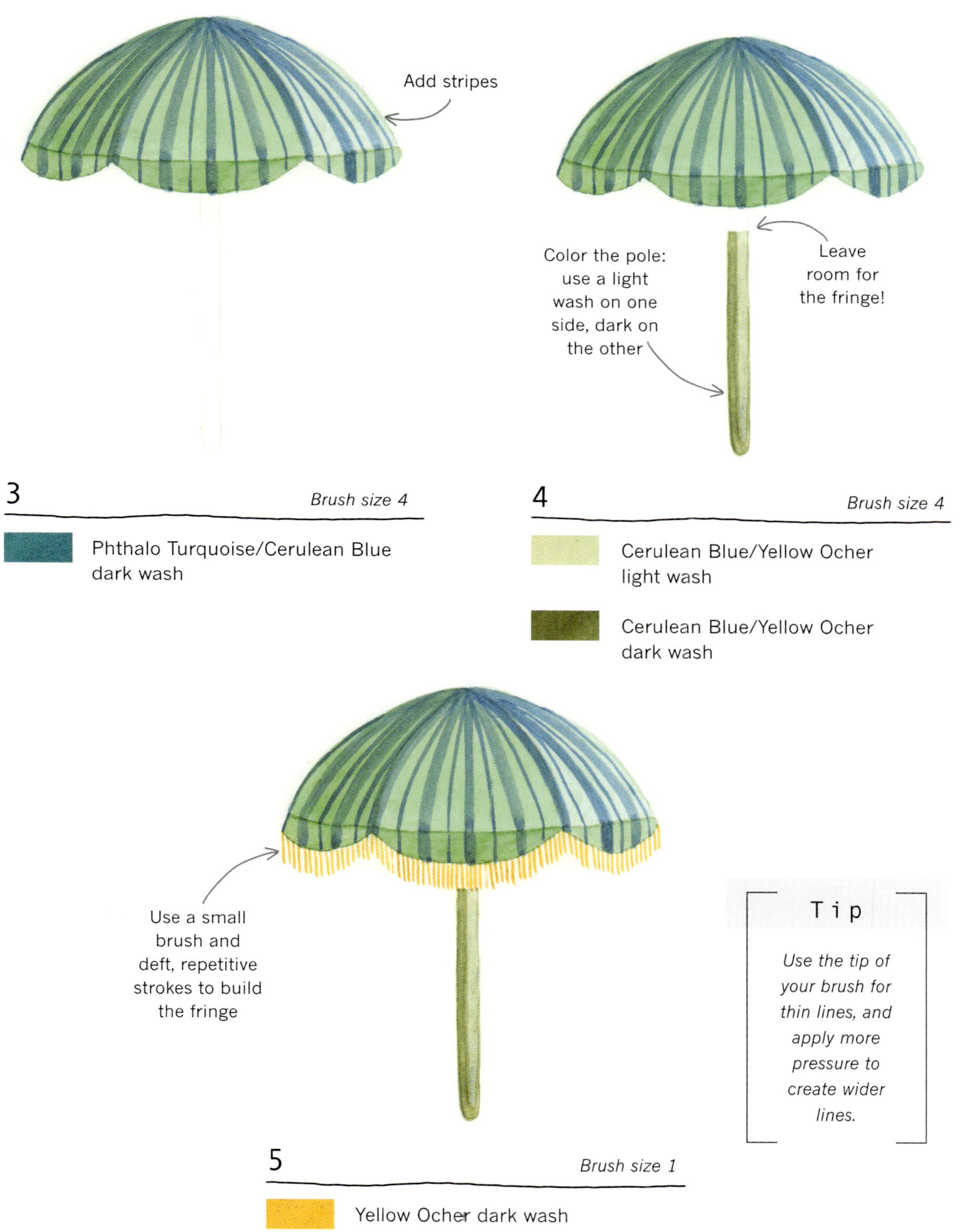

3   *Brush size 4*

Phthalo Turquoise/Cerulean Blue
dark wash

4   *Brush size 4*

Cerulean Blue/Yellow Ocher
light wash

Cerulean Blue/Yellow Ocher
dark wash

5   *Brush size 1*

Yellow Ocher dark wash

Tip

*Use the tip of
your brush for
thin lines, and
apply more
pressure to
create wider
lines.*

Journal Entry

Time for some creativity and reflection with this elegant project. The irregular wash across the journal pages is key to creating the papery, tactile effect.

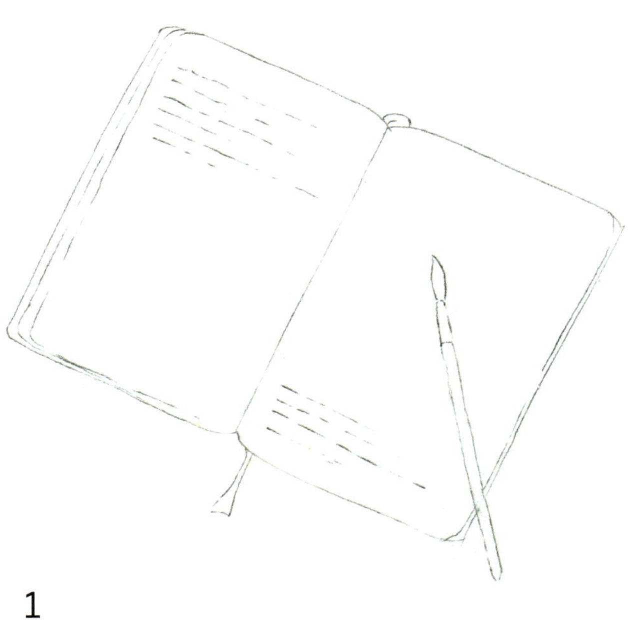

1

Begin with a simple pencil sketch.

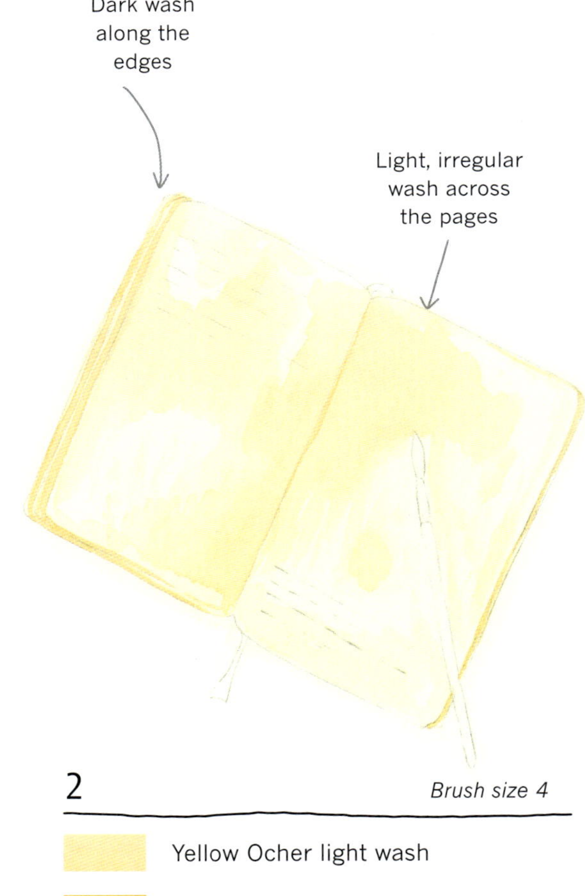

2

Brush size 4

Yellow Ocher light wash

Yellow Ocher dark wash

Tip

Don't be tempted to use a larger brush for the base wash in step 2. A size 4 brush will give you more control over the dappled effect, and will make it easier for you to leave the lighter areas—they would get swallowed up by a size 7 brush.

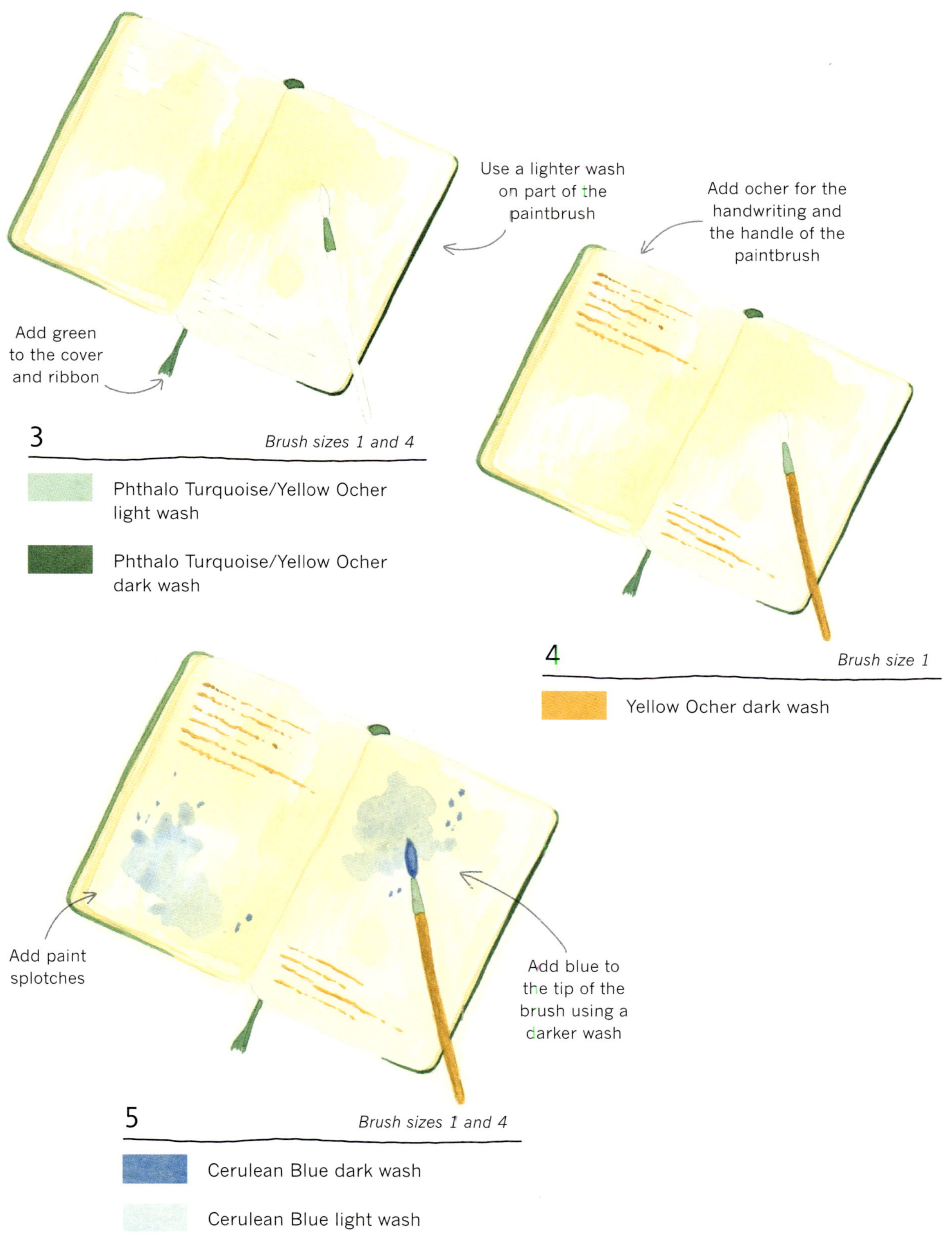

3

Brush sizes 1 and 4

Phthalo Turquoise/Yellow Ocher light wash

Phthalo Turquoise/Yellow Ocher dark wash

4

Brush size 1

Yellow Ocher dark wash

5

Brush sizes 1 and 4

Cerulean Blue dark wash

Cerulean Blue light wash

Autumnal Glow

This three-color palette is all about golden light. It has a gorgeous, swooning feel, bringing to mind afternoon sunshine filtering through fall leaves.

THE COLORS

Green Gold

Cadmium Orange

Buff Titanium

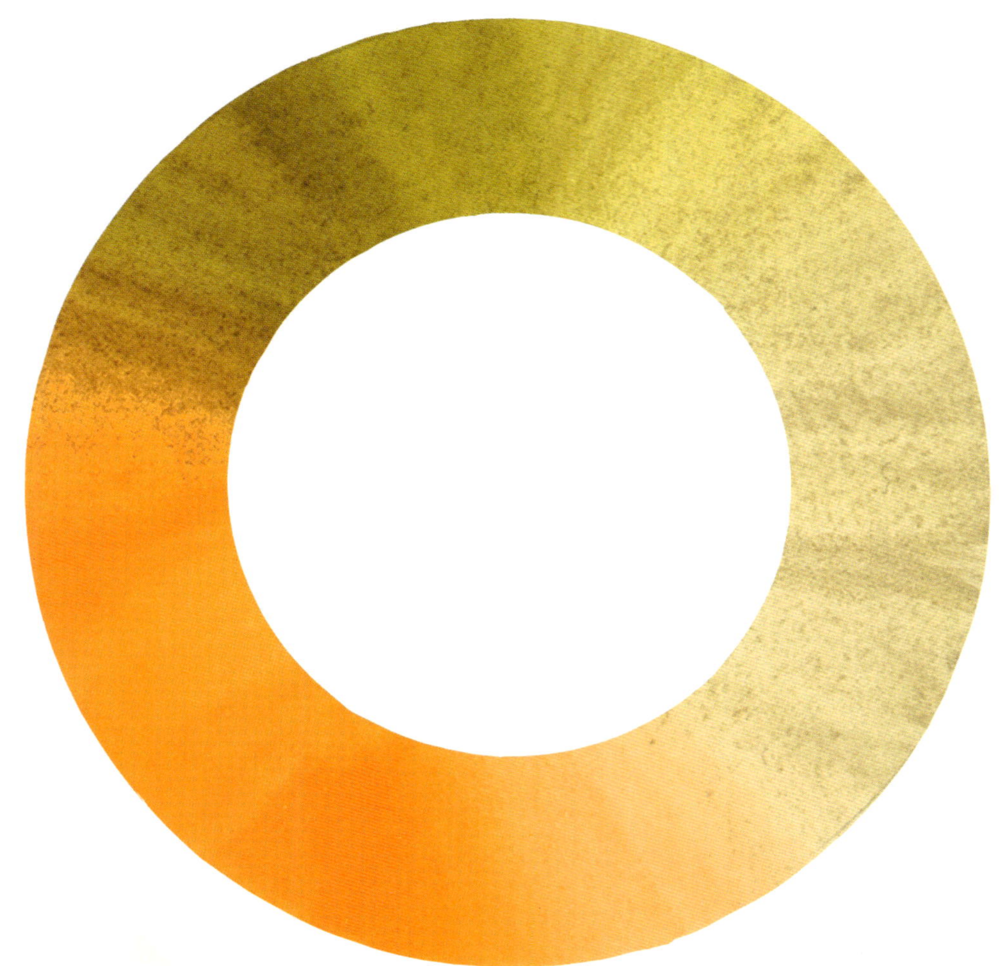

Mixing

The above shows the three colors on a simple
color wheel, each blending into its neighbor.
On the next page, you will see a chart showing
how the colors interact with each other.

COLOR CHART

Each color is shown at two strengths: a dark wash and a light wash. See p. 19 for more on washes.

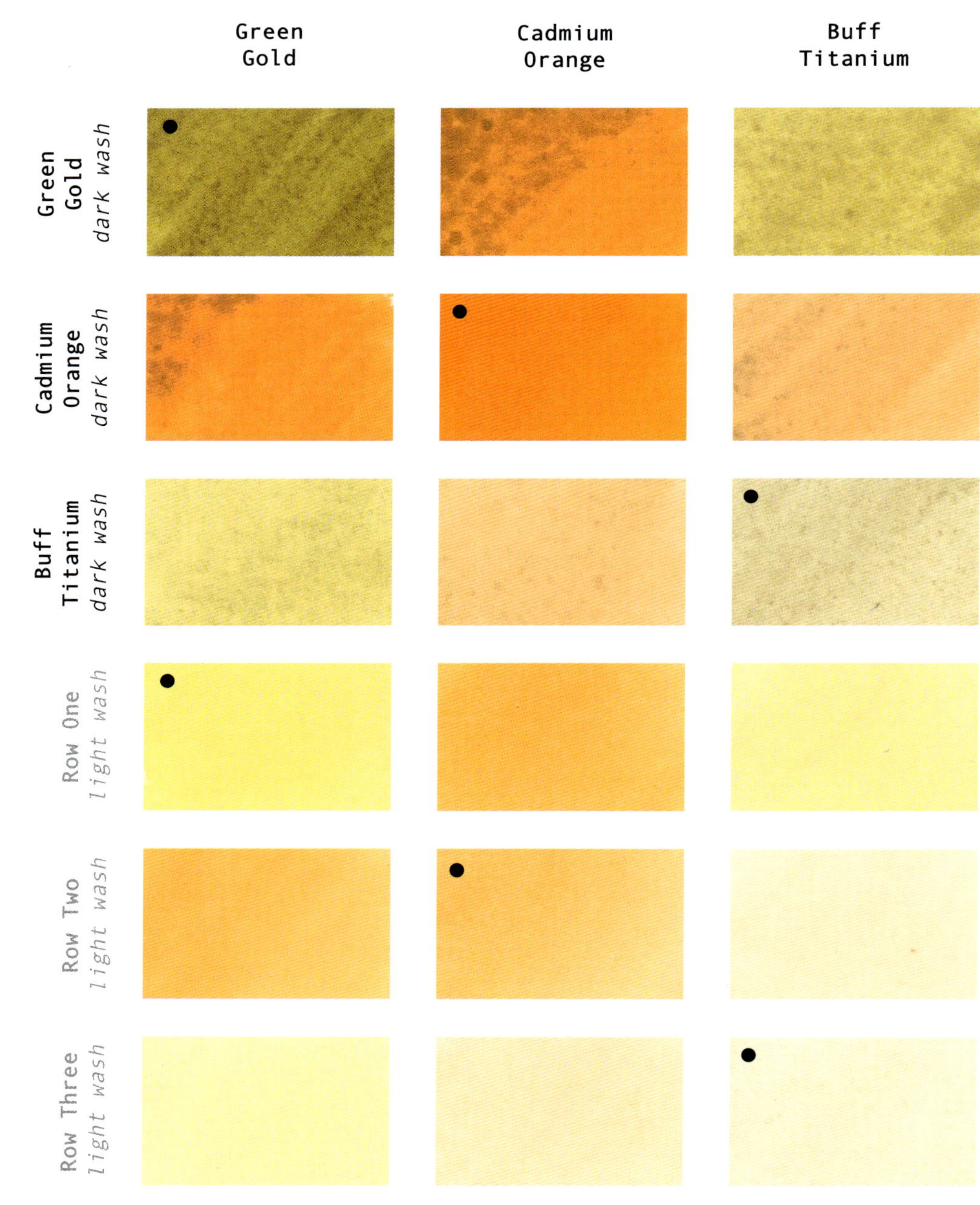

The Projects

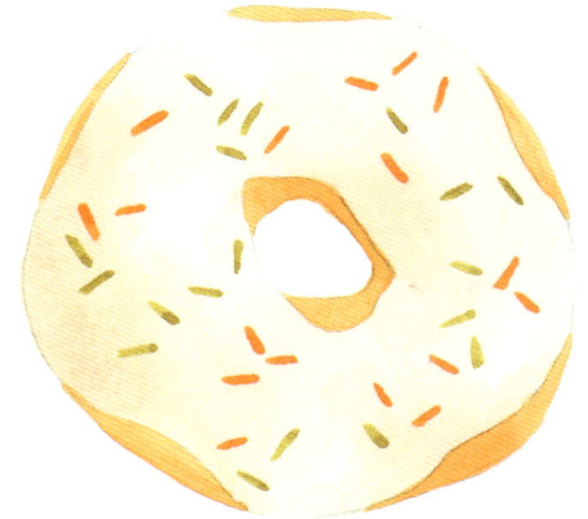

1. ICED DONUT

2. FUNGI

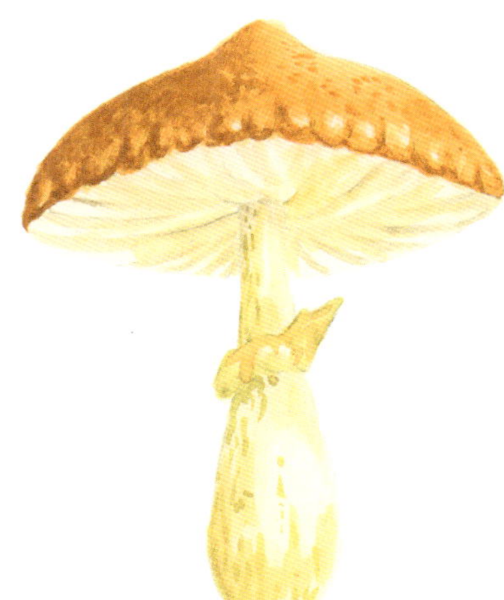

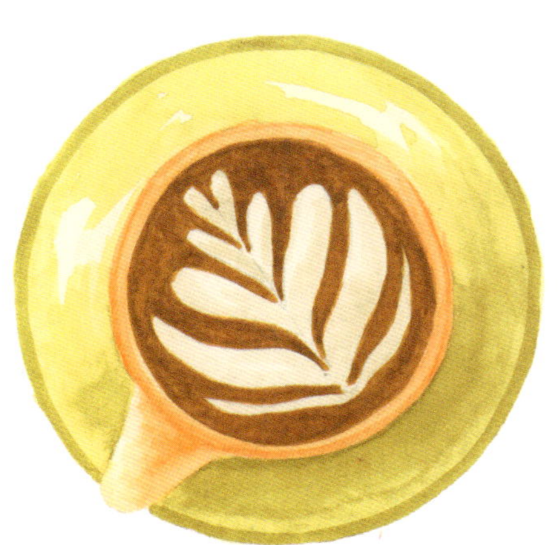

3. LATTE ART

Iced Donut

It's all about the simple pleasures in life. Take a break, gaze out of the window, take a sip of coffee, and bite into this sweet iced donut.

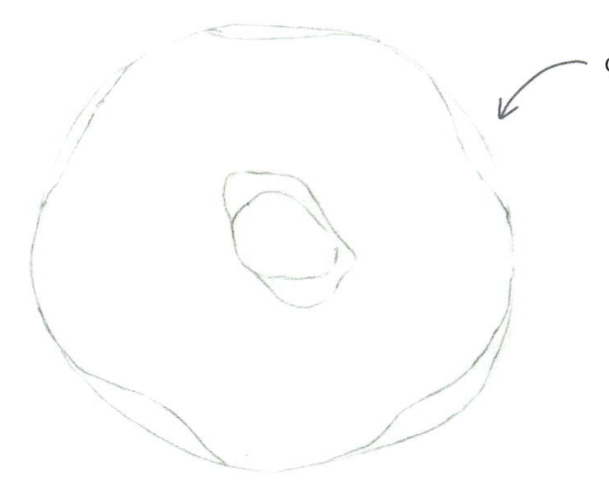

1

Begin with a simple pencil sketch.

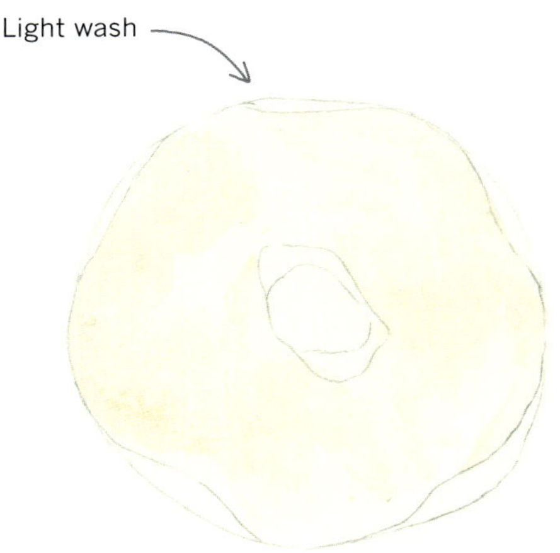

2 *Brush size 7*

Buff Titanium light wash

Add color to your dough

3 *Brush size 4*

Green Gold/Cadmium Orange light wash

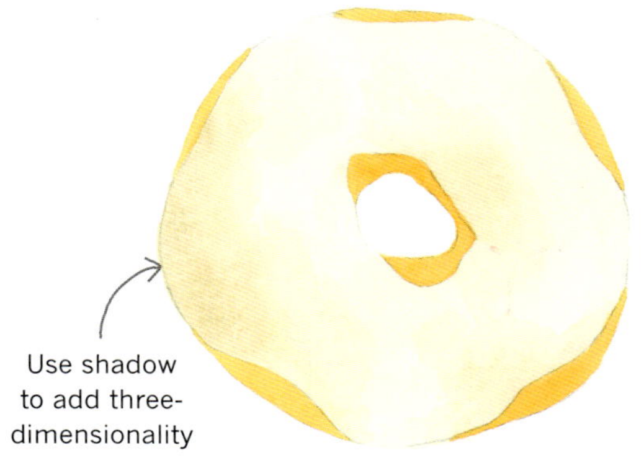

4 *Brush size 4*

Buff Titanium/Cadmium Orange light wash

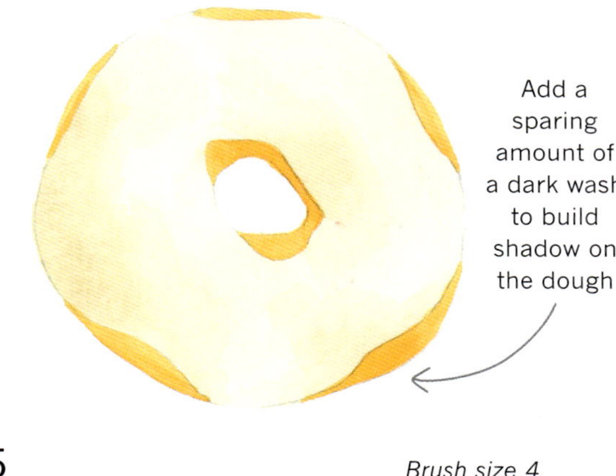

5 *Brush size 4*

Green Gold/Cadmium Orange dark wash

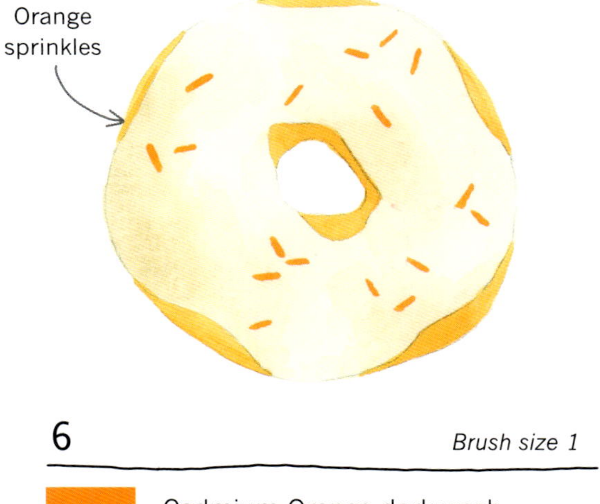

6 *Brush size 1*

Cadmium Orange dark wash

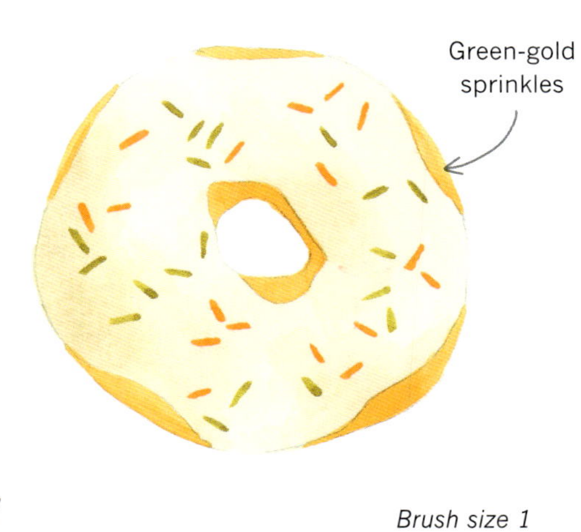

7 *Brush size 1*

Green Gold dark wash

Fungi

No need to go walking through the woods to forage for mushrooms: you can grow your own with this simple three-color palette. A small brush will come in handy for the speckles.

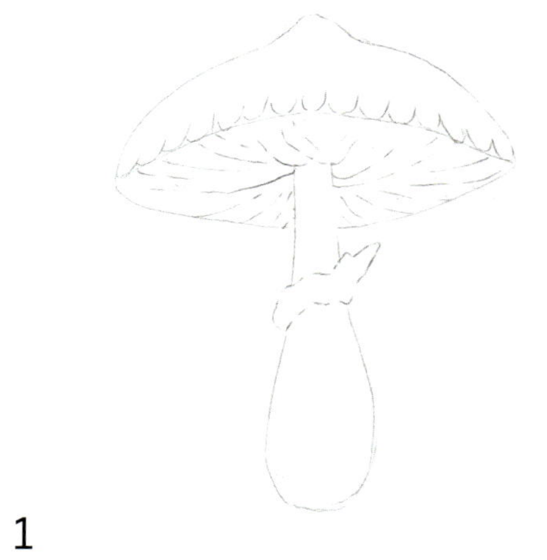

1

Begin with a simple pencil sketch.

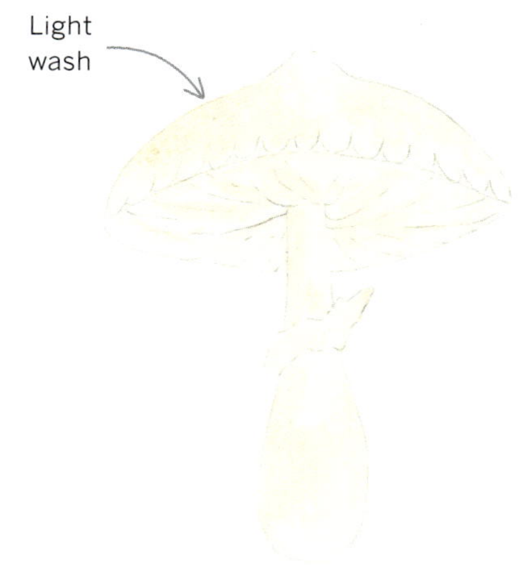

2

Brush size 7

Buff Titanium light wash

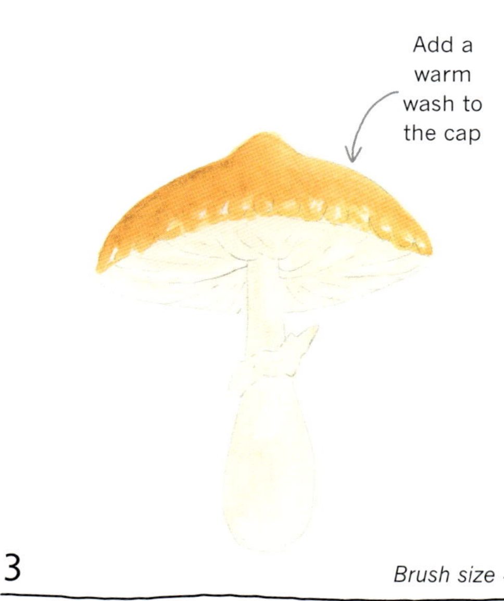

3

Brush size 4

Green Gold/Cadmium Orange light wash

Tip

Don't be tempted to rush it when adding shadow to the stalk and cap. One thick, concentrated layer of paint would be harsh and tricky to blend. Instead, slowly build these areas, layer by layer.

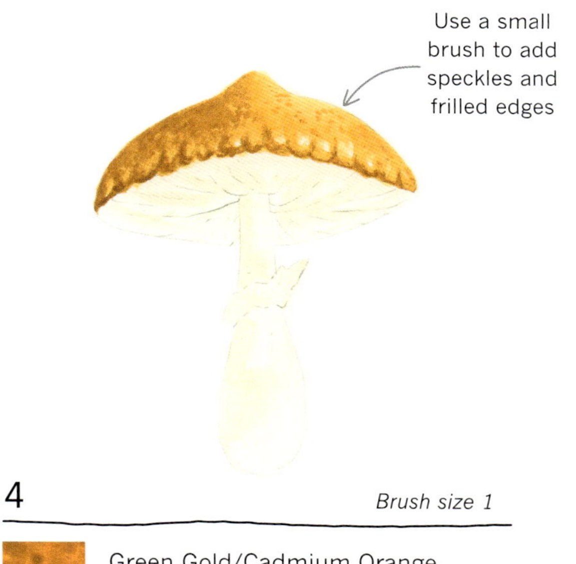

4 *Brush size 1*

Green Gold/Cadmium Orange
dark wash

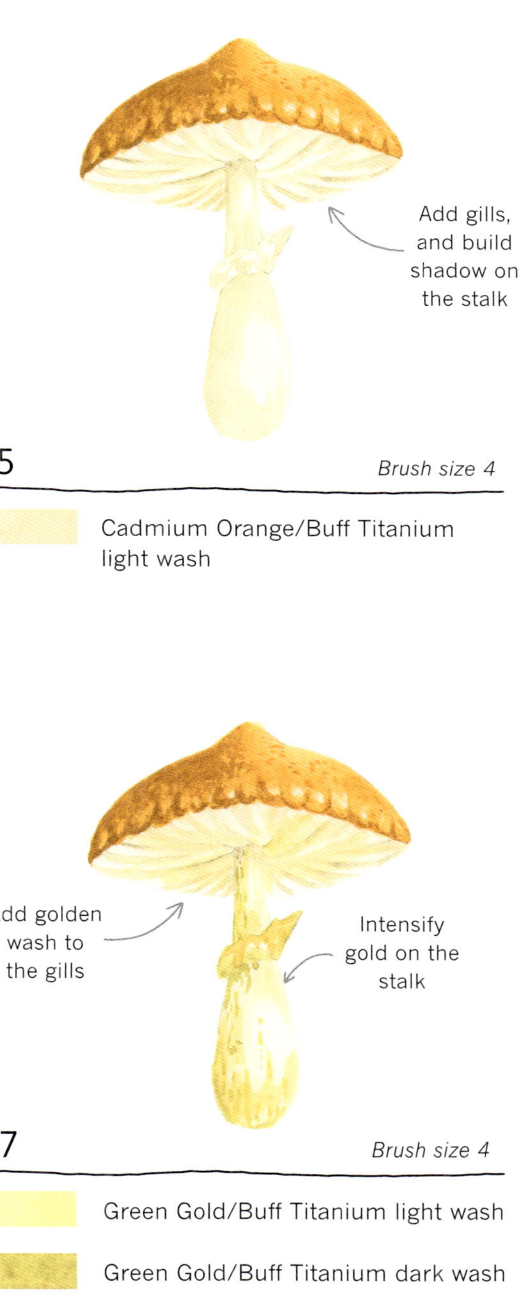

5 *Brush size 4*

Cadmium Orange/Buff Titanium
light wash

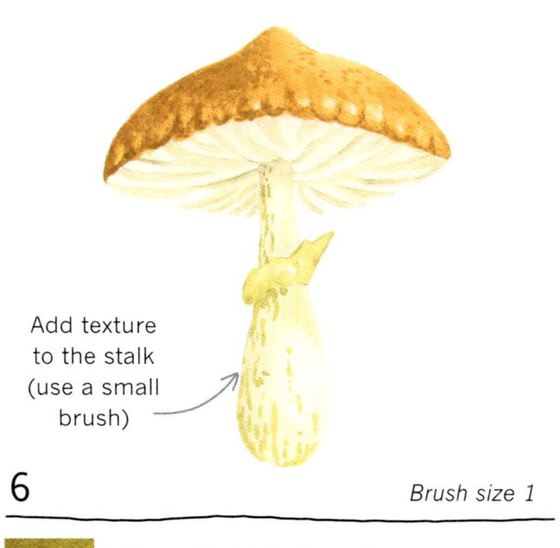

6 *Brush size 1*

Green Gold dark wash

7 *Brush size 4*

Green Gold/Buff Titanium light wash

Green Gold/Buff Titanium dark wash

Latte Art

Flat white or cappuccino, latte or mocha: whatever your preference, a hot mug of coffee is the best way to start the day. Practice your barista skills with this three-color latte art.

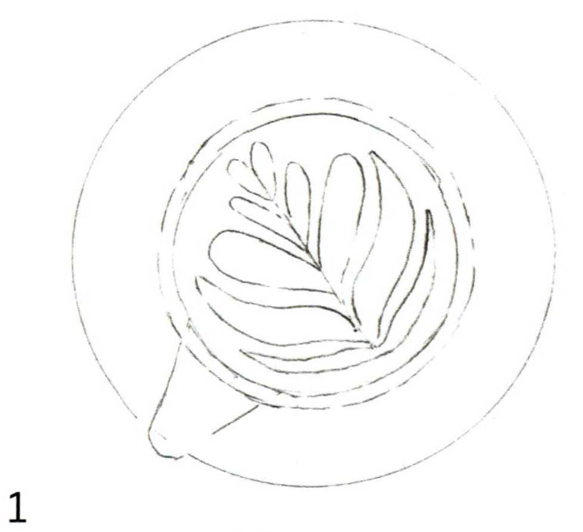

1

Begin with a simple pencil sketch.

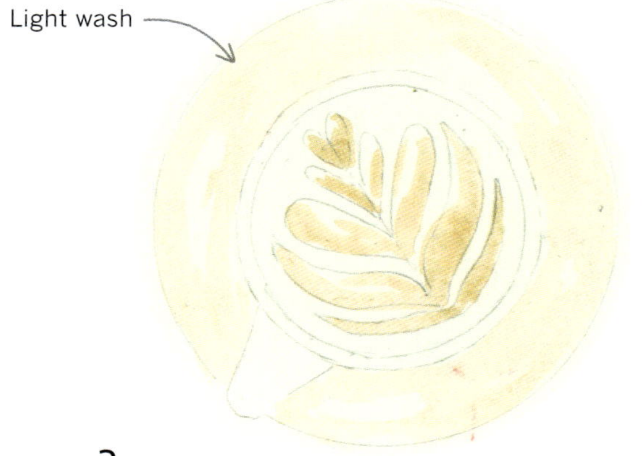

2 *Brush sizes 4 and 7*

Buff Titanium light wash

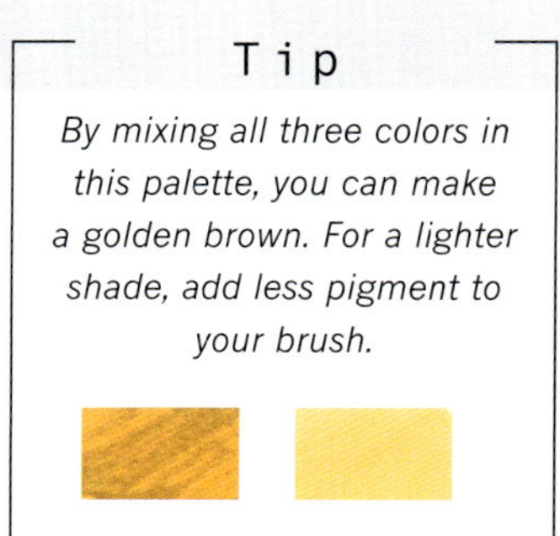

Tip

By mixing all three colors in this palette, you can make a golden brown. For a lighter shade, add less pigment to your brush.

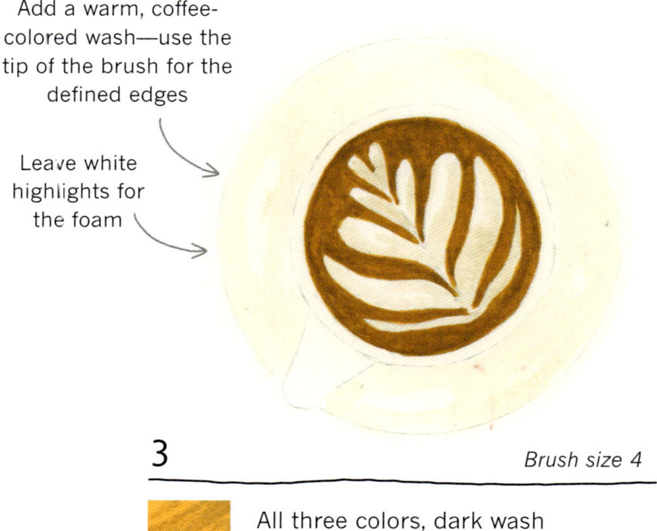

3 *Brush size 4*

All three colors, dark wash

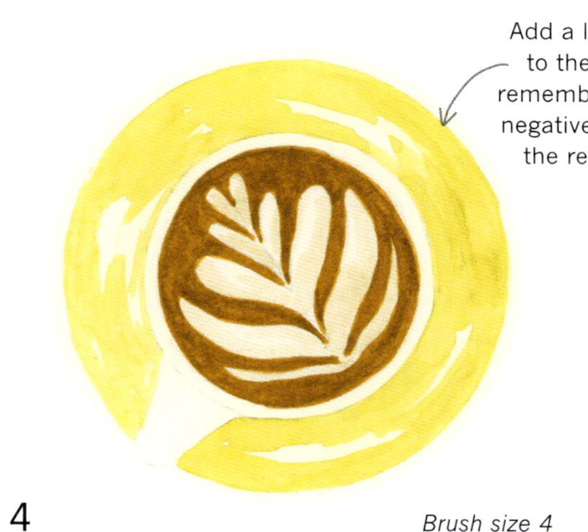

4   *Brush size 4*

Green Gold light wash

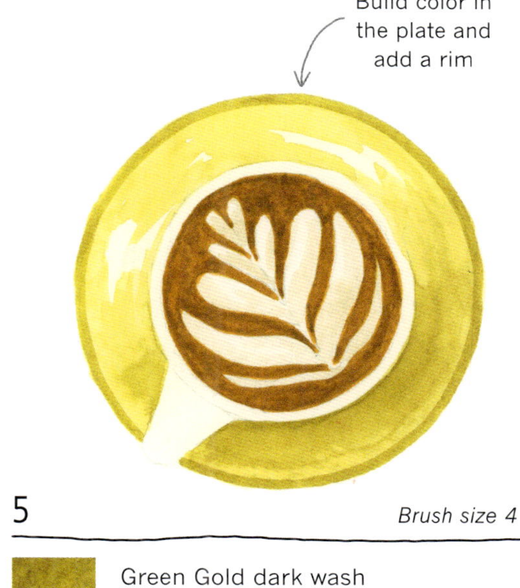

5   *Brush size 4*

Green Gold dark wash

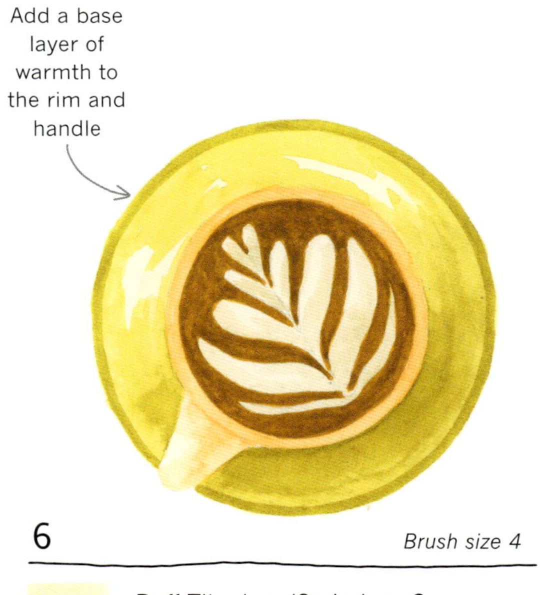

6   *Brush size 4*

Buff Titanium/Cadmium Orange
light wash

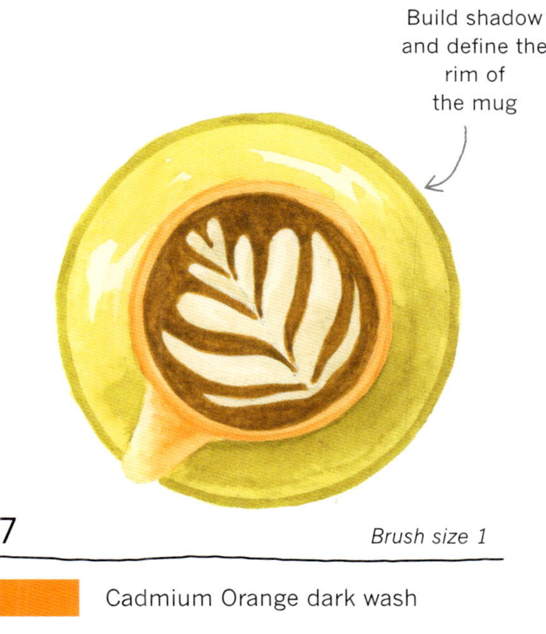

7   *Brush size 1*

Cadmium Orange dark wash

Festive Vibes

This three-color palette is cozy, rich, and sumptuous. It is
a festive mix that lends itself well to fruit and colorful
objects from around the home . . . it's beginning to
feel a lot like Christmas!

THE COLORS

Green Apatite Genuine

Alizarin Crimson

Cadmium Yellow

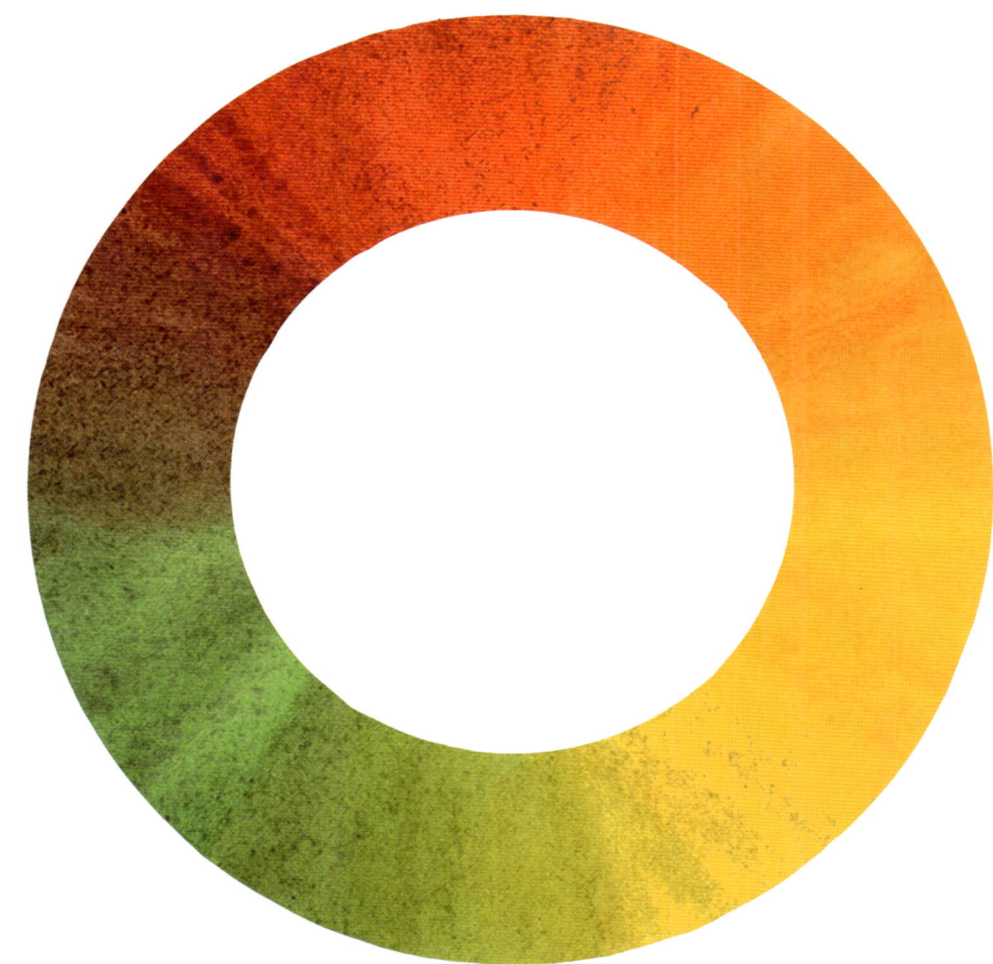

Mixing

The above shows the three colors on a simple
color wheel, each blending into its neighbor.
On the next page, you will see a chart showing
how the colors interact with each other.

COLOR CHART

Each color is shown at two strengths: a dark wash and a light wash. See p. 19 for more on washes.

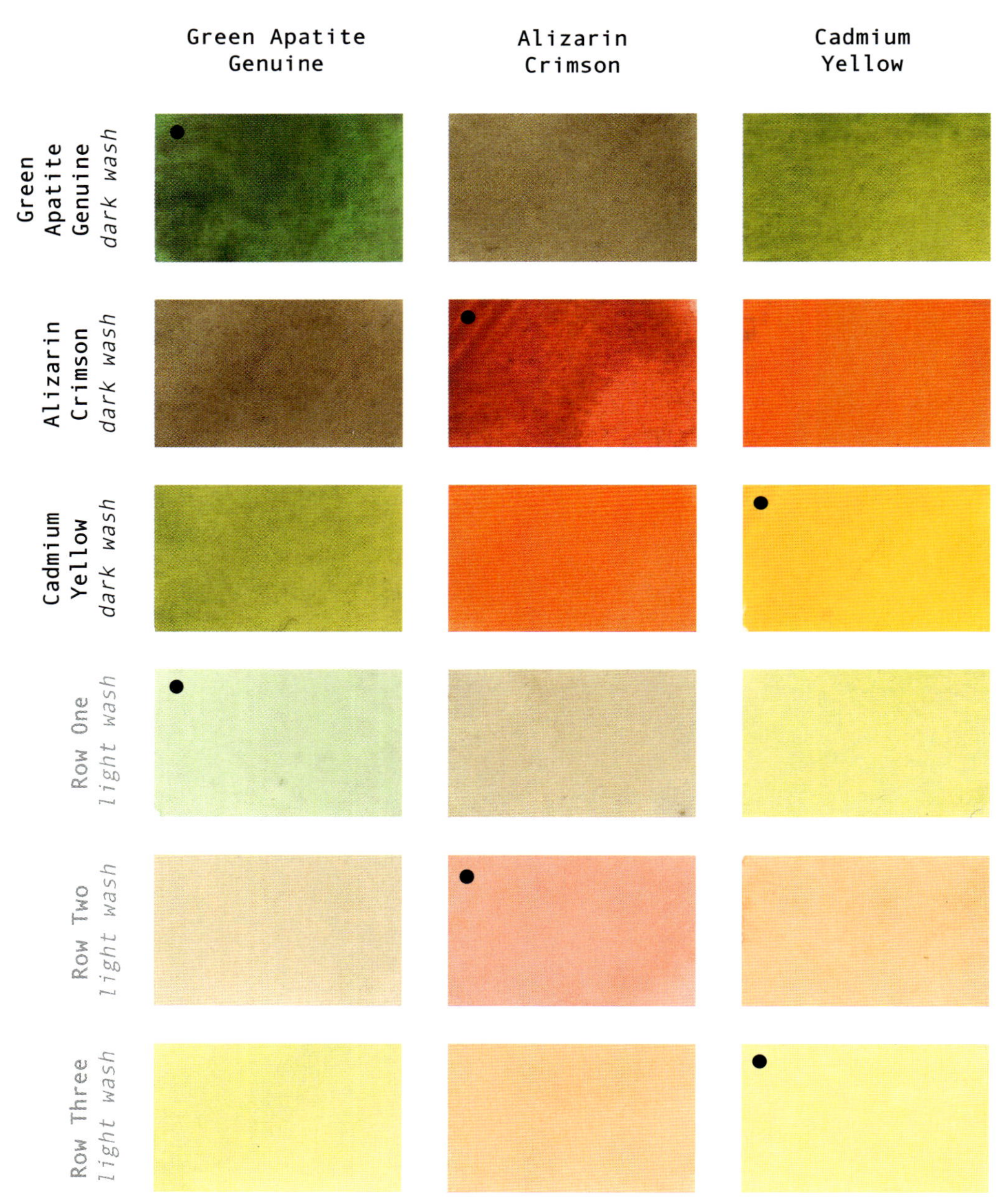

The Projects

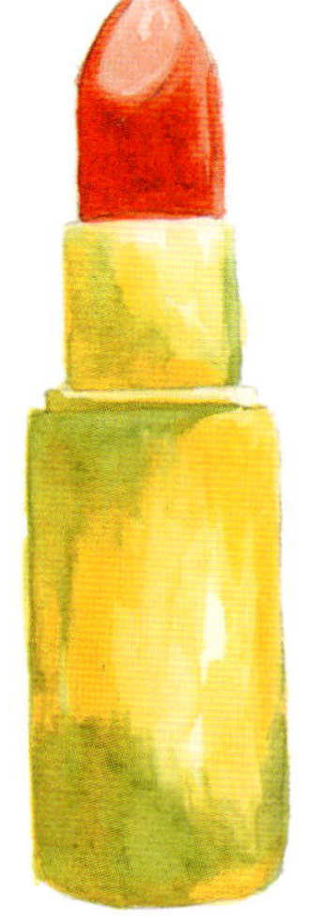

1. RED LIPSTICK

2. BEDSIDE LAMP

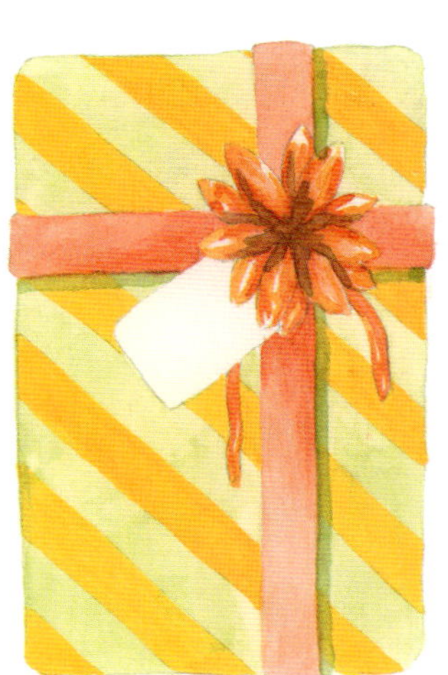

3. PRESENT

Red Lipstick

So simple, so glamorous: red lipstick says confidence like nothing else.
This pleasing project is an instant mood boost.

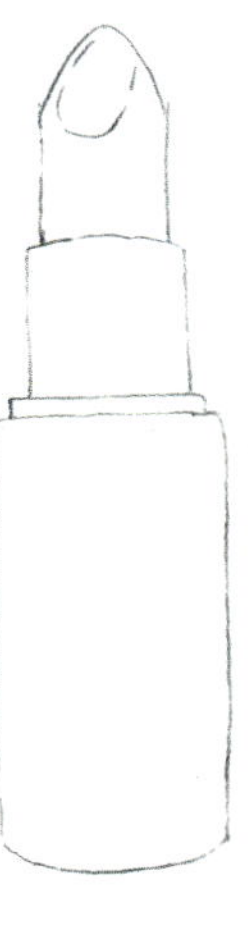

1

Begin with a simple pencil sketch.

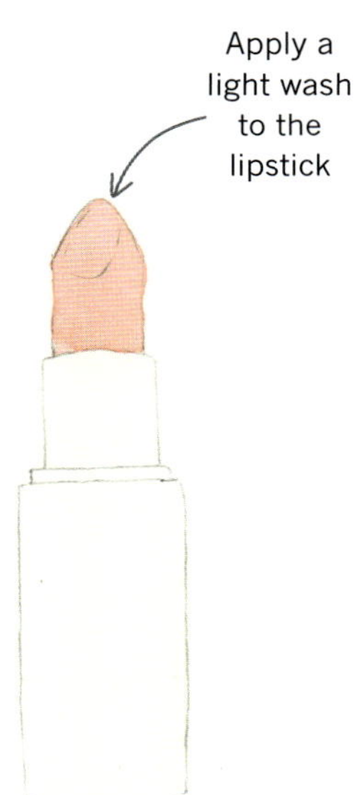

2

Brush size 4

Alizarin Crimson light wash

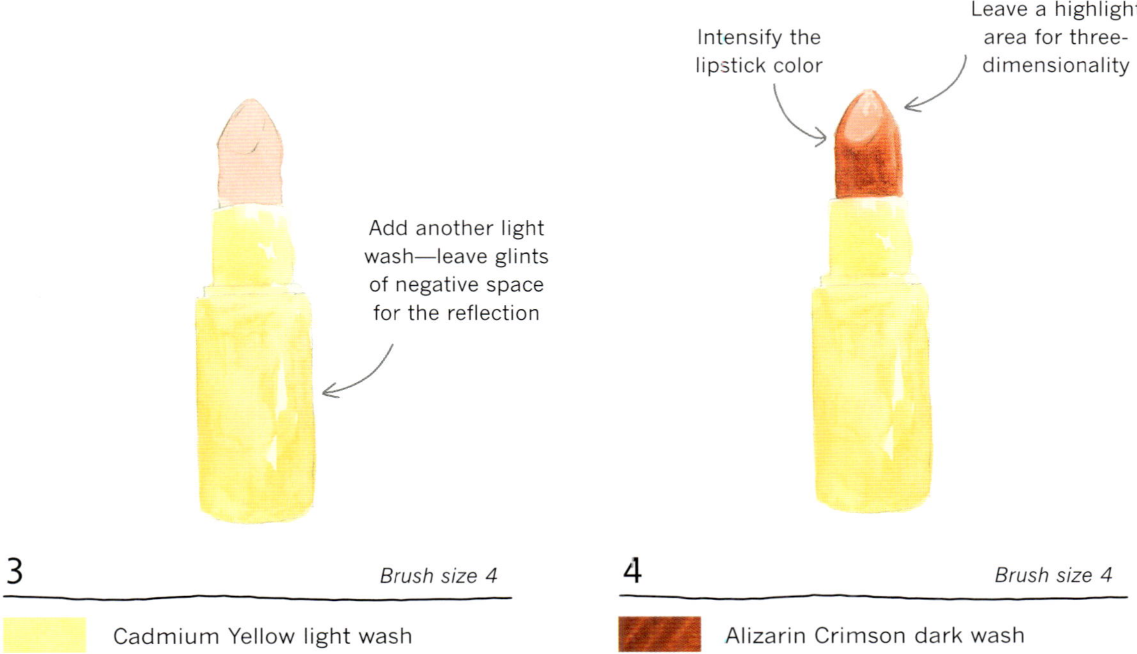

3 *Brush size 4*

Cadmium Yellow light wash

4 *Brush size 4*

Alizarin Crimson dark wash

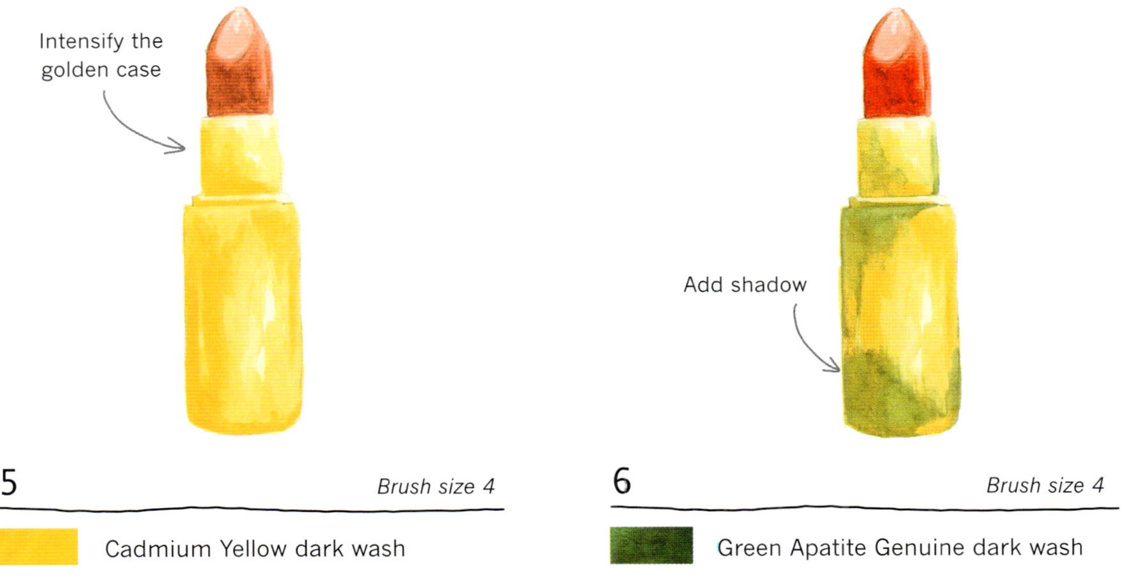

5 *Brush size 4*

Cadmium Yellow dark wash

6 *Brush size 4*

Green Apatite Genuine dark wash

Bedside Lamp

Have fun playing with texture in this project, where a textile lampshade contrasts with a smooth, ceramic stem. You'll end up with an item any interior designer would be proud to have on their bedside table.

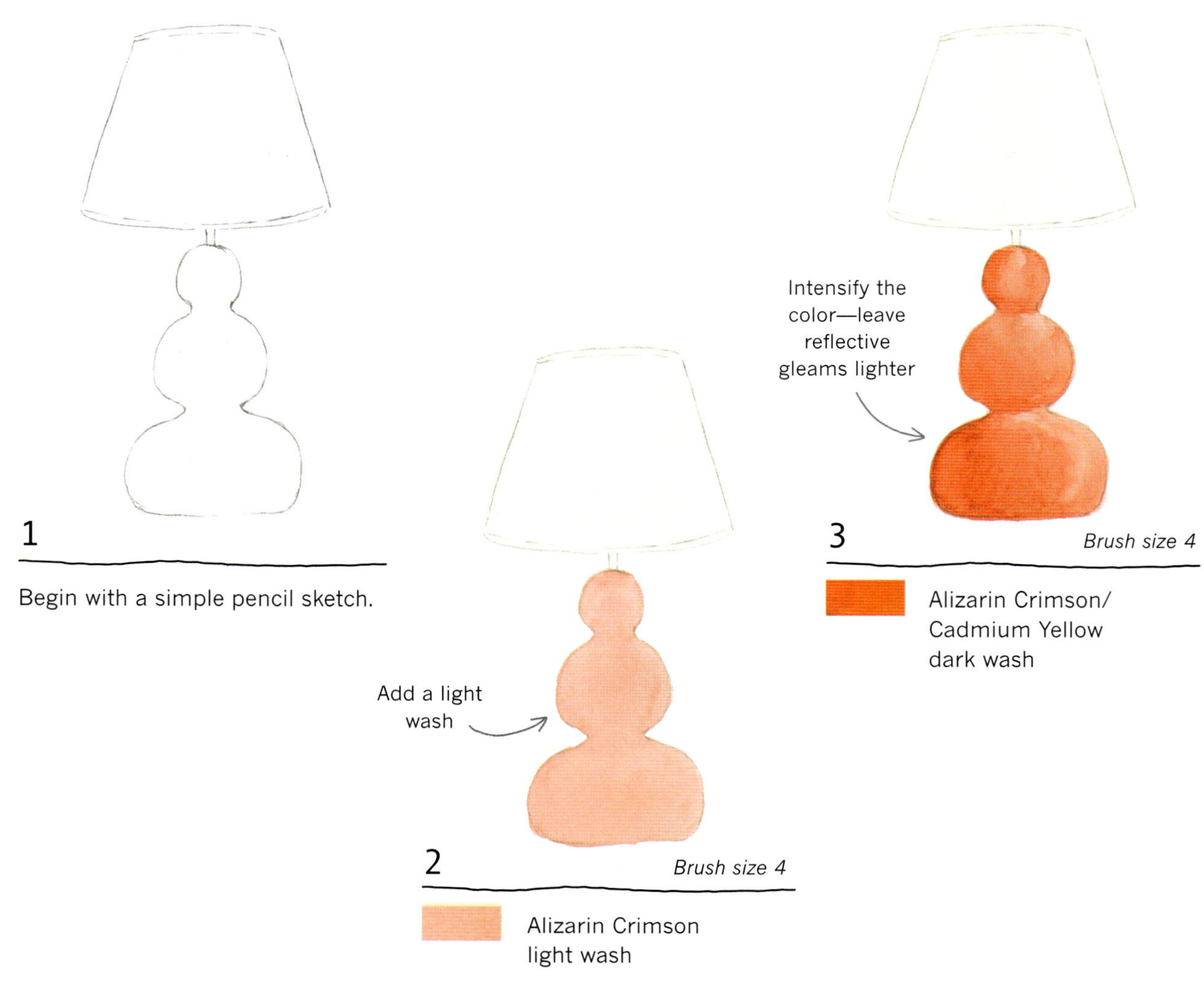

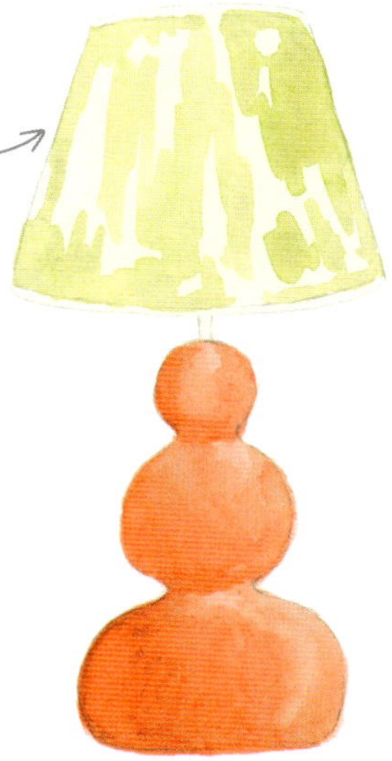

Add patches
of light green
to capture the
lampshade's
texture

Add a layer
with patches of
darker green, to
emphasize the
texture

4   *Brush size 4*

Green Apatite Genuine/
Cadmium Yellow light wash

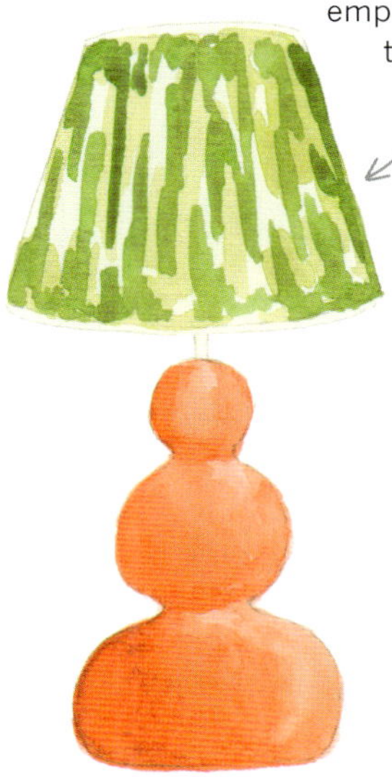

5   *Brush size 4*

Green Apatite Genuine dark wash

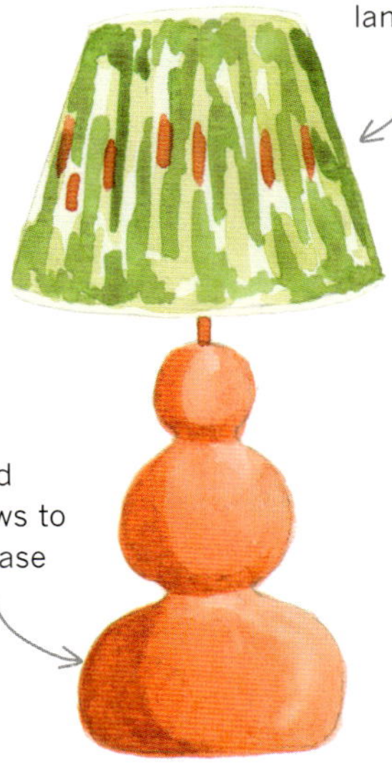

Add darts
of color to the
lampshade

Add
shadows to
the base

Add finishing
touches of
yellow to
the top and
bottom of the
shade

6   *Brush size 4*

Alizarin Crimson dark wash

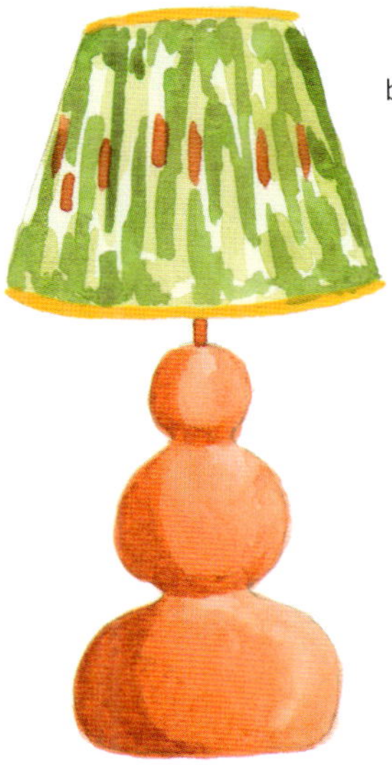

7   *Brush size 1*

Cadmium Yellow dark wash

Present

Let the festivities commence with this beautifully gift-wrapped present. Use just three colors to paint your own bold, striped gift wrapping and red ribbons. Why not go meta and gift your painting to someone when you're done?

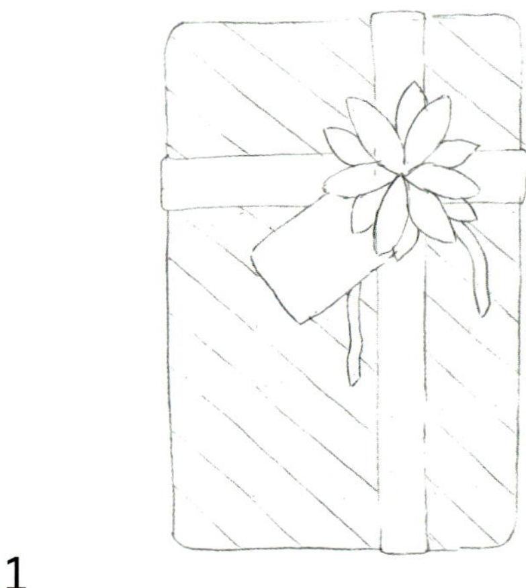

1

Begin with a simple pencil sketch.

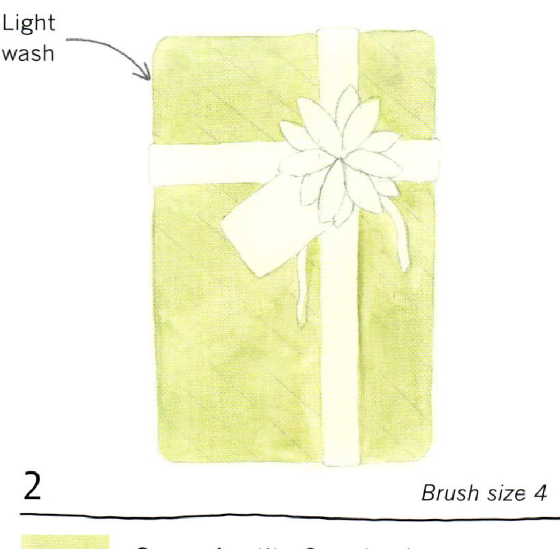

2

Brush size 4

Green Apatite Genuine/
Cadmium Yellow light wash

3

Brush size 4

Cadmium Yellow dark wash

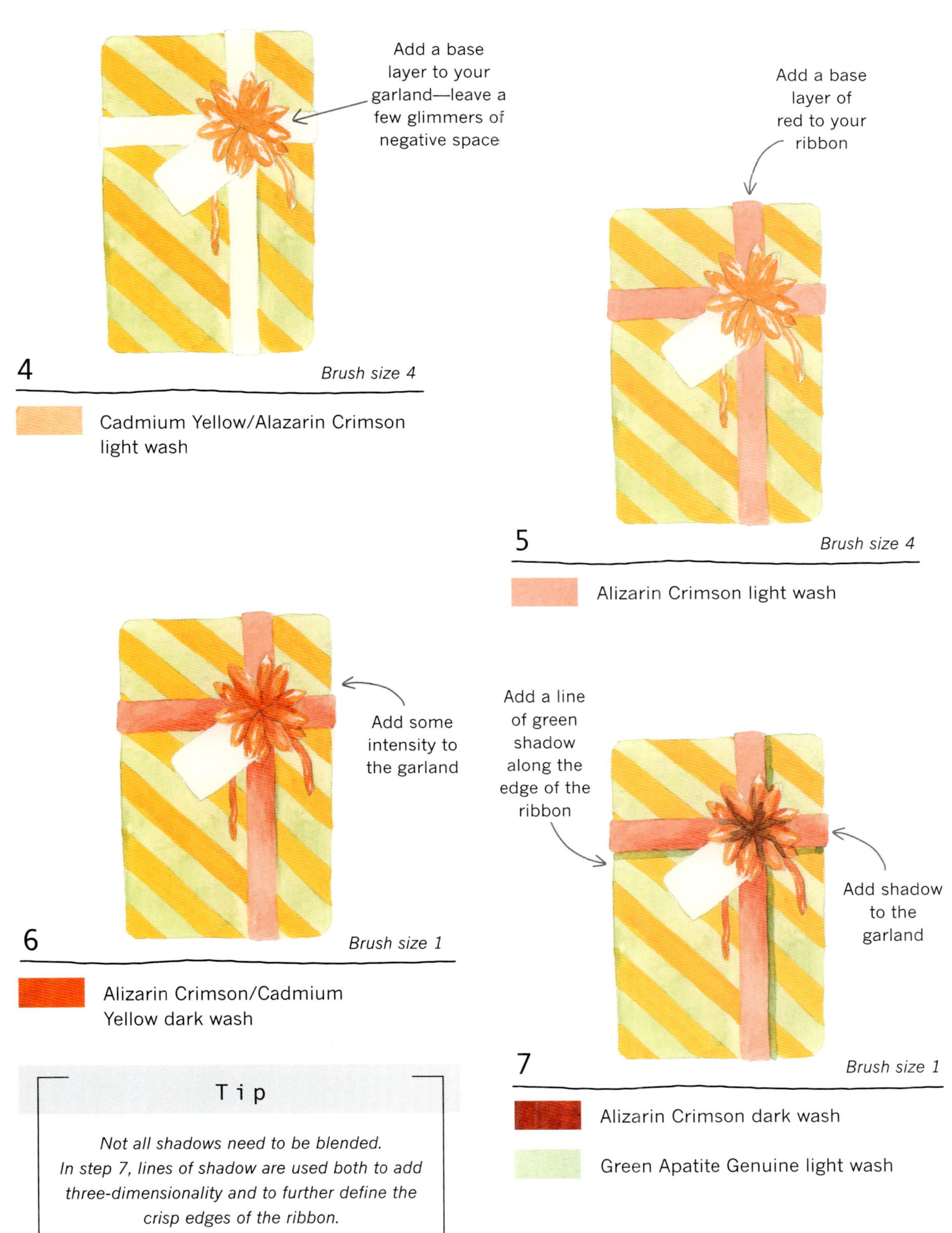

4

Brush size 4

Cadmium Yellow/Alazarin Crimson light wash

5

Brush size 4

Alizarin Crimson light wash

6

Brush size 1

Alizarin Crimson/Cadmium Yellow dark wash

7

Brush size 1

Alizarin Crimson dark wash

Green Apatite Genuine light wash

Tip

Not all shadows need to be blended. In step 7, lines of shadow are used both to add three-dimensionality and to further define the crisp edges of the ribbon.

Color Index

PERMANENT RED ORANGE

Shmincke: Horadam. Color index name: PO62/PR242. Color index number: n/a

ROSE MADDER

Winsor & Newton. Color index name: NR9; Color index number: 75330

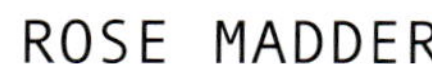

DELFT BLUE

Schmincke Horadam Aquarell. Color index name: PB60; Color index number: 69800

MANGANESE BLUE

Winsor & Newton. Color index name: PB15; Color index number: 74160

NAPLES YELLOW

Winsor & Newton. Color index name: PW6, PBr 24; Color index number: 77891, 77310

BEACH SPIRIT, P. 34

BUFF TITANIUM

Daniel Smith. Color index name: PW6:1; Color index number: 77947

SCANDI CALM, P. 44;
AUTUMNAL GLOW, P. 104

POMPEII RED

Daniel Smith. Color index name: PBr7; Color index number: n/a

SCANDI CALM, P. 44

PERYLENE GREEN

Winsor & Newton. Color index name: PBk31; Color index number: 71132

SCANDI CALM, P. 44

YELLOW OCHER

Winsor & Newton. Color index name: PY43; Color index number: 77492

TRUE ROMANCE, P. 54;
SUMMER SWOON, P. 94

PAYNES GRAY

Winsor & Newton. Color index name: PB15, PBk6, PV19; Color index number: 74160, 77266, 46500

TRUE ROMANCE, P. 54

CADMIUM YELLOW

Winsor & Newton. Color index name: PY35, PO20; Color index number: 77205, 77199

TROPICAL SUN, P. 64;
SPRING FRESH, P. 84;
FESTIVE VIBES, P. 114

ITALIAN DEEP OCHER

Daniel Smith. Color index name: PY43; Color index number: 77492

TROPICAL SUN, P. 64

COBALT TURQUOISE

Daler-Rowney 155 (RS series *** opaque). Color index name: PB36

TROPICAL SUN, P. 64

GREEN GOLD

Winsor & Newton. Color index name: PY129; Color index number: 48042

MAGIC TOUCH, P. 74;
AUTUMNAL GLOW, P. 104

ALIZARIN CRIMSON

Winsor & Newton. Color index name: PR83; Color index number: 58000

MAGIC TOUCH P. 74;
FESTIVE VIBES, P. 114

MOONGLOW

Daniel Smith. Color index name: PB29, PG18, PR177; Color index number: n/a

MAGIC TOUCH P. 74

PHTHALO TURQUOISE

Winsor & Newton. Color index name: PB16; Color index number: 74100

SPRING FRESH, P. 84;
SUMMER SWOON, P. 94

CERULEAN BLUE

Winsor & Newton. Color index name: PB35; Color index number: 77368

SUMMER SWOON, P. 94

CADMIUM ORANGE

Winsor & Newton. Color index name: PY35, PR108; Color index number: 77205, 77202

AUTJMNAL GLOW, P. 104

GREEN APATITE GENUINE

Daniel Smith. Color index name and number: n/a

FESTIVE VIBES, P. 114

About the Author

Katie Putt is an award-winning London-based
watercolor artist and illustrator. Her work combines
a traditional style with a relaxed, modern touch.
She is the author of *Boost Your Watercolor
Confidence,* and is an experienced teacher of
watercolor workshops. To view more of Katie's
work visit @studio.storey on Instagram.

Illustration Credits

The publisher would like to thank the following individuals and
organizations for their kind permission to reproduce the images in this
book. Every effort has been made to acknowledge the pictures, however,
we apologize if there are any unintentional omissions:

p. 12 top: Ann Yuni / Shutterstock; p. 12 below: Sooksan Kasiansin /
Alamy Stock Photo; p. 13 left: Ilze_Lucero / Shutterstock; p. 13 right:
Nikita Oskolkov / Shutterstock; p. 14: Azurhino / Shutterstock; p. 15
tertiary colors, left to right: Crystal Odenkirk / Shutterstock; Vesnin_Sergey
/ Shutterstock; Evgenii Skorniakov / Shutterstock; Silver Spiral Arts /
Shutterstock; Linda Armstrong / Shutterstock; Alx Yoel / Shutterstock;
p. 16 top: Asya Alexandrova / Shutterstock.
All other artwork is by the author.